Green Architecture

James Wines

Green Architecture

Edited by Philip Jodidio

TASCHEN

HONG KONG KÖLN LONDON LOS ANGELES MADRID PARIS TOKYO

Dedicated to my daughter Suzan Wines

To stay informed about upcoming TASCHEN titles, please request our magazine at
www.taschen.com/magazine or write to TASCHEN America, 6671 Sunset Boulevard,
Suite 1508, USA–Los Angeles, CA 90028, contact-us@taschen.com, Fax: +1-323-463.4442.
We will be happy to send you a free copy of our magazine which is filled with information
about all of our books.

© 2008 TASCHEN GmbH
Hohenzollernring 53, D–50672 Köln
www.taschen.com

Original edition: © 2000 Benedikt Taschen Verlag GmbH
Edited by Caroline Keller, Nicola Senger, Cologne
Design and Layout: Marion Hauff, Milan
Cover design: Sense/Net, Andy Disl and Birgit Reber, Cologne

Printed in China
ISBN 978-3-8365-0321-1

Contents

Man can hardly recognize the devils of his own creation.
Albert Schweitzer

Preface

Page 6/7
Hill town
Southern Italy
c. 1400

Page 7 and 8
Plan Voisin
Le Corbusier
Paris, France
Project, 1925

Architecture in the 20th century began as a celebration of the Age of Industry and Technology; but this is rapidly changing in response to a new Age of Information and Ecology.

This book is intended as a general exploration of one of the most complex and problematic issues facing humanity over the next century – that is, how to construct a human habitat in harmony with nature. The purpose is to set the stage for an expanding creative dialogue, but not pretend to offer utopian solutions for the damage wrought by construction technology and the waste of resources during the past 60 years. The text is really more about opening up ideas and issues for investigation and identifying new directions in green design.

The chapters include a review of 20th-century green architecture, a history of ecologically oriented shelter from Neolithic times to the present, and a survey of architects who are seeking to change the relationship between buildings and the environment. It is a compendium of these designers' constructed and proposed works that, with varying degrees of success, are dealing with such issues as environmental technology, energy conservation, sustainability, and the conversion of all these elements into architecture as art. Too often the problem with so-called green architecture is the conflict between having a strong sense of mission and an admirable commitment to ecological design principles, versus an overly righteous moral posturing and a failure to convert noble objectives into an equivalent artistic expression. For example, there is much talk of "sustainable architecture" as an alternative to the industrialized societies' wasteful legacy of short-term construction. However, without art, the whole idea of sustainability fails. People will never want to keep an aesthetically inferior building around, no matter how well stocked it is with cutting-edge thermal glass, photovoltaic cells, and zero-emission carpeting. While there are many publications today that cover the scientific and technological side of the eco-design revolution, this book approaches the subject from a conceptual, philosophical, and artistic perspective.

In 1923 the great Modernist pioneer Le Corbusier hailed a "new epoch" and proclaimed: "There exists a new spirit! Industry, overwhelming us like a flood which rolls toward its destined end, has furnished us with new tools adapted to this new epoch, animated by the new spirit." Today, 85 years later, we see this overwhelming flood as the enemy of nature and a problem of global magnitude that must be reversed – or, at the very least, radically modified – for human survival. The building of shelter consumes one-sixth of the world's fresh water supply, one-quarter of its wood harvest, and two-fifths of its fossil fuels and manufactured materials. As a result, architecture has become one of the primary targets of ecological reform. Oblivious to these sobering statistics, the majority of architects continue to design buildings rooted in the style, spirit, and industrial technology identified with Le Corbusier's once prophetic "new epoch." Unfortunately, it is an inspirational source that has become tarnished and discredited in the face of current environmental realities.

Whereas Le Corbusier referred to the house as "a machine for living in" – acknowledging his debt to industrial sources – there is a new generation of architects who regard the earth itself as the ultimate "machine" and the human habitat as an extension of the concept of Gaia, or the earth as a living organism. If the designers of this century's earlier machine age could forge convincing new paradigms for shelter out of the mechanisms of industrial production, then one can only imagine the potential explosion of future creativity in response to the ideas found in nature. The science of ecology has provided a radically expanded view of the natural environment, insights into its working processes that never existed before, and the inspirational foundation for a new architectural iconography.

This book explores how a heightened awareness of earth-centric information has influenced architecture in the 1990s. It is a preface for revised thinking about the relationships between construction and environment, an exploration of new sources of form and content, and a confirmation that the building arts are in the nascent stage of a revolutionary transformation that will ultimately change the way we live.

Strip architecture
Las Vegas, Nevada, USA
1970

Aerial view of Caracas
Venezuela
1993

Scheme for Bicentennial Celebration
Robert Venturi
Benjamin Franklin Avenue, Philadelphia,
Pennsylvania, USA
1976

The 'control of nature' is a phrase conceived in arrogance,
born of the Neanderthal age of biology and the convenience of Man.

Rachel Carson

Compared to the environmental crisis, all other social, political, economic, and scientific issues pale into insignificance. Obviously if humanity expires from global warming, over-population, pollution, starvation, and a lack of water, it will matter very little whether civil rights have been achieved, the Middle East is at peace, an Aids vaccine exists, or the national debts have been paid. In point, all of these threats to our survival are directly or indirectly related to environmental destruction.

Unfortunately, the cataclysmic predictions of some of our finest environmental specialists still go unheeded, or they are watered down for reasons of political expedience and corporate greed to a level where the public is deluded into a state of complacency. There seems to be no human enterprise that is not based on the premise of Man's dominance over the earth and the delusion of some spiritually ordained right to clog the rivers, pollute the air, foul the beaches, poison the soil, and impose general havoc on nature. Within this scenario I have written this book on environmental architecture, exploring the role of the building arts in a new Age of Ecology.

In many ways this publication could be considered both too early and too late. From a design perspective, it is too early. While there is brilliant work being done today that qualifies as "green" and "sustainable," most architects' actual choices of visual interpretation are still locked into timeworn 20th-century stylistic idioms which tend to confuse, rather than reinforce, a progressive image of earth-friendly architecture. On the other hand, from the standpoint of advocating some much needed environmental reforms in the building arts, this book is too late. A major proportion of the architectural profession has remained oblivious to the magnitude of its irresponsible assaults on the land and resources for many

decades. Furthermore, given the long-standing need for an environmentally oriented philosophy in architecture, the main messages of this book are actually a half century overdue.

There are many publications today that have examined the subject of green architecture as though it was simply one more set of problems to be resolved through advanced technology. While, obviously, the goal of sustainable living can be strengthened by such environmentally progressive innovations as the use of recycled materials, thermal (smart) glass, energy efficient construction methods, and photovoltaic solar collectors, most of these solutions tend to isolate the means from the mission. This 'mission' calls for a commitment by societies everywhere to unite in a common cause and connect to the natural environment on a more profound philosophical, psychological, and cultural level. Otherwise, the basic incentives for survival may be defeated by a diversionary proliferation of remedial mechanisms that do not address the deeper social conflicts caused by a collective state of denial.

Returning to the questionable choice of early Industrial Age imagery that still characterizes a great deal of green architecture, there are frequently some justifiable solar energy, resource conservation, and air quality related rationales for the continued use of expressed technological features – for example, expansive plate glass walls, skeletal steel construction, and exposed duct systems. But there also remains a lot of stylistic baggage that needs to be discarded – or at the very least, seriously re-evaluated – to accommodate the development of a new ecology-based architectural language.

This book is a modest endeavor to examine green design in this context. The origins of this critique began with an earlier book, entitled *De-Architecture*, that I published in 1987. It was written as a protest against the ubiquity of certain types of Modernist-derived structures and the oppressive anonymity of cities and suburbs resulting from this influence. It introduced some aesthetic propositions and critical thinking about the relation of architecture to context that I am expanding upon here.

In many ways *De-Architecture* was indebted to Robert Venturi's pioneering 1966 treatise, *Complexity and Contradiction in Architecture.* His seminal book opened designers' eyes to the parallels in communicative imagery to be found in historic civic and religious architecture, contemporary commercial structures, and American vernacular buildings which had been excluded from consideration among adherents of orthodox Modernism. By means of searing critique, trenchant insights, and radical design ideas, Venturi ripped through the heavily insulated walls of academia and let in a welcome blast of fresh air. He admonished architects for their inflexibility and enslavement to hand-me-down and derivative design vocabularies. He opened up new horizons by creating an awareness of the potency of an architecture of signs and symbols and revealed the deeper implications behind the popular culture iconography found in American main streets and commercial strips.

The initial triumphs of Modern Architecture were inspired by the industrial dream. From the turn of the century through the 1930s, architects passionately believed there was a direct equation between the combustion engine and a spiritual vision for shelter. Today one only has to observe the bleak and hostile legacy of this vision in cities around the world to see how these ideals have degenerated through endless repetition in the hands of mediocre followers of the Modern Movement. As long as buildings are conceived as isolated "big events," as monumental statements by their designers, all the same mistakes will be compounded over and over again. Venturi understood this problem perfectly and became a prophet of change; but the revolution has been slow in gaining a secure foothold.

The fundamental message of my book proposed that architecture in the 1990s should examine new ideas for the built environment, based on subliminal connections to what C. G. Jung referred to as society's "collective unconscious." My text supported a content-oriented departure from Modern Design conventions (which are still as rigid in their doctrinaire prescriptions as the formerly disdained Beaux Arts ever was), with the premise that Western civilization is now in the Age of Information and its architecture should conceptually and iconographically reflect this radical change of source material.

De-Architecture points out that, during the past decade, people's collective unconscious – in fact, their entire perception of the world – has been moulded by the supremacy of television, cinema, mass media, and the computer. This has resulted in a set of subliminal references that have little to do with the industrial and technological forces that shaped the economy, social structure, and habitat of the early part of this century. For example, Le Corbusier's sacred architectural geometry of "cubes, cones, and spheres" and his corresponding enthusiasm for mechanized wonders of automobiles, airplanes, and railroad trains, gained their original currency from a metaphorical association with the 1920s vision of a new Machine Age. Now, as a result of the total assimilation of a technology-based design language into architecture, the potency of this imagery has been lost. From our present information era viewpoint, the Modernist legacy has become too ponderously specific to reflect the ephemerality and exchange-of-information spirit of such influences as mass media, the Internet, and satellite communications.

My early arguments also suggested that the aesthetic value of buildings should no longer be seen exclusively as a sculptural art of abstract form, space, and structure, but should, rather, shift the focus to informational and contextual associations relating more to a dialogue in the mind. This conversion from physical to mental is consistent with the information revolution and it also opens up archi-

Indeterminate Facade
SITE
Houston, Texas, USA
1975

Aerospace Museum
Frank O. Gehry
Los Angeles, California,
USA
1982–84

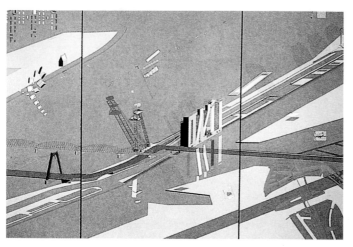

**Apartment Building &
Observation Tower**
Rem Koolhaas
Rotterdam,
The Netherlands
Project, 1982

tecture to a range of ideas and options that
have been closed off for most of this century.
These alternatives include buildings seen as
a means of critical commentary on the basic
definition of architecture, buildings as hybrid
fusions of representation and abstraction, and
buildings as "environmental sponges" which
absorb their imagistic clues from the widest
possible range of contextual sources.

Given the explosion of the information
revolution during the past few years, the principal message of *De-Architecture* for the 1980s
was its proposed shift of priorities in architecture from structures as self-contained abstract
objects, to buildings as "filtering zones" for
receiving, absorbing, and communicating outside sources of information. It is a concept that
can be regarded as a logical bridge to the ideas
proposed in the following text on environmental architecture. This book represents an evolution from the philosophical perspectives of
De-Architecture to the major concern of the
building arts in the year 2000 – that is, how to
design the human habitat with a sensitivity to
ecological principles and translate this message into a new architectural iconography.

While architectural discourse in the
1970s and 1980s (including my own contribu-

tions) tended to treat building art as an insular
subject, isolated by its own theoretical obfus-
cation, I now prefer to see my writing of this
period as transitional and leading toward the
far more urgent challenges of an ecological initiative. This hermetic situation in architecture
has been much like the tendency of psychology to base its analyses on an interpretation
of the mind as a sanctuary of introspection
and narcissism. Today, in contrast, the rapidly
growing field of eco-psychology is displacing
this limited perspective through the realization
that mental disorders are frequently the consequence of humanity's alienation from nature. In
a similar way architecture, as a fundamental
part of the matrix for human survival, can
hardly afford to remain separated from the
larger environmental picture.

The universal recognition of the power
of ecological forces is influencing all fields of
endeavor. Lester Brown, President of the Worldwatch Institute, describes this epochal moment
as "nothing less than an environmental revolution, an economic and social transformation
that ranks with the agricultural and industrial
revolutions." In critical terms, this suggests
dumping all of the ego-motivated excesses
associated with most architecture of the 20th
century in favor of a more socially responsible
and environmentally integrated approach. It
basically proposes that architecture has one
primary mission – to progress from "ego-centric" to "eco-centric." This evolution refers to a
mental state of transference where the habitual
notions of an insulated psyche (detached from
the natural environment) are exchanged for
the re-awakening of an expansive sense of
'oneness' with nature.

The supply of philosophically based literature dealing with ecological architecture is
still limited. This is partly a result of the obvious urgency of the environmental crisis and
the fact that most authors consider doomsday
warnings to be far more important than contemplative musings in architectural theory. It is
difficult to ignore the fact that industrialized
societies everywhere appear to be on an earth-
ravaging suicide course. In response, there are

now hundreds of publications on environmental reform and its relationship to every aspect of survival – including resource conservation, land use, waste disposal, government legislation, economic policy, and health care. Very little of this literature places the burden of responsibility on re-shaping contemporary societies' mental attitudes toward the earth and the awesome challenge of setting the stage for the possible emergence of eco-centric philosophies and religions. One notable exception is Charles Jencks' 1995 book, *The Architecture of the Jumping Universe.*

Jencks' basic thesis proposes that concepts in astrophysics – specifically quantum and chaos theories – as well as computer technology's cybernetic revolution, have given birth to an architecture of "cosmogenesis" that is being reflected in the design of certain contemporary buildings. Within a broad theoretical premise, he also includes eco-centric, anthropocentric, and morphogenic sources as an explanation for buildings demonstrating elements of disjointed geometry and convoluted organic shapes. Although acknowledging the ecological disasters surrounding us, his main focus is still within that inspirationally threadbare territory of formalist design, where architectural innovation is measured primarily by the familiar shape-making, space-making criteria identified with traditional abstract art. Jencks also attributes generous metaphorical associations to the work of architects such as Rem Koolhaas, Peter Eisenman, Santiago Calatrava, Frank O. Gehry, Coop Himmelb(l)au, Daniel Libeskind, and others, all drawn from his catalogue of cosmological references. Since he is preoccupied with labyrinthine formal strategies and the superficial similarities between astrophysical diagrams and Möbius strip influences in current architecture, the author makes very little evaluative distinction between buildings with admirable environmental contributions and those with only exaggerated sculptural features. In point, his favorite structures are too often fabricated in such ecologically offensive materials as stainless steel and endangered wood products, or sheathed

in obscenely toxic waste producing metals like titanium, copper, and aluminum. Jencks seems too easily satisfied with purely stylistic justifications for his cosmogenic metaphors, while neglecting the more urgent role of architecture to function as both an ecologically responsible and a symbolically communicative presence in the 21st century. As Jencks careens around the universe, he appears less interested in the fact that the earth under his feet is slipping away. By scanning the cosmos for exotic metaphors, he seems to be missing the dual capacity of architecture to translate the lessons of nature into a sustainable habitat and high art. Unlike many of my more obsessively practical green colleagues, who tend to underestimate the value of philosophical discourse, I am very supportive of Charles Jencks' quest for a new cosmology in architecture. The difference in my approach to this issue is to reverse the priorities – to advocate a "nature first" policy in the search for ideas right here on earth – and then move outward to the galaxies for additional sources of symbolism.

In addition to providing a survey of the past, present, and speculative future of earth-centric ideas and attitudes, my book is an analysis of recent architecture that has contributed to significant changes in environmental thinking. Rather than focus on technological innovations – as noted before, a major aspect of green architecture that has been extensively covered by other authors – I am looking at the subject from a conceptual, aesthetic, and philosophical viewpoint. In discussing contemporary work, my objective is to identify the motivational ideas behind each architect's approach that shows promise for the development of an ecologically inspired art of building in the Age of Ecology.

Life is right, and the architect is wrong.

Le Corbusier (toward the end of his life)

Nature's Revenge: A Brief Survey of 20th-century Green History

From an ecological perspective, mainstream architecture for the past two decades has sent out all the wrong messages. As a result of designers' obsessive desire to maintain the stylistic imagery identified with the 20th century's earlier industrial and technological dream, buildings have continuously displayed characteristics reminiscent of everything from factories to dirigibles, turbines, carburetors, oil derricks, ocean liners, rockets, and space stations – in fact, communicating a whole range of associations other than a connection with the earth itself. These Machine Age influences share one thing in common. They represent the profligate consumption of fossil fuel and a technocentric and anthropocentric view of the human habitat. Ask almost any architect to draw up his or her fantasies for a visionary building in the world of tomorrow, and the result will invariably look like a prophetic sketch that might have come from the hand of a Russian Constructivist in 1920. Particularly from the 1970s to the present, the celebration of such high-tech features as exposed structural systems, vast expanses of plate glass, and cantilevered, tilted, or skewed steel trusses has somehow become synonymous with a progressive look in architecture. As architect Michael Sorkin astutely observed in a 1990 critique of the Deconstructivist Exhibition at New York's Museum of Modern Art, the continuing craze to scavenge Constructivist imagery has resulted in "the reduction of an architecture of polemic, contention, and vitality to the necrophiliac realm of motif, the transmutation of research into fashion, the liberation of form from content so as to make it useful for appropriation by hacks." In addition to its negative environmental implications (and contrary to being progressive), this 90-year-old, industrially derived iconography has become the embodiment of a new academy

and the equivalent of a contemporary Beaux Arts.

The comparison of stylistic ubiquity in current architecture to the 1890s Beaux Arts is not inappropriate. By the turn of the century this institutionalized tyranny had become much reviled by the pioneers of Modernism for being a regressive pastiche of superfluous historical decor. Its academic constraints were rejected in the face of an explosive new era of seductive technology, utilitarian ideals, and social reform agendas. By taking an equally uncompromising critical position today, one might conclude that anything associated with industrial imagery, formalist design, Modernist or Constructivist derivations, the absence of landscape, and the lack of environmental commitment in the building arts could be seen – like the Beaux Arts – as evidence of a reactionary nostalgia for earlier times. Machine Age imagery is also the antithesis of relevant architecture at the threshold of an ecological revolution.

This does not suggest that architects should suddenly throw out the baby with the bath water (as the Modernists unfortunately did with the Beaux Arts) and abandon all evidence of high-tech features in their work simply to update their styles and try to look ecological. At the same time, it does mean that the profession is being compelled to face a radical re-evaluation of its priorities, and that soon the most progressive new voices in design will inevitably threaten the status quo. It can be safely predicted that, because of the urgency and increasing expansion of the environmental movement, architecture will probably change more radically over the next two decades than it has changed in the past 100 years. Far beyond the usual self-conscious motivations of style and theory, the shape of buildings will finally be forced to respond to the demands of

Compositional invention
Iakov Georgievich
Chernikhov
Project, 1933

ITT Building
Ludwig Mies van der Rohe
Chicago, Illinois, USA
1944

**Apartment Building &
Observation Tower**
Rem Koolhaas
Rotterdam, The
Netherlands
Project, 1982

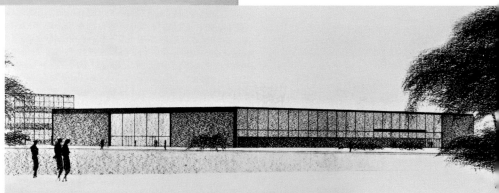

**Post Office Savings
Bank**
Otto Wagner
Vienna, Austria
1903–12

Palais Stoclet
Josef Hoffmann
Brussels, Belgium
1905–11

**Carson, Pirie & Scott
Store**
Louis Sullivan
Chicago, Illinois, USA
1899–1904

limited resources and earth-centric imperatives.

This is potentially one of the most challenging periods of architectural innovation in history. While many of the established architects today are intimidated by the accelerating momentum of change – fearing their stylistic commitments may be under attack – there is no reason why this revolution cannot be optimistically approached as the threshold of a great creative era. Here, for the first time in seven decades, is an opportunity to invent the future on terms that are sociologically and ecologically responsible. The industrial and technological influences that launched this century were rooted in cultural and economic change; as a result, rarely did the architects of early Modernism ever consider such issues as environmental impact, or the related psychological effects of their work on city dwellers as a consequence of this loss of contact with nature. They were committed to formalist and functionalist invention and new technologies, pure and simple. If people didn't appreciate the results, their negative reaction was dismissed as evidence of the public's philistine ignorance or conservative values. It is this profound misjudgment on the part of the architecture profession that is at the root of the environmental problems we face today. By insisting on a set of design standards divorced from ecological responsibility, architecture has forfeited its richest source of ideas, caused incalculable environmental damage, and failed to communicate with the very constituency it is obligated to serve.

Environmental architecture is now in an evolutionary stage that parallels the growth of early Modernism, before all the stylistic elements of the past had been totally eclipsed by the more iconic purity associated with a Machine Age aesthetic. For example, the work of architects such as Josef Hoffmann, Otto Wagner, Adolf Loos, Peter Behrens, Auguste Perret, and Louis Sullivan in the early 1900s still retained many of the stylistic references and deference to a metropolitan scale reminiscent of the 19th century. While distinctly mod-

Schröder House
Gerrit Rietveld
Utrecht, The Netherlands
1924

ern in feeling, their buildings still did not amplify the new age message with the same aggressive impact as later works by Le Corbusier, Mies van der Rohe, Theo van Doesburg, and Gerrit Rietveld. When mature Modernism achieved a dominant influence, the parallels between industrial production and its expression in form became definitive and easily perceived. In a similar way, the next decade will surely produce consistently more dramatic evidence of environmental technology, the earth sciences, and natural landscape expressively transformed into an unmistakable architectural iconography for the Age of Ecology.

Since the earth can be seen as the ultimate "machine for living in," Le Corbusier's classic description of the functional habitat applies with even broader implications to the environmental era. If designers of the 1920s and 30s could develop a persuasive architectural language out of the rather limited (by comparison to nature) inventions of industry, imagine the wealth of ideas to be found in the complexities of terrestrial and cosmological phenomena. Why, for example, aren't the natural wonders of ecology, hydrology, geology, or the revelations of biophysics and astrophysics, even more of an inspirational resource for the building arts than the structural geometry of a crane, or some Cubist-derived design conventions? Likely opposition to this proposal would come from those insular reactionaries within the current architectural scene who invariably protest any hint of narrative or referential content as anathema to the purity of traditional abstract form. Yet it is precisely this content-deprived, technologically driven, and environmentally irresponsible resistance to change that is at the basis of most regressive architectural thinking today.

Even the most advanced advocates of ecological design are still struggling with ways to integrate environmental technology, resource conservation, and aesthetic content. Without all three components in place, there is little chance for a truly enduring architecture. A major factor contributing to the longevity of buildings that have survived from the past is their fusion of nature and art. They had to be both earth friendly and beautiful to be worthy of preservation in the first place. There is much talk of sustainability in buildings these days; however, this discourse tends to center around the state of permanence as a desirable feature – followed by speculative methods, materials, and structural systems that have no track record of extended durability. Under this long-term endurance definition, the most reliable model of sustainable architecture would have to include any 600-year-old structure, still in excellent physical condition and active use today. A good demonstration would be certain Italian hill towns, where magnificent 13th-century buildings are filled with the latest computer technology and operationally accommodate international communications industries. The reasons for this longevity are simple. These picturesque villages were ideally situated for defensive security when originally constructed, their thermally efficient walls were built of regionally available materials, and their interior spaces – uninterrupted by today's proclivity for sculptural excess – have proven adaptable over hundreds of years of changing uses. Finally, the main key to the hill town's continued success has been an artistic value worth preserving. In contrast, there are many admirable examples of contemporary green buildings, crammed with cutting-edge environmentally favorable features, that have neither met the test of time nor demonstrated much aesthetic value. In point, it is a normal experience to visit a well publicized 'ecological

building' and be handed a checklist brochure of its earth-friendly virtues, while there is no visible evidence of any attempt on the part of the designer to resolve these contributions in terms of art. It may be green, but it is boring architecture.

This matter of sustainability cannot be looked at from the limited perspective of durability alone, even though one of the main arguments of this book is to defend the value of art in overcoming the tendency of societies to discard buildings with unreasonable frequency. Sustainable architecture basically comes down to three purposes – first, to advance the purely selfish motive of survival by a cooperation with nature; second, to build shelter in concert with ecological principles as part of this objective; and third, to address the deeper philosophical conflicts surrounding the issue of whether we really deserve the luxury of this existence, given our appalling track record of environmental abuse. A further, and ultimate, question remains: if we convince ourselves that we really merit nature's blessings, what does the notion of sustainability have to do with the soul and its relationship to a spiritual eternity?

In its earliest primal state, sustainable habitat simply referred to mankind's use of caves capable of being passed from one generation to the next, without disturbing the ecosystem. A later interpretation is reflected in certain aboriginal cultures' belief that any hand-built dwelling must defer to nature's need for reclamation; therefore, it should be conceived from the outset as part of a seamless dematerialization back into the environment when its sheltering functions are no longer required. Sustainable architecture in ancient cities usually meant construction technology developed out of regionally accessible materials which satisfied the demands of climate, topography, and agriculture as the principle means of survival. The quest for eternal life in most religions – particularly as manifested in ancient tombs and commemorative monuments – established a premise for buildings with exceptional durability, plus a choice of indestructible materials to guarantee this permanence. Sustainable architecture in the 1990s includes certain practical earth-centric features; for example, buildings that can be recycled in perpetuity for reasons of construction technology and functional design, structures that use the sun's energy efficiently, and all forms of shelter that respond to regional climate and materials limitations.

The philosophy of sustainability is also associated with various societies' perception of eternity. It has been inseparable from historic architecture ever since early religious connections were made between the concept of an 'eternal soul,' the need to honor this spirit by offering provisional housing en route to paradise, and the construction of awesome monumental sanctuaries to symbolize the mission (as in the ancient Egypt of Tutankhamen). In today's world, there doesn't seem to be much call for architecture as a spiritual depot. Religions now exert far less ritual power over the mass of people than, for example, Catholicism imposed during the 12th century, and they have lost a great deal of theological credibility to the more persuasive picture of eternity described by science. This revised view is being reconstructed (some say, "deconstructed") by the conceptual breakthrough of time and space theories. Astrophysics has charted a new geography of the heavens, leaving considerable doubt concerning the whereabouts of a paradise beyond this world where the soul can rest in peace. Instead, science describes everything in the universe as unfathomable electromagnetic forces, composed of particles, waves, explosions, inversions, expansions, and contractions, all trapped in a bleak and hostile void. Contrary to most religious doctrines, which promise greater rewards in a heavenly afterlife, these unpleasant scenarios characterize the greater unknown as nothing more than convulsive clusters of energy, trapped in endless chaos. Physics elaborates on this rather bothersome concept by proposing that our very being is nothing more than an equivalent composition of particles – a speculation which tends to discourage much hope of a spiritual fulfillment

Tomb of Tutankhamen
Thebes, Egypt
c. 1323 B.C.

elsewhere. These doubts raised by science, would seem to suggest that our chances for happiness may be more reliably terrestrial than paradisiacal. While speculative in any case, this kind of debate reinforces the insurance value of humanity's investment in an earth-bound existence. At the same time, the affirmation of nature's power does not preclude believing that sustainable architecture still has a role to play in celebrating the eternity of the soul.

Leaving the spiritual realm of sustainability for the more focused applications in green architecture, it is strange that even the individual components of environmental technology are rarely interpreted by architects as artistic raw material. Ecologically favorable hardware like thermal glass, solar collectors, photovoltaic panels, air filtering systems, and recycled construction materials, which could all be used to enhance the final building-as-art statement, are usually treated indifferently as "installed" rather than "expressed" elements of design, with no clues to their sources in nature or contributions to the expanded life and communicative content of buildings.

Like the confusion surrounding sustainability, the whole environmental issue suffers from problems of definition, terminology, and treatment in media exposure. The word "green" itself is in danger of becoming as over-publicized and meaningless as passé terms like

The Hay-Wain
John Constable
National Gallery, London,
England
1821

"post-modernist" and "deconstructivist" became a few years ago. For architects long involved with ecological design, the growing surge of popular hype (and its frequent misunderstanding of the real issues) has forced a need for environmental advocates to distance themselves from an omnivorous press that can so rapidly convert fertile ideas into impotent rhetoric. On the other hand, today's green movement needs a supportive media voice to continuously remind the global community of its precarious plight if the assaults on our fragile eco-systems continue unabated.

These fears over mankind's abuse of the environment are hardly new. They have been preceded by a history that can be traced back to the laments of Plato, agonizing over the loss of verdant hills and forests that surrounded ancient Athens as a result of relentless deforestation for shipbuilding and fuel. He wrote: "What now remains, compared to what was, is like the skeleton of a sick man, all the fat and soft earth wasted away and only the bare framework of the land being left." He was describing a situation where the once fertile Mediterranean basin had become a man-made desert. Formerly prosperous ports were abandoned to marsh land, as the harbors filled with silt wastes and the peripheral towns around Athens became landlocked, arid, and no longer able to support habitation.

In much of the ancient world, nature was regarded with awe and fear, since people were presumed to be helpless in the face of its power. After the major scientific discoveries of the 16th to the 18th centuries, Western societies, with their greed-driven economies, began to believe in the illusion that nature could be conquered through science for the exclusive benefit of commerce. This led to a reliance on technocentrism, which replaced the formerly deferent relationship between people and their environment. By the 19th century an apprehensive group of artists, writers, and philosophers, fearful of the consequences of rapacious industrial growth, began to idealize past civilizations – inclusive of ancient Greece – as the models of a more sympathetic communion with nature. Shelley and Blake, followed by Emerson, characterized the romantic view in literature, while English gardens celebrated a nostalgia for antiquity through the orchestration of artificial ruins wrapped in lush vegetation. Henry David Thoreau endeavored to weld the links between nature and society, and painters like Gustave Courbet, William Turner, and John Constable reminded audiences of the mysteries of landscape that were being endangered by the technologically based ravages of industry. John Ruskin admonished technocrats for their callous disregard for human identity in a machine-dominated world, and John Muir gave eloquent support to nature's gifts by defending the preservation of America's great forest lands. Toward the end of the 19th century, the Arts and Crafts Movement and Art Nouveau became the last architectural styles to celebrate the relationships between the building arts and natural forms. After that, the battle was lost. Modern Design swept the slate clean with its persuasive arguments about the relevance of industrial imagery, the provision of an easily imitated kit of parts, and a seductive manifesto for the future.

The strongest voice of resistance – and the singular innovator whose work shaped the fundamental principles of integrating architecture with its context in this century – was that of Frank Lloyd Wright. This awesome genius was a prophet of the entire environmental movement as far back as 1910, long before the word "ecology" was even in common use. He grasped the whole potential for buildings to become extensions of their environments by means of forms reflecting the contours of surrounding topography and the use of construction materials drawn from regional resources. He also connected the functional purposes of architecture to those processes in nature that parallel human behavior in the way they seek light, darkness, nourishment, and protection.

Wright was also the pioneering force behind "organic architecture" (which has served as a general frame of reference for many arguments in this book). In his view "Modern architecture is merely something – anything – which may be built today, but organic architecture is an architecture from within outward. Organic means intrinsic, in the philosophical sense, entity – wherever the whole is to the part as the part is to the whole and where the nature of materials, the nature of the purpose, the nature of the entire performance becomes clear as a necessity. Out of that nature comes what character in any particular situation you can give to the building as a creative artist."

For reasons that can only be explained by the fickleness and superficiality of stylistic vogue, Wright's ideas fell out of favor when Modernism gained its ascendancy. Perhaps this was due in part to the fact that his work, like that of such artists as Picasso and Matisse, could not be successfully copied without falling into banal caricature. This decline into parody was inevitable and spawned several generations of Wrightian pastiche. At the same time, his crusade for organic architecture got

"Falling Water"
Frank Lloyd Wright
Bear Run, Pennsylvania, USA
1935–39

Farnsworth House
Ludwig Mies van der Rohe
Plano, Illinois, USA
1946–51

German Pavilion
Ludwig Mies van der Rohe
World Expo, Barcelona,
Spain
1929

buried under the quick and easy cubes, cones, spheres, and nine-square grids of academic design and the indifference of the architectural profession to environmental alarm signals. The work of architects like Le Corbusier, Mies van der Rohe, Rietveld, and Melnikov seemed more neatly packaged, more accessible to imitation, more rigorously formal, and tidier in theoretical terms than the earth-oriented, multi-dimensional, rough cut and romantic prairie philosophy of Frank Lloyd Wright. This philosophical gap is best articulated by Wright's retort to Le Corbusier's aphorism describing the house as a "machine for living in": "Yes," Wright quipped, "just like the human heart is a suction pump."

As early as the 1920s and 30s the impact of technocentric overkill was being attacked by some leading critics of the day, but very few architects were listening. By then, the antiseptic industrial appearance of building and absence of such distracting amenities as landscape became inseparable from the whole idea of progressive design. This minimalist approach also conveniently found favor with bottom-line developers who were always looking for building technologies that were cheap, functional, and fast. The destructive effects of this proliferation of purity on human psychology and ecological stability got buried under the architects' ideological rhetoric and the development companies' profit motives. Only occasionally, as in 1938, when Lewis Mumford published the *Culture of Cities*, was forceful opposition voiced. Mumford reprimanded the builders of America: "As the pavement spreads, nature is pushed farther away; the whole routine divorces itself more completely from the soil; the slaughterhouse and the cemetery are equally remote and their processes are equally hidden." Taking aim at suburbia, Mumford sardonically touched on the psychological effects of rampant dreariness: "Standardized materials and patterns and plans and elevations – here are the ingredients of the architecture of the machine age: by escaping it we get our superficially vivacious suburbs; by accepting it, those vast acres of nondescript monotony. ... The chief thing

needful for the full enjoyment of this architecture is a standardized people."

In 1962, Rachel Carson's book *Silent Spring* essentially launched the popular concern with ecology. While some scientists and a few courageous politicians had warned of the dangers of environmental neglect, she managed to etch the threat of an eco-Armageddon and an industrial and military conspiracy into people's minds with greater impact than all other authors. Her grim record of the effects of pesticides, industrial wastes, and air pollution

Lollipop Trees outside the Lincoln Center
New York, New York, USA
1990

Aerial view of suburban housing
USA
1970s

on human survival alerted an entire generation to the perils at hand. Carson's book became one of the motivating alarm signals for the environmental youth movement that followed.

The first national wave of green consciousness in America started with the youth movement of the 1960s. At that time the cause unfortunately became associated in the public's mind with political radicalism, unreasonable measures to protect nature, and the endangerment of job security if land was preserved instead of plundered. For conservative citizens, the image of isolated communes, sheltered under geodesic domes, and populated by what the press disdainfully referred to as "naked eco-freaks" growing organic vegetables, became an alienating vision of the environmental revolution. Also, the confrontational rhetoric of the 60s portrayed the government and industry as greed-driven and irresponsible conspirators, destroying people and plant life for their own nefarious ends. Whether accurate or not, this hostile invective was interpreted by mainstream Americans as threatening to their traditional lifestyles and calling for personal sacrifices to save animals and trees. The radicals of this era, swept along by their anti-establishment politics, failed to realize that by segregating themselves in remote compounds (all of the solar panels and earth-covered shelters notwithstanding), they ignored the first principle of ecology – that is the law of "integrated systems." This concept of interactive cooperation, based on the way nature actually functions, is obviously the antithesis of individualism and isolationist behavior. As a result, while the youth movement enjoyed a lot of publicity for their beliefs, they tended to lose sight of the larger ecological picture. The typical "Drop City" refuge was not really a viable answer for a green habitat – although the incentives were admirable – so, for this and other assorted reasons, the 60s environmental movement never really succeeded in gaining its desired influence on government and the public.

During the 1970s and 80s, as a result of America's swing to a conservative and exploitative politics of "supply side" economics and its recklessly self-serving environmental policies, the green movement floundered for a while. It was revived again in the late 1980s as a result of a favorable press and an increasingly concerned population who had, by then, witnessed a succession of environmental dis-

asters in the form of nuclear waste leaks, flooded cities, and crop failures. It occurred to even the most obstinate detractors of the ecology movement that Mother Nature was going to have her way and it was wiser to cooperate than resist. At the same time high-profile administrations, like the Reagan presidency in the USA and the Thatcher administration in Great Britain, were plagued by widespread criticism of their resource-wasteful environmental policies. This, in turn, provoked an effective public outcry and offered tangible targets of blame for a series of well publicized ecological mishaps related to governmental negligence. It also fueled a new generation's environmental activism.

By the early 1990s, the citizenry of every nation began to personally experience unusually severe environmental devastation in the form of heat waves, soil pollution, droughts, oil spills, and the increased incidence of disease. Somehow the information revolution finally managed to communicate the threat of "unseen forces" in nature and persuade increasingly larger portions of the global population to acknowledge both the visible and invisible threats described by science. Whatever the sacrifices required in terms of remedial action to save the environment, the world community began to see these penalties as far less painful than the prospect of total extinction.

A cohesive global ecology movement and a unified course of action have not yet been established, since so many of the destructive residuals of the 1980s still remain. The main obstacles to progress can obviously be blamed on conservative political and economic agendas; but, at the same time, there is considerable pressure being brought to bear on governments from grass-roots movements, activist organizations, and green parties. All across Europe, green parties increasingly win ground and are responsively participating in the political process. Also, the number of environmental advocacy societies has increased to staggering proportions compared to the 1970s, and such groups as Greenpeace, Environmental Action, The Sierra Club, Friends of

the Earth, and The Nature Conservancy all claim burgeoning memberships. Most encouraging of all, a recent Gallup poll indicates that 77 percent of adult Americans define themselves as pro-environment.

Other areas of progressive activity in the green revolution have been related to the fields of philosophy and eco-psychology. The influential psychologist Theodore Roszak calls for an expansion of the environmental movement to include a "psychological impact statement" that can trace mental disturbances – and even a larger scope of societal dysfunction – directly to people's loss of contact with the earth. This relatively new focus in psychology has moved away from Freudian psychoanalysis, with its anthropocentric view of the id as a guarded sanctuary and its defense strategies against the hostilities of nature. In the 1930s Freud claimed that: "Normally there is nothing of which we are more certain than the feeling of our self, of our ego ... marked apart from everything else." His concepts of the ego and libido as exclusive gateways to the uncovering of emotional aberrations are now being challenged by an expansive type of analysis where the human psyche is never separate from the larger web of environmental forces. Carl Jung as well, while more open than Freud to external influences on the mind, saw his concept of the collective unconscious as moulded by a range of culturally based symbols, with very few references to the earth. It is curious that

"Aegean Sea" oil spill
La Coruña, Spain
1992

Page 26
Portable Architecture
Cohos Evamy Partners
Alberta, Canada
1967

Commune life
1960s

Strip architecture
Los Angeles, California,
USA
1990s

Jung diagnosed his patients' dreams involving references to buildings and interiors as indicative of their desire to regain the lost security of the womb, or as evidence of their tendency to construct protective walls in the mind. Why, instead, didn't he interpret their visions of dwelling spaces as part of a universal instinct to find sanctuary again in the sheltering crevices of nature, or as evidence of a subliminal need to return to the primordial origins of the human habitat?

The basis of eco-psychology is to help people see the magnitude of their alienation from the natural environment and guide them toward finding ways to bridge this gap, rather than pursue a self-indulgent search for answers within the dead-end zone of the ego. This expansive horizon for the mind parallels the territories now being explored by radical ecologists, who declare that unless mankind re-connects in the most profound way with the integrated systems of nature, our species is doomed. This sinister overview is not mere apocalyptic hyperbole for dramatic effect. It is the product of a widening philosophical and scientific conviction that, if the technological world persists in its seemingly irreversible expansion of consumerism and its measure of all success in terms of financial rewards alone, the end may be nearer than we think.

In the face of this scenario, it has been a peculiar characteristic of Structuralist, post-

Structuralist, and Postmodernist philosophical discourse that virtually no hint of environmental awareness has appeared in the theoretical work of our leading voices in literary criticism and philosophy. Considering the much heralded quest for new definitions of meaning in linguistic analysis, it seems strangely insular that the principal coding mechanisms continue to be based on Freudian psychology and the stockpile of referential sources are still extracted mainly from consumer culture and politics. For example, the Structuralist theories of Jacques Lacan and Claude Lévi-Strauss have challenged the capacity of language to accurately communicate thought by using the relationships between "surface structure" (the signifier) and "deep structure" (that which is signified) as analytical tools in understanding the rituals of social interaction and the underpinnings of psychology. Post-Structuralist writers like Jacques Derrida and Michel Foucault have also questioned the nature of meaning and continuity in human communications by identifying inversions of language that, in some ways, parallel the investigations of chaos theory in science. Derrida has used the tactic of deconstruction to shatter the conventional surface readings of literature in order to question the reliability of language itself. Along a parallel course of reasoning, psychologist Foucault has analyzed confusing and misleading flaws in the "systematicity of discursive practices" by calling attention to the contradictions of interpretation between continuity and discontinuity, between saying and doing, reason and madness. In the semiotic studies of Roland Barthes and Jean Baudrillard, the signifier/signified concept embraces the pop culture iconography of signs, symbols, rituals, and systems as a threshold to understanding the ambiguous territory between real and imagined. Baudrillard describes a world where consumer culture has created a perilous state of illusion and detachment from reality, thereby producing a universal condition where simulation becomes the new reality. With the prodigious growth of the mass-media and cybernetic revolutions – the ultimate manifestations

You can create desolate wastelands of the spirit as well as of the environment.
You can scar people as well as land.

Ada Louise Huxtable

of his notion of ecstatic hopelessness in the face of excessive stimuli – the deterioration of meaning threatens to become an apocalypse of language debasement. The primary omission in this provocative argument is its failure to account for that day when the plug is pulled on the power systems. From the larger perspective – referring to that inevitable time when fossil fuel runs out (optimistic predictions estimate 100 years), when the electrical grids shut down, and when nature takes its just revenge – this kind of intellectual gamesmanship could come to be seen as quaintly myopic. In summary, the propositions of these major thinkers are drawn from such anthropocentric sources as popular culture (particularly fashion, advertising, and films), and the politics of racism and gender discrimination. From a literary perspective they have failed to connect with what poet Jay Parini has identified as the "actual universe of rocks, trees, and rivers that lies behind the wilderness of signs." While the argument could be made that all human endeavor is an extension of nature and therefore a part of the larger ecological picture, the fact remains that Post-modern philosophy has not focused on ecologically based paradigms and their connections to language and psychology as major sources of ideas for comparative analysis and theory. The key philosophical luminaries have remained narrowly confined within a typically ego- but not ecocentric frame of reference.

A totally opposite view is proposed by the "deep ecologists." Similar in some ways to structuralist theory in language (referring to the surface structure/deep structure concept), the deep ecology movement is based on radical propositions developed in the early 1970s by Norwegian professor Arne Naess. With his controversial claim that the human race is no more deserving of respect, protection, or continuity than any other organism, he has unleashed legions of eco-advocates functioning somewhat like shock troops for environmental action. The deep ecologists spare no one from responsibility and blame all humanity for the current crisis, pointing out that indus-

try could not prosper and pollute without the support of consumer choices; so, the entire solution to a potential ecological cataclysm is a massive propaganda campaign to reverse the global state of mind and expose the truth about technological delusion.

The foundations of deep ecology can be traced back to the nature-oriented religions of Zen Buddhism and Taoism, as well as environ-

View of Caracas slums
Venezuela
1970

**Aerial view
of mega mall**
USA
1996

Excessive drought
Senegal
1997

mentally friendly philosophers like St Francis, Spinoza, and, more recently, Rachel Carson. The major purpose of the movement is to change the paradigms which have distorted contemporary society's value systems, economies, and relationships to nature. For example, in 1967, prophetic writer Lynn White anticipated deep ecology's forceful critiques by identifying Christianity as the archetype of an anthropocentric religion and a prime illustration of the arrogant hypothesis that nature exists for man's convenience. From White's viewpoint, this global faith has done more to promote the 'dominance of the earth' folly than any other philosophical influence, and it shares, with the cult of consumerism, a voracious campaign to brainwash people into believing that more is better. He has proposed that Christianity, like any product-marketing industry, endorses the equation that more people means a larger constituency, increased power, and greater profits. Meanwhile every environmental expert on earth has warned that over-population is at the top of the list of aberrations leading to an ultimate apocalypse.

Part of the strength of deep ecology lies in the convincing checklist of facts and figures to support its doomsday theories and the avenues of practical and spiritual options that it offers to society as part of a sustainable life package. On one hand, Arne Naess paints a grim picture of humanity's chances of survival by proposing that a dread disease like Aids may simply be the beginning of nature's way

of trimming population and eliminating Homo sapiens (regarded, in the larger eco-scenario, as the earth's own cancer). At the other extreme, he heralds a new age of intelligent stewardship for the earth, where man returns to his appropriately humble role as only one small component of the total eco-system. To accomplish this, Naess sees the need for a radical revision of social structure and the introduction of what he calls the "ecological self ... in and of nature from the very beginning of our selves." He continues: "Society and human relationships are important, but our self is much richer in its constitutive relationships." Reflecting aboriginal cultures' seamless identification with the environment, Naess maintains that "my relation to this place is part of myself; if this place is destroyed, something in me is destroyed."

Deep ecology has defined the most radical and persuasive intellectual position of the 1990s. Its fundamental difference from the 60s tendency toward isolationism and individualism as a defense against environmental destruction is its plea for a decentralized, participatory, global eco-democracy. One ominous threat to this new paradigm is the popularity of the old one. There is alarming evidence that most of the optimistic events of the late 1980s – the liberation of Eastern Europe, the unification of Germany, the reduction of nuclear armaments, and the rise of Third World economies – may now have become nothing more than an exaggerated caricature of the familiar Western-style clamor for consumer products, wasteful technologies, and an ever-proliferating glut of mega-malls and fast food outlets. It is paradoxical that the same information explosion which led to universal awareness of the virtues of democracy did not manage to separate the concepts of human rights and environmental initiatives from the evils of Capitalism. An over-effective merchandising of freedom has backfired to become the cancerous spread of consumerism.

Arne Naess, forever the optimist, feels that a new wave of the "eco-philosophical" (or "ecosophy") may replace the merely ecological,

In our hearts we know there is something maniacal about the way we are abusing the planetary environment.

Theodore Roszak

which he sees as a limited science. He states: "By ecosophy I mean a philosophy of ecological harmony or equilibrium. A philosophy is a kind of sophia wisdom, is openly normative, it contains both norms, rules, postulates, value priority announcements, and hypotheses, concerning the state of affairs in our universe. Wisdom is policy wisdom, prescription, not only scientific description and prediction." He seems to be suggesting that deep ecology will be involved less with doomsday pronouncements and more with the development of a new earth-centered cosmology – approximating, perhaps, a new religion that is closer to the revolutionary ideas, beliefs, and policies that can bring humanity into alliance with nature and closer to the answer for survival.

This summary of ideas and issues in the ecology movement only touches the surface of a vastly complex dialogue, with an infinite variety of emotional reactions, philosophical theories, political positions, and proposals for remedial action. The bottom-line concession seems to be a worldwide agreement concerning the magnitude of the problem. As a counterpoint to the tendency toward euphoric optimism and as a general reminder of the reality at hand, it is sobering to be reminded of the magnitude of environmentally related problems and some of their statistics. These include:

■ Water supplies

Water tables are falling globally and, in major portions of the Middle East, Africa, and India, most communities consume more than half of their renewable water supplies. Over-population and economic expansion in these regions exacerbate the crisis. Other disturbing statistics include such facts as one-fifth of humanity consumes water that is not fit to drink and the construction of all forms of shelter consumes one-sixth of the world's water supply.

■ Lead in gasoline

Most of the developing countries of the world have not cooperated in reducing the lead content in motor vehicle fuels. In virtually all of China, Africa, and Eastern Europe – where automotive traffic is growing at alarming rates

– the lead percentage can be as high as 0.15 per litre. Depending on topographical features and climate conditions, this can cause serious physical and mental disorders.

■ Soil erosion

Naturally vegetated land surface – the best insurance policy against erosion – is being radically decreased worldwide each year as agricultural and industrial incursions reduce the soil's ability to restore its nutrients and maintain a stable structure. For example, China is the most affected by this crisis, where 3,500 million tons of eroded soil each year are deposited into riverbeds and lakes. One ominous result is the annual loss of 390 million cubic meters of its water storage capacity, causing an incremental increase in the construction of more dams and reservoirs.

■ Tropical rain forests

It is universal knowledge that rain forests are essential for global climate control and the survival of all living species. The clearing of these precious resources for reasons of farming, timber, and cattle ranches over the past decade alone has removed more than 8 percent of the world's tropical forests – reducing the area from 1,900 million hectares in 1980 to 1,700 million hectares in 1990.

Deforestation
Tofino Creek, Canada
1993

- Nuclear energy facilities

There are more than 430 operating nuclear reactors globally and all must be decommissioned at some point during the next 35 years at a cost of approximately $900 million per unit; and this refers to the cheapest available technology. In Great Britain alone, there are 54 reactors that will have to be shut down by 2060 at a price of £16 billion. As of this writing, there is no safe storage plan or adequate dump facility for nuclear waste anywhere in the world, while more than 10,000 tons of contaminated discard are being produced annually. It takes more than 150 years to successfully decommission a power station, and the most potent level of waste – plutonium – has a 29,000-year half-life. This means that no living creature can go anywhere near this radioactive garbage for a longer period than the entire history of civilization. To add a few more gloomy statistics: plutonium is still produced illegally and could easily serve some terrorist cause; there are increasing nuclear stockpiles being assembled as additional countries demand military parity in the world arena; industries and governments continue to advocate the construction of new nuclear plants; and, as a final footnote, the minuscule amount of nuclear waste from Enrico Fermi's original experiments has still not found a secure resting place.

- Population growth

The world's population is now 6 billion people, with an average annual growth of approximately 90 million. According to U.N. estimates, the population will continue to expand to a level of 11.9 billion by the year 2050 – adding, in effect, the population of three new Africas. Under this scenario, the demands on water supplies, land surfaces, and natural resources will be so overwhelming that some form of mass extinction may take place.

- Global warming

The potentially catastrophic rise of global temperatures, as a result of increasing greenhouse gases (CO_2), is another favorite candidate in the worldwide scenario. Scientists presently predict a global increase in temperature of 3.5 degrees Celsius by 2100. This warming tendency would cause ocean waters to expand through the melting of polar caps, raising sea levels 6 cm every ten years, and would essentially wipe out most major cities at sea level. General climate changes would destroy vast parts of the ecosystem, reduce the food-producing countries to a level far below demand, radically increase disease and famine in desert areas as water supplies disappear completely, and activate a greater frequency of floods, droughts, hurricanes, and tidal waves.

Returning to the topical concerns of this book – and in the face of the unstable future outlined above – the big question for the human habitat remains, what is the role of architecture? Most noticeably in the 20th century, the built environment has been more a part of the problem than the solution. The irresponsible wastefulness associated with construction technology, heating, and cooling have only been the beginning of architecture's assaults on natural resources. For reasons of its association in the public mind with aggressive intrusions on the land – blasting out holes, leveling forests, paving wetlands, befouling the soil – the architectural profession has been targeted by critics as one of the most culpable of the environmental enemies. But this high profile can be converted to an advantage. By advancing the argument that architecture has the dual responsibility to help solve environmental problems, as well as visually celebrate the results, it can become the quintessential public herald of eco-centrism and ecosophy. The environmental revolution can only succeed realistically one small step at a time, and architecture is one of its most visible chroniclers of progress. This role of the building arts confirms the now more restrained views of Arne Naess who, today, feels "impatient with the doomsday prophets and confident that we have a mission, however modest, in shaping a better future that is *not remote*."

Nuclear Power Station
Sir Basil Spence
Trawsfynydd, Wales
1959

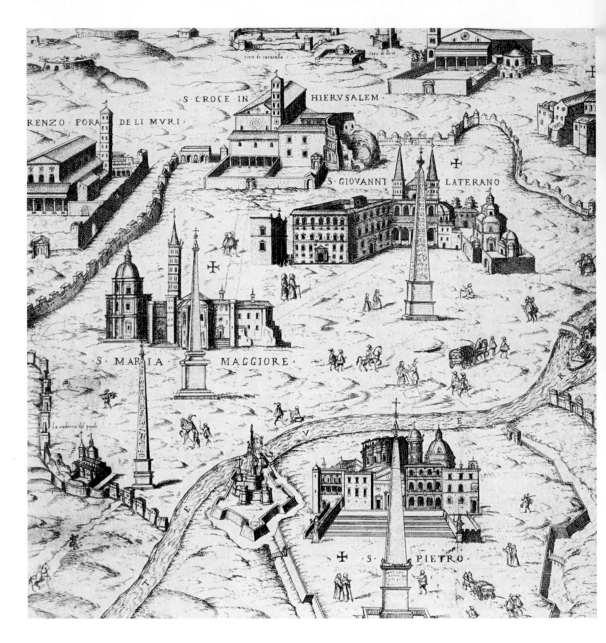

**Sisto Quinto's plan
for Rome**
G. F. Bordino
Rome, Italy
1588

It is one thing just to use the earth: it is quite another thing to receive the blessing of the earth and to become at home in the law of this reception, in order to shepherd the mystery of being and to pay attention to the inviolability of the possible.

Martin Heidegger

We know that the white man does not understand our ways. He is a stranger who comes in the night and takes from the land whatever he needs. The earth is not his friend, but his enemy, and when he's conquered it he moves on. He kidnaps the earth from his children. His appetite will devour the earth and leave behind a desert. If all the beasts were gone, we would die from a great loneliness of the spirit, for whatever happens to the beasts happens to us. All things are connected. Whatever befalls the Earth, befalls the children of the Earth.

American Indian Chief Seattle

Eco-Philosophy and Early Green History

Architecture is one of the most dependable reflections of a civilization's philosophical foundations. This is not to say, simply because some past municipality has built impressive monuments, paradisiacal gardens, and a sustainable habitat, that this society somehow represented a paragon of spirituality, benevolence, and ecological enlightenment. To the contrary, certain notoriously despotic monarchies have constructed the most aesthetically magnificent and ecologically responsible civic works, while some admirable democracies have left only oppressive architectural voids and environmental devastation. For example, this paradox is amply illustrated by the tyrannical Pope Sisto Quinto in 16th-century Italy, whose consummate urban designs for Rome still define the beauty of this city; versus the interminable and featureless wasteland of middle America's "land of the free" tract houses and merchandise malls. The point is that, even if the true motivations or political policies of sponsorship are not directly reflected in what is built, the ultimate story of a society – hidden or disclosed, truthful or hypocritical – is there to be read by future generations. The most impressive examples of architectural iconography and municipal planning usually relate to a fully resolved integration of social structure, governmental policy, religious rituals, and people's relationship to the environment. It invariably reveals a strong motivating philosophy that has inspired and sustained a culture; whereas, conversely, the least convincing examples of building imagery and city planning generally reflect a weak or corrupted ideology.

There is an endless litany of apocalyptic scenarios being predicted by ecologists, scientists, economists, politicians, and self-appointed doomsayers today. It is based on their collective view that humanity has failed in its commitment to an ecologically favorable philosophy. As mentioned earlier in a review of the disturbing observations of eco-psychology, 20th-century societies universally lost contact with the earth on a level unprecedented in history. The opportunities for a reversal of this catastrophic trend are usually lost to political expedience, popular ignorance, and environmental programs biased in favor of economic advantage. From a policy-making perspective, governments will now admit to the magnitude of environmental destruction, but rarely even think about the level of philosophical and tactical reversal needed to find solutions. As evidence of this limited commitment, now that the issue of global warming is a confirmed fact (and not just a controversial theory), the international business and government communities are holding a series of urgent conferences to seek global remedies. While the intentions are admirable, the inevitable compromises are still based on maintaining the status quo in terms of the definition of 'progress.' The bottom line is always focused on adjusting environmental reform to accommodate the insular objectives of profit margins, stock values, interest rates, employment levels, gross national product, etc. – seldom on considerations of fundamental change in the entire structure of economic values and the re-training of large segments of the work force in preparation for growth industries like waste management and environmental technology.

Simultaneously, there are some reasons for optimism. International government organizations now favor the establishment of a binding worldwide policy where industrial and

Mega mall interior
Ohio, USA
1996

national economic success can no longer be measured purely on productivity and monetary growth. Instead, progress must be evaluated in terms of ecological impact. In this way, the costs of environmental restoration resulting from the depletion of resources, quantity of pollution produced, and other forms of damage must appear as deductions from profits on all balance sheets as both an immediate deficit and a long-term liability.

All such environmentally friendly actions tend to be only temporary technological and economic band-aids applied to the ever-increasing potential for an imminent doomsday. On the most profound level there is the challenge of developing a worldwide ecological philosophy and, with this incentive in place, a potential for the most revolutionary change in the way human society functions since the invention of agriculture. At the risk of attaching too much importance to this issue, it is probably not an exaggeration to predict that humanity's ultimate salvation may rest on finding the equivalent of an eco-religion which governs environmental responsibility and offers salvation through a philosophy of "connectedness." This total fusion of mind and nature is at the root of any true earth-oriented experience. With a few isolated exceptions found in aboriginal cultures, most of the world today lives in a linear state of compulsive profit motive and consumer-based technocracy. These conditions are trapped within an illusion of progress and a reality of traumatic

"disconnectedness." In his environmentally concerned writings, Heidegger has seen the dangers of this alienating condition and has described a more desirable state of connectedness as follows: "The experience of earth yields transformation. Put another way: to focus one's thinking on earth recycles the energy that flows through the earth – and through humans as part of the earth – and transmutes human energy such that we know our being-one-with-the-earth, or more generally; our being-connected, connectedness as such, interbeing. Parenthetically, it is my contention that only this experience of connectedness will save the earth – and us with it. Any attempt, however grandiose and with however much commitment to its cause, will fall short if it does not have at its root this transformation of human experience in which human thinking knows connectedness as such and itself within that."

Returning to the focus on architecture, this need for a philosophical grounding is at the foundation of any hope for a sane ecological approach to design. Given the seemingly irreversible consumption of fossil fuel, expansion of consumer markets, and unbridled technological advancements, the search for alternatives is severely compromised. Under these circumstances, any suggestion of a new philosophy in the building arts that might contradict these rapacious forces and radically alter entrenched design criteria is not likely to find widespread sympathy. At the same time, an earth-centric approach is the only option for the human habitat to regain its iconographic and functional relevance.

One obvious source of environmental enlightenment is to turn to those ancient and/or still existing cultures that have been predicated on a state of connectedness with nature. The danger of this choice is a tendency toward nostalgic glorification of some isolated, eco-responsive, aboriginal society that is totally removed from today's high-tech world. On the other hand, the lessons of these civilizations and their cosmologies reveal a wealth of insights into the evolution of the human habitat that cannot be ignored. They also provide instructive examples of how to deal with climate and demonstrate ideas, attitudes, and low-tech solutions that can still be incorporated into contemporary shelter. Most importantly, these cultures offer the basis for re-thinking our relation to the earth.

It is sobering to acknowledge that organized societies – meaning those based on some kind of shared resources and governing system – have existed for less than 30,000 years. Any form of shelter that can be regarded as "designed" architecture has been around only 10,000 years. And, finally, this entire intricate structure we call civilization has evolved primarily as the beneficiary of a 15,000-year freak phenomenon of ideal climatic conditions. Nature's more consistent character is typified by a brutal and inhospitable scenario of volcanic eruptions, tidal waves, ice ages, and lethal chemical emissions. The human species, in its more advanced state, has experienced nature only as a condition of rare paradisiacal interlude; as an Eden-like sanctuary, functioning on its atypical best behavior. In a dangerously naive way, we take this condition for granted.

Certain ancient civilizations, and a few existing cultures we condescendingly refer to as "primitive", have understood the unique blessings of the earth. This means they have feared the loss of its endowments sufficiently to create insurance policies in terms of ceremonial gratitude to help guarantee nature's continued benevolence. Present day Western societies have neither the environmental appreciation, nor the ritualized observances. Instead, the earth is erroneously seen as an endowed bank account. There seems to be a universal illusion that resources can be infinitely withdrawn without re-investment (and usually without even paying the interest rates). When this profligate excess is occasionally thwarted by nature's revenge – in the form of global warming, the spread of disease, or other ominous warnings – the industrialized societies' reaction is a resentment of the reprimand and the pursuit of some diversionary,

but usually even more destructive, alternative tactic.

While the ecology movement today can be credited with raising public consciousness concerning the perils of technocentrism and the folly of trying to "conquer nature", we have no equation in industrial societies for that infinite state of connectedness that is at the foundation of an ecology-based philosophy in aboriginal cultures. For example, anthropologist David Croft describes the basis for this spiritual void as related to the definition of soul: "While Western traditions used the concept of the soul to divide humans from non-humans, aboriginal groups such as the Aranda used the concept of soul as a bond between themselves and other species. ... Several interesting points can be made about the intimate relationship between traditional aborigines and their environment: First, contrary to the dominant Western social paradigm, the Wik's and the Aranda's [tribal groups] moral realms do not stop with the human species. Other species and the landscape are part of it. ... While they do not attribute to other species anything approaching what may be called inherent value, they do recognize that other species have their own interests and that other species are entitled to

Neolithic hut
c. 3000 B.C.

Cave dwellings
Cappadocia, Turkey
c. 1000

pursue these interests. While ritual participation may not be the form Western commitment to the environment and other species would or could take, the lesson to be learned is that of intimate involvement, rather than an affected air of superiority."

Expanding on this issue of environmental ethics in the industrialized world, author Holmes Rolston III asks: "How far are humans so continuous with nature that they must accept environmental limits? Is the steady state, for instance, compatible with unending progress? Does it compel a no-growth economy, or even a reduction of our standard of living? To answer we need an inventory of potential resources in materials and energy, but we also need to employ axioms about an ever-advancing technology, limitless scientific development, what counts as betterment, and the wits of man in bypassing nature's limits. The presumption of ecological spokesmen are strikingly reminiscent of the debate about geographical determination – the belief that the physical environment significantly limits and fixes the character of a society. Humans must

submit to and operate with certain natural, ecological givens." Furthermore, these givens must be regarded as spiritual connections to the entire infrastructure of ecology, as universally shared survival mechanisms, as earth celebration rituals, and as the source of a living iconography. These commitments assume that the concept of the soul is seen not as separate from nature, but as a part of it.

Looking at architecture as a chronicler of man's relation to the environment, it is useful to trace its evolution throughout the millennia. Strangely, there is no consistent record of steady improvement or evidence that, because one previous culture was environmentally accomplished, the succeeding generation learned from its model. To the contrary, depending on the strength of its philosophy (or relative fear of nature's revenge), each past civilization seems to have risen and fallen based on its capacity to achieve a balance with nature. It is a history without logical chronology or rational structure. The only consistent pattern seems to be based on the fact that the most exploitative cultures usually committed some form of environmental suicide.

The origin of all habitats is troglodyte living (cave dwellings), and it is a tradition that wisely continues in some parts of the world. There is a wrongful assumption among some architectural historians that Homo sapiens did not take command of his full mental and organizational potential until the development of free-standing buildings and the social hierarchy such independent structures represent. Certainly the advent of the house and its evolution into the village, aligned with the discovery of agriculture (history's first truly radical innovation), represented cultural progress; but this had more to do with expedience and the first assertions of control over nature – not necessarily a philosophical or environmentally friendly commitment.

Now that sophisticated cave paintings in France have been found to be more than 17,000 years old, one can surmise that these extraordinary works performed a function not unlike the Internet of prehistoric times. This suggests that caves had all of the iconographic significance of free-standing houses and even the status of ritual monuments. This further indicates the existence of an enormously progressive and organized society that saw shelter as an extension of nature's provisions, not as an imposition. The definition of architecture as an independent and intrusive object in its context is not necessarily synonymous with cultural advancement. On the other hand, once this definition became the criterion for a perceived control over nature, it marked the beginning of buildings being used as propaganda vehicles for governmental power, environmental conquest, religious doctrines based on human superiority, and ego-centric deities forged in Man's own image. From these ancestral origins, architecture became the single most potent messenger of anthropocentrism – a role it has served ever since.

On the most essential levels, troglodyte dwellings and structures made of sun-baked mud and other indigenous materials are ecologically friendly. Caves and underground habitats – including the subterranean villages of Shensi and Kansu in China, Cappadocia in Turkey, the Malmata area of Tunisia, and the Siwa region in Egypt – take advantage of virtually all that nature provides. They do not impose unreasonably on their environment, they do not negatively affect regional ecology, and they do not require high levels of energy consumption for heating or cooling since their consistently comfortable interior temperature is guaranteed by earthen enclosure. Similarly, mud-brick architecture relies on solar heat for hardening and strength. As opposed to the burning of fossil fuel or wood to harden masonry, the raw material of mud is abundant and its insulating value to a finished building in a hot and arid climate is exceptional. The origins of underground and mud architecture are pre-historic and originally based on pure expedience by their builders, who simply used their intelligence to construct accommodations out of locally available resources. In time, however, each of these forms of habitat became more and more ritualized and consciously

designed, resulting in overwhelmingly beautiful examples, such as the fresco-covered cave churches of Cappadocia, or the tower mosques of Mali in Africa. In these examples, the fundamental aesthetic power derives from the sense that every architectural detail is an extension of context. While their pragmatic elements of functional shelter are obvious, contrary to the orthodoxy of Modernist design, the relationships between form and service never seem to

Cave paintings
Lascaux, Dordogne, France
c. 17000 B.C.

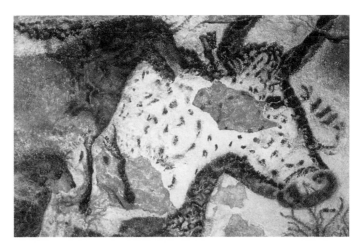

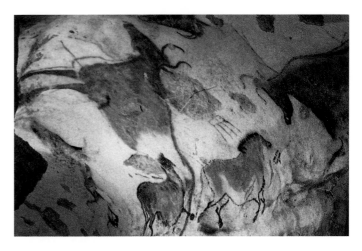

The Great Mosque
Djenne, Mali
c. 1400, rebuilt 1906–07

have been the primary motivation. In a strange way, this kind of architecture suggests the opposite of those contemporary conceits related to sustainability (which frequently means some form of ecological camouflage disguising long-term investment ambitions). Even though these structures are built with durable materials and ecologically sound principles, they project the mystical impression of being in a state of metamorphosis. They appear to be simultaneously emerging from and returning into the earth, suggesting a capacity to be absorbed and recycled in perpetuity as a condition of pure spirit.

The premise of this discussion – the proposition that without a consensus green philosophy architecture is doomed to a pattern of environmental delinquency and iconographic irrelevance – must be addressed on contemporary terms. The economists and politicians are probably right; the first stage of change in any field is to start with the world as

it is (not as compared to the idyllic perception of some past culture that has no bearing on current realities). Relative to architecture, their claim would be that the priority systems and cosmologies of nomads, aboriginals, and low-technology civilizations, however environmentally instructive, simply cannot be applied to today's industrial world with its alarming population explosion and universal dependence on fossil fuels and international communications. At the opposite extreme of this argument, many advocates of deep ecology propose that it is only through a massive reversal of technocentrism and anthropocentrism that humanity has any hope of survival. There is persuasive evidence to support this contention, as global warming increases, natural disasters take an ever greater toll, and technological operations break down with greater frequency. Ominously, while the relentless acceleration of economic growth continues unabated, the electrical power systems that run the show are more vulnerable to failure and the news of generator and distribution grid breakdowns in various parts of the globe is becoming commonplace. If the electricity goes out, the world basically grinds to a halt. If this happens, as most religious prophets have predicted, "the meek will inherit the earth." The radical ecologists envision a sooner-rather-than-later "earth reduced to its primal state" scenario and have proposed extreme (but essentially unworkable) measures to prepare for this impending day of reckoning.

Somewhere in between the options of continuing the great techno-onslaught and retreating to a simple nomadic lifestyle there is probably some kind of rational and workable approach to the future. The task is not without its radical demands. From the perspective of architecture, these challenges become the combination of a total re-evaluation of educational process and conventional design criteria. For instance, just as commerce and industry must decide that the profitability of environmental protection and recycling is greater than unchecked expansion, the building arts must totally embrace the ecological initiative at the expense of holding on to unproductive traditional values. Like business, the vested interests in architecture are so entrenched and the reversal process so demanding that revolutionary action is the only viable choice.

This revolution is unlikely to take the form of humanity's en masse return to the wilderness, or a popular craze for living in grass huts; still, there will probably be some clear-cut ecological standards and an ethical and philosophical frame of reference from which the new architecture will emerge. While these standards should not be prescriptive in terms of aesthetic choices, the ethical issues could become another matter. Throughout history, and in almost all societies, architects have undertaken even questionable assignments, regardless of the environmental or moral consequences. The most debased manifestations of this willingness to accommodate political authorities were the competitive design bids for detention centers and concentration

camps, even torture facilities and gas chambers. It is a grotesque legacy made even more incomprehensible by the record of architects' solicitous letters to the authorities in response to requests for change orders that made the intended process more efficient. On a less overtly savage level – yet also morally reprehensible, given designers' ultimate contribution to an environmental Armageddon – there is the fervent jumping through hoops architects are willing to perform for a commission to erect the world's tallest skyscraper (the most anti-ecological of all building types) or the opportunity to bulldoze an indigenous natural landscape in favor of a gambling casino. Part of the new eco-morality will rest with architects and their capacity to persuade clients to make responsible environmental choices (at the very least, for economic reasons); but also to convince builders of the future to see the value of an earth-centered philosophy, based on connectedness.

**Aerial view of
Singapore City**
Singapore
1990s

Aboriginal shelter
Northern Territories,
Australia

Returning to the lessons of history, this continued review of past architecture is useful only as a demonstration of choices in philosophical principles, as an assessment of archetypes that have proven to be environmentally successful, and as a means of evaluating earth-centered models that still have currency today. The premise here is that architects presently face a daunting negative reality which will progressively force them to change their role and their product. Obviously, if a massive power failure occurs, this argument becomes academic and the warnings of the deep ecologists will become vindicated prophecies. Taking a more positive position, it is equally possible that electricity will prevail through wise choices in alternative energy sources, toxic damage of the past 100 years will be reversed as environmental technology becomes one of the highest profit enterprises of the 21st century, and the information revolution will serve the cause of eco-centrism by expanding knowledge of the ecological crisis and its solutions. Hopefully these assumptions are not a product of unwarranted optimism.

The history of a true eco-philosophy in architecture can be seen as a contradiction in terms. Certainly the most environmentally responsible shelter was developed by nomadic cultures where, in some cases, it barely existed at all (referring to simple clusters of tree branches and palm leaves which blew away in the next strong wind), or choices where protection from the elements meant a retreat into the nearest available cave or rock formation.

These choices made no commitment to architecture as an aesthetic or iconographic entity in itself and no demand on natural resources. Expedience, more than philosophy, motivated this approach, and tribal cosmology was usually expressed through totemic rituals, rather than associated with permanent structures.

The appearance of the dolmens and earth mounds – characteristic of Paleolithic and Neolithic monuments – represents the earliest evidence of true organized cosmologies and ceremonial recognition of nature's capacity to bestow or withhold its blessings. While little is known of the true intentions of these early monuments, it is interesting to note that habitats in Neolithic cultures were relatively primitive: just webs of bones and branches covered with animal skins or woven thatch, while their commemorative sites were impressive. Anthropologists seem united in the view that these societies had relatively sophisticated interpretations of nature, successful agriculture, and a complex set of rituals that responded to astrological influences, burial rites, religious beliefs, and what the 18th-century philosopher Edmund Burke has referred to as "a terror of the sublime." In a remarkable 1757 treatise, *A Philosophical Enquiry into the Origin of our Idea of the Sublime and Beautiful*, Burke's observation that "all edifices calculated to produce an idea of the sublime ought to be dark and gloomy" perfectly characterizes virtually every awesome monument from Stonehenge to the Gothic Cathedral. This universal condition of a subliminal awe of the unknown and a fear of nature's vengeful forces became a hinge point in eco-philosophy, where human response can basically take one of two directions – humble cooperation or aggressive resistance. In the most ancient societies, the fear element probably prevailed. Evidence from remaining fragments of oral history (the best example being Australian Aboriginal accounts of "Dream Time") seems to confirm that the earliest mythologies were dominated by tales of natural catastrophes, where an insurance against such events was based on ceremonial appeasement of the gods.

Stonehenge
Salisbury Plain, England
c. 3200–1600 B.C.

Druid ceremonial circle
Avebury, England
c. 3000 B.C.

Let us a little permit nature to take her own way, she better understands her own ways than we.

Michel de Montaigne

Less than two decades ago aboriginal society was considered, by Western standards, to be populated with uninteresting primitive people, wandering around in an inhospitable environment, worshipping totems, and conditioning their behavior in deference to some metaphysical fantasy. With the rising importance of the ecology movement and the expansion of interest in survival through communication with nature, the aborigines have become the primary focus of intense anthropological study and the heroes of sane environmental policy. As the realization increases in the West that our fundamental way of life may be doomed by profligate excess, there is a desperate exploration of alternative lifestyles that may hold some answers. The aborigines' spiritual view of their place in nature is the polar opposite of everything technocentric culture stands for. It graphically illustrates just how far the so-called civilized world has distanced itself from the integrated processes necessary for survival.

Western society's usual response to disruptive environmental occurrences, like earthquakes, floods, fires, and hurricanes, is to express disbelief over the effrontery of nature's assaults, identify targets of blame (political

inaction or engineering incompetence), demand that technology find solutions, and condemn the event as a "natural disaster." These reactions represent prime examples of a dangerously uninformed environmental detachment. An aborigine would not even begin to understand the absurdity of this victim mentality. Furthermore, he would probably draw the simple conclusion that these dreaded catastrophes are not necessarily natural, but instead, man-made, disasters. From this perspective, it becomes blatantly obvious that if the community had not paved over the wetlands, the flood waters would have been absorbed and the township would not be submerged. If people had not built flimsy dwellings on the hillside over a fault line, an earthquake would not have tumbled their houses into the valley. If developers had not erected sub-standard condominiums on tropical beaches in a hurricane zone, the buildings wouldn't be blown into the sea on an annual basis.

One remarkable aspect of aboriginal culture is the concept of "totemism," where the tribal member at birth assumes the soul and identity of a part of nature. This view of the earth and its riches as an intrinsic part of oneself – called animism – clearly precludes mistreatment of the environment because this would only constitute a destruction of self. Totems are more than objects. They include spiritual rites, oral histories, cult societies within tribes, and the organization of ceremonial lodges where records of the past travel routes of the soul can be exchanged with others and converted to mythology. The primary motivation is the preservation of tribal myths and a consolidation and sharing of every individual's origins in nature. The aborigines see their relationship to the environment as a single harmonious continuum, through a hierarchy of totems that connect to their ancestral origins, a cosmology that places them at one with the earth, and behavior patterns that respect ecological balance.

The most complex concept in aboriginal culture – and the one virtually impossible for

Stilt houses
Hollywood Hills,
Los Angeles, California,
USA
1995

an outsider to completely understand – is the condition known as "The Dreaming." It does not refer, in any conventional sense, to the Western definition of a dream as some form of hallucination, apparition, or means of access to the sub-conscious, as in psychotherapy. In a study of non-Western cultures James Cowan describes it thus: "The Dreaming is, first and foremost, a metaphysical condition denoting the working of the divine principles dressed up in the garb of totemic heros. The myth is their expressive vehicle. ... No other condition more poignantly expresses an aborigine's relationship with the Dreaming than his totemic identity. For it is an act of identifying with 'something other' than himself that allows a tribesman the opportunity to transcend ordinary reality in an act of union. His totem is both his alter ego and a metaphysical landmark which orients him while he lives. ... Not to have a double or shadow in the world is to be condemned to an inferior existence governed by the here and now, rather than by the mysterious plausibilities said to have occurred during the time of The Dreaming."

This phenomenon of "Dream Time" seems to have both metaphysical and ecological implications. There are parallels to ideas in modern science and philosophy, where concepts of time include conjecture about the condition of being – proposing that we are knots of energy brought together by the laws of physics – and that our real existence may be only as clustered particles recycled in perpetuity. The Dreaming also appears somewhat like the Western scientific description of a curving space which runs into itself and thus fuses past, present, and future into an endless continuum. To the credit of the Aboriginal sense of correctedness, their concept of parallel existences in both the immediate world and as part of a timeless infinity has a marked similarity to some of the most sophisticated propositions of astrophysics today.

The system of totemic identity, as a condition of dualities where one's soul is shared by the self and an alter ego in nature, has intriguing implications for ecology. "All possi-

ble human temperamental variations can be embraced in the act of symbolic identification with nature," explains James Cowan. "It is a remarkable system. ... What is at work here is, if in an obscure way, a form of ecological classification linking all nature into an overall pattern. It is this ecological classification that might bear further investigation, in the interest of discovering whether there may be a pairing in nature designed to preserve its balance and harmony between species. If this is so, then aboriginal thought may have provided us with an important new system of classification that can be used as a part of environmental protection." Certainly one of the most useful lessons evident here is the fact that the aboriginal totem acts as a conscience, guiding tribal and individual relationships with the natural environment. It is an excellent model of a societal monitoring system built into the culture and its collective unconscious. This system is the opposite of Western civilizations' response to ecology, which can usually be characterized as some kind of self-conscious compromise or begrudging concession to duty.

Unfortunately, the levels of environmental sensitivity and resourcefulness represented by a few rare aboriginal groups only provide a checklist of admirable standards against which our Western ecological track record can be unfavorably compared. The groups also represent vulnerable and residual societies, seemingly left over from prehistory, that have somehow miraculously survived in isolated areas of

Aboriginal cave painting
Northern Territories,
Australia
Repainted annually

Mud brick buildings
Berber Village, Tunisia

times to the present, this heritage appears to include a consistent pattern of increasingly obsessive anthropocentrism. Depending on regional climate, topography, access to resources, and religious and political influences, there have been some outstanding examples of cultures in balance with nature. Unfortunately, these sustainable successes are few and far between. We tend to admire the poetry and mystique of those mud brick cities of Africa and the Middle East, the garden architecture of Persia, and the hill towns of Italy with the view that their builders might have been early emissaries of an ecological mission. True, the masterful fusion of buildings with context, the consummate invention with local materials, the innovative uses of low-level technology, and the imaginative conversion of all these factors into art offer much to admire. The reality of history, however, indicates that these exemplary communities were more often the product of expedient construction techniques than any attempt at environmentally conscious design. Much of their compelling beauty – although rooted in religious and civic celebration – was simply a result of the lack of fossil fuel-driven machinery, the unavailability of industrially manufactured (meaning impersonal) building products, and the inherent appeal of hand-made architecture.

The anthropocentric concept of Man at the center of the universe and the parallel manufacture of deities forged in the human image could only have come out of the luxury of an extended period of relative atmospheric and geological stability. It reinforced the conceit that nature exists for the convenience of humans. Naturally, this vision has undergone an infinite number of definitions and revisions throughout history; but the underlying theme has remained relatively constant, producing such extremes of environmental success and failure as civilizations that have scripted their own demise in less than a few decades to others that endured for thousands of years.

In most of the ancient world, a generally benign climate reinforced the illusion of mankind's power over nature, and the occasional

Australia, Africa, South America, and North America. But they are now fast succumbing to the various corrupting influences of Western invasion (and, in a few cases, headed toward cultural extinction). In a perverse way, nature seems to be offering us these archetypes of sane environmental policy, but making it impossible to access them for reasons of our own blinding aggressive behavior. This fundamental conflict of the modern world was accurately predicted by Søren Kierkegaard in 1854: "Destroy your primitivity and you will most probably get along well in the world, maybe achieve great success – but Eternity will reject you. Follow up your primitivity and you will be shipwrecked in temporality, but accepted by Eternity."

Returning to the more linear and familiar heritage of Western societies from Neolithic

disruptions caused by natural disasters – earthquakes, hurricanes, volcanic eruptions, etc. – could be explained away as expressions of displeasure by the gods. These occurrences were used as convenient evidence that the deities really existed and deserved the respect of fear and worship. From this simple hypothesis, the entire superstructure of early civilization was born. The civilizations of Mesopotamia, Egypt, Sumeria, and Greece needed emissaries to appease the gods and function as messengers of divine intervention for the people. This led to the building of social hierarchies where priests and monarchs took charge of keeping the deities happy through spiritual enforcement. Since appeasement demanded cash flow, massive economies and tax structures were developed to pay for all the sacred monuments and administrative overheads. This ingenious premise for social order had the dual advantage (primarily for those in charge) of creating an elite class in command of the environment and an underclass subjugated by the fear of divine retribution. It was a rather paradoxical situation, since religion combined with politics to pay tribute to the powers of nature. This hierarchy demanded awe and supplication from the populace and, at the same time, permitted the ruling classes to violate the land in any way deemed profitable or expedient.

Our confused ecological policies today are simply a legacy of these ancient priority systems; with the additional problem of an unprecedented growth of industrial "conquer-the-earth" mentality and its folly of absolute sovereignty over nature. Whatever the ecclesiastical prescriptions and fears of divine reprisal that kept earlier societies in check, these restraints have all but disappeared in the contemporary world.

A major flaw in most organized faiths today, like the deceptive fetishism of consumer culture, is their provision of pacifying therapy and feel-good absolution based on strictly introspective indulgences. People will listen distractedly as ecologists and a few concerned religious leaders weave grim tales of an immi-

Persian garden drawing
c. 1400

nent environmental Armageddon; but, in general, these messages don't enter the collective unconscious as a code of survival. Instead, they are treated as peripheral fragments of information to be filed away. They are seen as descriptions of futuristic scenarios that do not affect daily life and as bothersome reprimands for wasteful behavior like failing to conserve fuel oil or recycle old newspapers.

Scenes from Genesis
San Marco, Venice, Italy
Mosaic, c. 1200

The Parthenon
Phidias
Athens, Greece
447–432 B.C.

The earliest archaeological records of an agriculturally and politically well-developed civilization can be found in Jericho of 8000 B.C. It is regarded as the first documented example of a truly permanent community and center of trade. Jericho was a major supplier of grain in the ancient world and invested those leaders who controlled its production and storage with godlike characteristics (probably evidence of an emerging anthropocentricism); and, in fact, the granaries were considered to be temples of worship. The culture apparently did have a well-developed sense of environmental stewardship, and there is physical confirmation that the community built an elaborate – but discretely controlled – system of irrigation canals, kept a sustainable balance between farmland and natural vegetation, and understood the principles of soil conservation.

When Jericho was taken over by the Sumerians around 3000 B.C., the foundations were laid for ecological cataclysm. Through economic greed and a desire to radically increase the marketplace for grain, the invaders expanded the network of canals to a point where arable land was reduced and no provisions were made to filter out the saline deposits left by seasonal rains and overflow activity. As a result, essential drainage was eliminated, the canals filled in with silt, and vast areas of fertile soil were rapidly depleted. In a very short time a once flourishing agricultural economy came to a halt, and the entire culture went into decline. It must be remembered that these mistakes were made by a community that understood the bounties of nature, planted elaborate gardens and arcades to demonstrate this appreciation, built an economy around the value of water, and then sacrificed everything for short-term profits. It is a familiar scenario. The entire history of civilization is pock-marked with these ecological black holes, usually growing out of situations where one society has demonstrated a remarkable capacity to build, plant, harvest, irrigate, and use resources prudently, while the following generation has committed environmental suicide.

Domestic architecture in the ancient world was rarely responsible for ecological problems (other than those associated with sanitation and disposal of wastes) and, in fact, much of its heritage of innovation has become a paragon of environmental intelligence that continues to be studied today by contemporary architects. The guiding philosophies behind the urban plans and houses were relatively simple, and their lingering influence on green construction processes and artistic standards was mostly the result of a consensus set of aesthetic choices refined over the centuries. They also reflected the collective interests of the community in terms of imagery, respected the limitations of nature, and utilized sustainable construction techniques. On the other hand, the ambitious visions of religion and government were more problematic, since these forces determined the larger societal priorities and controlled the economies. This leadership also established – whether by purposeful policy or neglectful default – the philosophical context through which any civilization's ecological legacy can be judged.

Continuing this comparative overview of ecological links in the religions and societal behavior patterns of ancient cultures, it simply confirms a steady, if erratic, trend toward anthropocentric theology. At the same time, the concept of one god as the alter ego of man appeared as a hit-and-miss choice among different nations over a few thousand years' period. A great deal seems to have depended on how much reliance on nature the ruling classes and priests felt their society should acknowledge, versus the benefits of crediting the monarchy with transcendental powers and thus maintaining control through divine association. Some cultures preferred to have a complex heavenly bureaucracy representing all the beneficial features of nature in the form of separate gods for the sun, wind, rain, fertility, etc. These deities could capriciously bestow or withdraw their blessings if not appeased, thus keeping the people in a state of anxiety and supplication. Another choice was to endow a single ruling figure with the status of god-king, consolidating all of the religious and political sovereignty in one place. To complicate these definitions, sometimes the god-kings would embrace a form of animism – meaning a concession that other creatures in nature possess a soul – and then assume anthropomorphic identities themselves, where iconography would depict them as supreme beings suspended somewhere between animal and human.

Egyptian societies from about 4000 to 2000 B.C. appear to have had a productive program of environmental conservation, based on a keen understanding of how the Nile Valley functioned and a realization that unless commercial interests respected its seasonal rhythms the entire society would collapse. It could be speculated that if mechanized cranes and earth-moving equipment had been available to the ancient Egyptians, all of this deference to nature would have been converted to re-routing the waterways, dredging the Nile, building bridges, and constructing dams. To the contrary, the Nile Valley flourished for mil-

Excavations of Tel al-Sultan
Jericho, Israel

lennia primarily because land and water were well managed without advanced technology, and cities deferred to the climate by constructing buildings in protective clusters based on solar principles. At the opposite extreme, the more ostentatious Pharaohs built pyramids and temples to themselves that brought the display of commemorative excess to a level never attained before or since.

The anthropomorphic associations in Egyptian religious life seem to have worked well for this ancient society since it provided the bridge between a multitheistic mythology rooted in nature and a monotheistic structure essentially placing the monarchy above nature. The representative god system paid homage to every major environmental force (assuring the continuous fertility of the Nile Valley); at the same time, it invested the Pharaoh with all of the transcendental qualifications needed to rule the kingdom as an unchallenged divinity. Philosophically complex, the rationales for this hierarchy must have developed out of a 'take-no-chances' approach to theology. It was organized to function simultaneously as an acknowledgment of nature's demand for respect and as a vindication for the profligate indulgences of the ruling class. Additionally, this mythology's vast range of narrative imagery – depictions of anthropomorphic gods, fantasy gardens, astrological charts, battle scenes, feats of heroism, domestic life, and Nile Valley commerce – spoke of a society that helped sustain its power through the richness of its iconography.

The Egyptian resistance to changing this highly workable and iconographically potent system was readily demonstrated by a short-lived flirtation with monotheism during the reign of Pharaoh Ikhnaton (1385 B.C.), when this ill-advised ruler tried to establish Amon, the sun-god, as the single deity. Even though this choice probably paralleled other monotheistic religions – especially the rise of Judaism – the Egyptians rejected his theology in less than one generation and all of the former deities were restored during the subsequent reign of Tutankhamen.

The educational value of examining cultures of the ancient world in the context of today's ecological politics offers an opportunity to identify remarkable similarities between these communities and our contemporary equivalents in capitalist economies. There is also the challenge of trying to sort out some useful philosophical models that might influence the future of architectural design. In the case of the Egyptians, the religious connection to animism and the multiple deities associated with natural phenomena were decisive factors shaping their sense of ecological responsibility. The Egyptians placed an obligatory cap on environmental exploitation, creating a series of ceremonies and icons that served as everyday reminders of the parameters and the penalties. In the present day, we have no equivalent of this cap. The persistent warnings of science and some compromised industrial clean-up programs represent our only environmental acknowledgments – and these are strictly remedial, not spiritual.

Virtually all the religions of the world had some association with animism and, if not exactly representative of the strong eco-centric connectedness found in aboriginal cultures, at least gave plants and animals an important place in their hierarchic structure. In a few cases, this meant divine status and translated into the familiar anthropomorphic images of human bodies that have metamorphosed into the bulls, lions, and falcons which we associate with Assyria, Sumeria, and Egypt.

There were other iconographies, however, that focused more on cosmological and geomorphic references. One of the supreme examples was the ancient Celtic practice of constructing massive circular monuments composed of erect dolmens, earth mounds, and tombs in the form of piled boulders, called "cromlechs." The most outstanding megalith, Stonehenge on Salisbury Plain in Wiltshire, is assumed to have been some kind of astronomical observatory. Originally constructed by a Neolithic cult group in c. 3200 B.C., it was continuously expanded and refined in stages over the next 1,500 years. Very little is known of

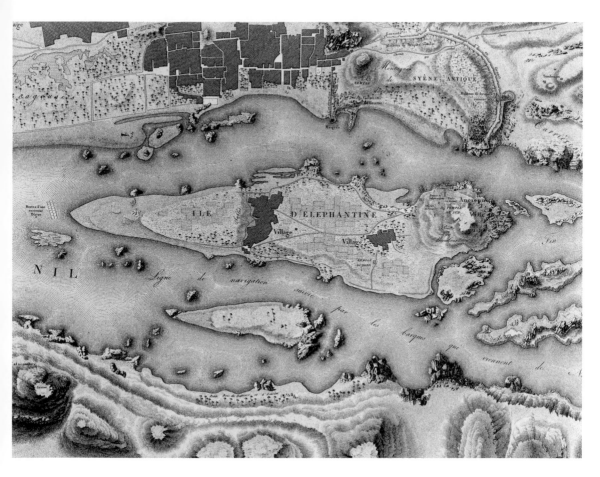

Nile Valley civilization
Island of Elephantine,
near Aswan, Egypt
In: *Description de
l'Égypte*, 1809

Anubis
Egypt
Papyrus, c. 1500 B.C.

Stonehenge
Salisbury Plain, England
c. 3200–1600 B.C.

**Frieze from
the Pergamon Altar**
Pergamon-Museum,
Berlin, Germany
180–160 B.C.

the civilization that built this ambitious structure; but it has been erroneously attributed to the Druids even though there is no real evidence that this society even existed at the time when Stonehenge was erected. What does seem certain is the revelation of a culture that had developed an extremely advanced picture of the universe and probably understood a range of abstract concepts about the cosmos

that anticipated modern astrophysics. There has been endless anthropological and scientific speculation about the level of scientific sophistication associated with Stonehenge – noting the uncanny alignment of the upright stones with respect to positions of the sun and stars – and attributing to its builders everything from mystical powers to the early practice of alchemy. This is architecture of the most compelling kind in terms of its environmental implications, and (as previously mentioned) it is also the most haunting expression of what Edmund Burke characterized as a "terror of the sublime." The metaphysical dimensions inherent in this structure are persuasive testimony that its builders saw the ecological experience as much more than a direct response to tangible evidence of connectedness in nature. It seems to be an acknowledgment of cosmic forces, a symbol of the totality of integrated systems, and a monumental example of eternal deference to the fearful unknown.

If we look at other examples of eco-philosophical commitment throughout the ancient world, we see that the Greeks seem to have played a decisive role in the tendency toward a more confirmed anthropocentrism. Leucippus and Democritus in the 5th century proposed the concept of atomism, which basically states that the physical environment is not as we see it and that matter is composed of atoms – thus, with great prophetic insight, laying the groundwork for modern physics. It was also the beginning of the mechanistic view of the universe and the assumption that science, by taking a non-empirical view of the world, represented a superior (and hence more accurate) threshold of phenomenological insight. The human brain, in this context, was seen as the center of the universe, and mankind's role on earth was then deemed primarily analytical and custodial. Greek philosophy seems to have been the origin of the imperious single-track Western idea of Man over nature.

For the Greeks, the interpretation of atomism proposed that all matter is built out of regular constituents and that the state of change is nothing more than a rearrangement

of stabilized parts. From this hypothesis grew the assumptions that the energy particles comprising humans (as the only creatures possessing a soul) would endure forever in a constantly revolving state and not be subjected to the creation and destruction of matter characteristic of the rest of the universe. As a progressive version of eternal life, supported by scientific theory, it is understandable why this concept became popular as the ideal justification for Man's superiority on earth. Even though the Greeks, like the Egyptians, had a host of deities with various attributes, the notion of atomism became the basis for a new field of philosophical science. The Classical atomists believed that the structure of atoms was only space, form, and weight – not color, temperature, light, and smell – and therefore denied some measure of status to what were probably considered the inferior elements of the natural environment.

The superiority of mind over matter was reflected in all aspects of Greek culture: the building of massive temples where form, scale, proportion, and geometry became the ultimate measure of aesthetic standards; the treatment of landscape as a functional surface to be exploited (thereby causing one of history's first recorded ecological disasters through the deforestation of Athens); and the establishment of a social and political agenda that expanded ego-centrism to much larger segments of the population. As authors of the original concept of democracy, the Greeks paved the way to such future liberties as private ownership of property, freedom of expression, parliamentary procedure, equity under law, and the cult of the individual. These entitlements – however admirable from the perspective of our current preference for representative democracy – have also heavily contributed to our detachment from nature. It is ironic that the very freedoms we value most are those inextricably associated with environmental decline. To add to this paradoxical situation, the contributions of ancient Greek civic architecture are generally regarded as one of the pinnacles of Western artistic achievement and democratic sym-

bolism; so it has always been assumed by subsequent generations that these structures were purposely built as a dialogue with their surroundings. In certain respects, this was true. The majestic presence and flawless site orientation of the Acropolis confirm an exemplary aesthetic response to context; yet this assembly of buildings has also provided a power-centered architectural iconography that has been adaptable to endless citadels of anthropocentric authority in the form of banks, stock exchanges, courthouses, museums, and government headquarters.

After the Greek contributions to mechanistic philosophy, the concept is primarily

The Acropolis
Athens, Greece
5th century B.C.

**New York
Stock Exchange**
George Browne Post
New York, New York, USA
1901–04

**The Ancient of
Days Striking the
First Circle of Earth**
William Blake
Library of Congress,
Washington DC, USA
1794

Page 55
Cathedral
Siena, Italy
begun in 1250

Detail of Cathedral
Lorenzo Maitani
Orvieto, Italy
c. 1310–30

identified with Réné Descartes, the 17th-century French philosopher who felt that scientific analysis should deal with quantifiables, instead of qualities. He proposed that, in looking at the natural environment, one should not rely on teleological explanations – for example, studying only the surface laws of nature to explain why plants seek the sunlight – but, instead, should examine the molecular structure of the leaf, which explains its preference for solar energy. Mechanism rejects what it considers the vagaries of qualitative evaluation in favor of deductive mathematical and mechanical models. As an influence on philosophy and science, it tends to be empirical and takes a condescending view of analysis growing out of interiority, subjectivity, or the instinctual response to nature. Descartes also authored the most famous quotation in philosophy: "I think, therefore I am," thus laying the groundwork for Existentialism and a host of later egocentric philosophical positions.

At the beginning of the early Middle Ages in Europe, the Greek contributions to philosophy and science had mostly disappeared in deference to the rise of Christianity. Atomism and the analytical approach to phenomena posed a danger to the doctrines of the Church and were openly opposed for centuries until the rise of Humanism during the Renaissance. By the 10th century, the secular influences of Greek science had also declined or had

become so dissipated they held no threat. As a result, the medieval Church's suppression of ideas had less to do with a hostility toward Plato and Aristotle, multitheism and natural philosophy, and more to do with the power implicit in controlling mass ignorance. The Church required a constituency held in check by a fear of damnation and the wrath of an all-powerful God. In this context, the knowledge and promotion of science became heresy.

During the 13th century there was a great revival of interest in Platonic and Aristotelian philosophy, and this is when the Church decided to invest all of its power and resources in cathedrals and ceremony. With the rise in popularity of Greek science, Christianity countered the movement with a tyrannical absolutism and a promotion of anthropocentrism which basically established the level of disregard for the environment we practise today. In this sense, the Middle Ages represented the apex of a separation of Man and nature. It was also the end of a millennia-long progression toward this dubious goal, starting with the deification of nature in Neolithic religions, shifting to its rationalized status in Greece, and ending in its de-sanctification as the reinforcement of an all-encompassing God and the supremacy of monotheism.

The medieval version of anthropocentrism was drawn from a theology where everything was conceded as subject to the will of God. He was seen as the supreme architect of all that exists and, hence, whatever earthly benefits humanity enjoyed were his rightful property. Man was not expected to be the caretaker of nature, but merely a beneficiary who had no particular responsibility (other than tacit appreciation) to maintain or respect its presence. Humanity's only duty was to praise God, bow to the will of the Church, and reject any ideas in conflict with these purposes. In *Religion and the Rise of Modern Science*, author Reijer Hooykaas explains this custodial role of God: "The Bible knows nothing of 'nature,' knowing only 'creatures' who are absolutely dependent for their origin and existence on the will of God. Consequently, the natural world is

54

admired as God's work and as evidence of the creator, but never adored." This became amplified justification for early Christians to hold nature at a distance and explain whatever happens in relation to the environment as "God's will."

Some daring critics during the height of the medieval Church's power must have asked the obvious question: "Why should the population undermine benefits we see everywhere and worship something that no one can prove exists?" Such heresy was usually dispatched with severe punishment. At the same time, it was also an incentive for the Church to sponsor some of the world's most persuasive iconography, calculated to dispel any doubts and function as the mass media of its day. The Gothic cathedrals, with their narrative surfaces and impressive devotional spaces, were perfect vehicles to convey the big message. Since most of the population was illiterate, agrarian, and indentured under serfdom, the miracle of these buildings' scale alone must have overwhelmed and commanded devotion. In addition to their sheer mass, the feats of engineering and the fact that every surface could be read as a compelling story inspired the believers and assured a total supplication. These magnificent structures are the best possible evidence of what a combination of consensus iconography, psychologically engaging art, and a seemingly unlimited budget can achieve in terms of mass communication. It is intriguing to speculate, in global terms today, what it would be like to experience the same level of dedication to the environmental movement as the church gave to the marketing of Christianity in the 13th century and then use contemporary architecture as its primary means of spiritual representation.

Moving from Western civilization to the Far East, the Chinese and Japanese interpretations of humanity's connections to the environment were based on Taoist and Zen philosophies. They believed that the practice of living should be a reflection of nature's infinite harmony. Whereas the ancient Greeks saw the world through a filter of mechanistic analysis

and revered geometry as an indication of Man's superiority over nature, the Oriental religions embraced anthropomorphism and a view of earth's treasures as the mirror of an even greater paradise beyond terrestrial life. Taoism, from the 3rd century B.C., is based on a belief that all living forms can be resurrected on a higher level. This religion proposed that

considered to be of a lower order, inclusive of architecture. The best that buildings could achieve was to engage landscape in a reverent way, reflecting the organic and asymmetrical characteristics of a perceived paradise. While geometric forms were a part of traditional Chinese architecture – usually as a reinforcement of landscape or a visual counterpoint to the indeterminacy of natural growth – these structures were the philosophical opposite of the Greek concept of geometric order imposed on the terrain. The Taoist idea was to fuse architecture and landscape as scenographic fantasies and symbolize a theological concept which saw the mind as a metaphor for nature.

In historic Japan, the Zen Buddhist vision of the entire universe as a system of interrelated parts, translated into architecture as an expression of the relation between inside and outside. This concept, similar to Taoism, refers to the structure of the mind as an extension of all the components of nature and the universe. The Zen Mandara (a theological coda) proposes a doctrine of dual realms – one being "the principle and the cause," the other being "the intelligence and the effect." The Mandara was the symbolic reference to a psychic state in which the mind became a landscape, achieving a fusion with nature and a perfect peace and spirituality. This psychological symbiosis was important. Zen was not about gardening, or relating to nature from a purely observational perspective, but rather it was about the act of being nature.

The early followers of Zen could not have understood the Western idea of conquering nature. In their conception, one only "conquers an enemy," and, since there is nothing to be feared in nature, the earth was regarded as the ultimate friend and benefactor. As described by Zen scholar Daisetz Suzuki: "The idea of conquest is abhorrent. If we succeed in climbing a high mountain, why not say 'We have made a good friend of it'? To look around for objects to conquer is not the Oriental attitude toward nature."

In the famous Ryoan-Ji shrines and rock gardens of Kyoto, for example, Paradise was

Japanese Summer drawing
Sesson Sukei
National Museum,
Kyoto, Japan
mid 15th century

Drawing of house and garden
Peking, China
c. 500

an animal could be reborn as a human (reinforcing, naturally, the supremacy of Man); but then Man could be resurrected as a god. For this reason it was important, during a believer's sojourn on earth, to seek simplicity in accord with nature and reject worldly pursuits in preparation for a possible deification through infinite connectedness.

In Taoism the objective was to live beyond conventional moral and social standards, believing that such limitations alienated one from nature. In this context, all the routine activities and constructions of civilization were brought to the living world as a group of imaginary islands represented by Horai stones, which were assumed to be populated in their "other-world" setting by blissful and immortal beings. This imaginary archipelago was perceived by Zen followers as "borrowed scenery" and as a symbolic representation of the believer's ultimate passage into the eternity of a transcendental garden.

Translated into traditional Japanese architecture, this theme of "borrowed scenery" combined with a concept of "inside/outside" was responsible for some of the most profound relationships between buildings and their sites in human history. The space organization of the traditional Japanese house reflected the theology of dual realms and was designed as a constant flow from interior to exterior. Walls were treated as tissue-like membranes separating, but informing, the two domains. Just as the interior was like a garden, the exterior was like a living room. In this way the architecture was seen as conversing with nature. In the traditional dwelling, all of the rewarding experiences of life and a communion with landscape were presented in microcosmic form. The enclosure and its integrated gardens were based on the assumption that the inhabitant could stay in one place, travel the world in spirit, and, as a bonus, enjoy an aesthetic prelude to Paradise.

The ultimate Zen experience was far removed from both teleological and mechanistic views of life in that it asserts the supremacy of "purposelessness." Daisetz Suzuki explains that "to be thus free from all conditioning rules or concepts is the essence of religious life. When we are conscious of any purpose whatever in our movements, we are not free. When teleology enters our life, we cease to be religious and we become moral beings." Needless to say, this idea is tantamount to anarchy from a Western perspective; but it also proposes nagging questions concerning all of our rigid commitments to technocentrism and anthropocentrism from ancient Athens to the present day. Relative to current architecture, one can readily see how notions of purposelessness

and its counterpart of oneness with nature would collide with the obsessive dogmatism of formalist and functionalist design and its high-tech stylistic commitments.

While contemporary Japan reflects very little of its classical Zen Buddhist environmental philosophy (and, in fact, has become a grotesque and hyperbolized version of Western technocracy), this legacy lives on in a limited number of preserved monuments and protected regions of the country. It is also a living religion in major parts of Asia and the closest equivalent to a true spiritual (and workable) version of eco-centrism today. Although we can perhaps dismiss the spiritually unfathomable ecological virtues of aboriginal culture as being too far removed from our context to have any relevance, it is more difficult to ignore the Zen experience. This faith is still a powerful force in highly sophisticated societies that fit our definition of progressive and, even in very recent history, has brought peace and spiritual harmony to vast segments of humanity in Asia.

Zen influence is growing internationally, and it is probably an appropriate subject with which to end this survey. This philosophy has many new followers who endorse its concept of oneness with nature as humanity's only hope. The premise of this entire examination of ecological architecture has been to try to identify some promising signs of universal concurrence – perhaps even a re-vitalized or re-interpreted religion – that could form the basis for a global environmental commitment. Zen offers a substantial promise of fulfilling this objective – at least from the standpoint of its ethical and ecological principles. However, in assessing its actual impact in the world today, Zen seems more naturally intrinsic to the East, cult-like in the West, and unlikely to sweep the world to enlightenment in the foreseeable future.

This overview of past cultures and the philosophical principles that shaped their relation to nature and the building arts is only intended as a summary of the more significant historical differences of attitude toward the

Garden at the Royal Palace of Katsura
Kobori Ershu
Kyoto, Japan
1625–50

environment. There have obviously been major omissions – for example, the entire Islamic world, the Incas, the Mayans, and the American Indians – but the main purpose here has simply been to identify clear-cut points of change by examining archetypal situations. In reviewing the results, there seems to be an equation between the degree of personal liberty afforded by a society and the translation of this freedom into a negative impact on the environment. As noted at the beginning of this chapter, there is no evidence that autocratic and oppressive governments have necessarily caused greater ecological damage than benevolent democracies; in fact the reverse appears to be more often the case. But this is obviously a statistic that has to be measured against the historical periods and geographical locations being discussed. The bottom line remains – at least in the 20th century – that it has mattered very little whether the governments have been despotic or liberal. In terms of environmental impact, the means of destruction have been the most diverse, the boundaries of restraint

have been the least defined, and the recognition of reality has been at its lowest level of acceptance.

When one acknowledges the spectacular conceptual advancements identified with the 20th century – especially in physics and astronomy – the idea of maintaining a purely technocentric perspective is absurd, anachronistic, and probably fatal. In view of the effects of Einstein's Theory of Relativity on astrophysics, and the exploration of such concepts as black holes and new insights into the thermodynamic laws of entropy, it is hard to believe that humanity's entire social, economic, and environmental policy structure is still based on an empirical, Man-against-nature, vision of the world. In defining the limitations of technocentrism (still dominant in science as well as commerce), environmentalist David Popper breaks down this limited perspective into three categories: "One level is 'ideological': science now provides a major element of our basic presumptions about the world and man's relationship to it, and, in coming to do so, classic sci-

House with dry garden and membrane walls
Kyoto, Japan
1990s

Dry Garden at Ryoan-Ji
Daisho
Kyoto, Japan
1509–13

ence has displaced alternative ways of understanding our world. It has displaced alternative bodies of natural knowledge, such as myth, folklore, and natural magic, and the completeness of this displacement is represented by the pre-eminent position which our society accords the scientific expert. A second level is 'theoretical': in its theories science explicitly or implicitly embodies particular concepts of the man-nature relationship – for example in evolutionary theories in biology. Thirdly, in its practice of 'methodology' it involves the scientist in particular methodological positions which describe especially the relationships between himself and the subject – the observer of nature – and the object under observation. Thus in this process – in the very act – of gaining knowledge of nature, the scientist defines his relationship with nature in a particular way."

These constraining influences may be too deeply embedded in the motivational structure of present-day societies to allow for any radical changes. The interdependent economic interests of the world and their equally profit-motivated governments are still inextricably bound by the classic principles of mechanistic science. Popper's summary proposes that empirical thinking, which deals primarily with exteriors and systems theories, has overlooked the value of interiority and subjectivity as valid means of connecting with nature.

Returning to the basic premise that initiated this discussion of the relationship between eco-philosophy and the building arts, it was proposed that the illusions of unbridled economic growth have continued to determine the means and the messages of architecture in this century. For example, in a newly booming marketplace like Singapore, the most tangible

Spiral galaxy M83
Hydra Constellation

demonstrations of business vitality are measured by record-breaking building heights and acreages of plate glass. This merely indicates that "progress" has a subliminal definition in the corporate mind and a corresponding architectural vocabulary to match its aspirations. If everything is inseparable from this definition, it only reinforces the myopic view that a society's forward momentum is attained by understanding only economic laws, not nature's laws. Inevitably, this destructive fantasy threatens to live on in perpetuity.

A more realistic approach to the future will be defined by looking for avenues of escape from a purely mechanistic view of humanity's relation to nature. If successful, this objective may liberate architecture from its habitual constraints – particularly its obsession with industrial style, wasteful technology, and obsolete notions of functionalism – and open up the profession to new heights of ecological awareness. The following survey of contemporary green architects is, in part, a search for promising threads of a unified eco-philosophy and evidence of a reduction of those traditions of technocentrism and anthropocentrism that have dominated this century more than any other.

Aerial view of Singapore City
Singapore
1994

The building as architecture is born out of the heart of man, permanent consort to the ground, comrade to the trees, true reflection of man in the realm of his own spirit. His building is therefore consecrated space wherein he seeks refuge, recreation and repose for the body but especially for the mind. So our machine-age building need no more look like machinery than machinery need look like a building.

Frank Lloyd Wright

Environmental Architecture Today

Page 62 and 63
Taliesin West
Frank Lloyd Wright
Phoenix, Arizona, USA
1938–42

Habitat '67
Moshe Safdie
World Expo, Montreal, Canada
1964–67

Any balanced review of the environmental movement in architecture today is both an affirmation and an apology. There has been some exceptionally creative work accomplished in the cause of ecological design that deserves applause; at the same time, there has also been much to regret as a result of the minimal effect of these efforts on any change in societal awareness as a whole. The only explanation for this impotency is the lack of a consensus philosophy – or, as cautiously suggested earlier, the absence of a new earth-centric religion that might lend communicative power and credibility to these efforts. Even though the strength of environmentalism is increasing, the concept is still treated as a thing apart from the demand for what are considered inalienable entitlements in consumer societies. In a dutiful way, most people approve of the changes prescribed by environmental reform ... as long as the changes do not change anything. Given this prevailing attitude and its delusory state of inaction,

green architecture has remained a curiosity in the corner, instead of a force in the main-stream.

Certainly one of the major problems facing environmental architecture, aside from the absence of a strong societal endorsement, is a professional choice to over-emphasize the technological advantages and undervalue the social and aesthetic aspects. There is an unbalanced amount of effort currently being spent to create a sanctimonious mythology around what is basically a collection of admirable engineering innovations. These techno-remedial solutions – often promoted by architects as challenges to public conscience – tend to discourage potential sympathizers by their reproachful tone and the sententious way the message is delivered. Although people are rather fascinated by end-of-the-world scenarios and fantasy cures, there is nothing particularly compelling about technical reports on photovoltaic cells, solar panels, and thermal glass, all of their admirable green intentions notwithstanding. As a point of comparison, imagine how indifferent audience response might have been if the medieval Catholic Church had invested its entire ecclesiastical resources in obscure liturgical dogma, to the exclusion of inspirational ceremony, exalting music, and a richly narrative visual iconography. Similarly, for architects to interpret today's environmental advocacy exclusively in terms of mechanical hardware and conservationist databases – without including the vastly more interesting sources of imagery found in nature – is to miss an extraordinary opportunity.

While it is not the purpose of this text to provide an exhaustive review of green design options, it is still important to outline the key ecological building procedures available to the architectural profession. It is equally important to keep this information in perspective. There

is already a danger that technological obsessions are distracting designers from understanding their place in the larger picture of interconnectedness – a role that, in addition to artistic leadership, includes a heightened awareness of cultural diversity, societal change, and the growing significance of eco-psychology. A more balanced objective now is to view environmental technology as a valuable tool kit, and natural science as a primary source of inspiration.

Many of the contemporary architects featured later in this book have made innovative use of environmental technology – contributions to be reviewed in detail later – still, there is a fairly routine catalogue of guidelines for ecological accountability that seem to appear in every publication on the subject. In fact, it is now being predicted by science and government that most of these responsibilities will soon be written into law, and building permits will be issued depending on compliance.

Briefly described, the standard eco-friendly checklist includes:
- Smaller buildings

The construction of modestly scaled architecture is a logical alternative to mega-structure assaults on land and resources; but the looming problem of global overpopulation and the need for mass housing throws this solution into question. In any event, the preferred choice is clustered, low-rise (fewer than six stories) dwelling spaces that maintain the close-knit integrity of the cityscape and do not bleed endlessly into suburban sprawl.
- Use of recycled and renewable materials

This directive proposes that a great deal of attention should be paid to the original selection of construction materials – guaranteeing intelligent choices which have recycling potential as a result of their production technology –

and thereby assuring a built-in potential to be used over and over again in perpetuity.
- Use of low-embodied-energy materials

The objective here is to select construction materials with attention to the entire biography of their production. While, for example, a certain choice of masonry product may appear to be environmentally favorable from a manufacturing standpoint, it may still fail in its ecological standards when further research shows that it contains harmful chemicals, deposits toxic wastes during production, and requires energy-consuming cross-country transport to get a supply.
- Use of harvested lumber

With the voracious destruction of the world's

Mud brick architecture
Southern Yemen
1980s

Balcomb Residence
William Lumpkins
Santa Fe, New Mexico, USA
1970s

Wind power
Australia
1980s

virgin forest regions to gather wood and prepare land for agriculture, every effort should be made to use only harvested lumber in construction and furnishings and avoid all imported exotic woods as much as possible.

■ Water catchment systems

While water is essential to all life on earth, it is also the most mindlessly wasted resource. The responsibility for a clean water supply does not just refer to the maintenance of a few regional reservoirs. It should also include the recycling of grey water and a commitment by cities and individuals to building-by-building catchment facilities, as insurance against extended droughts (an increasing possibility with the advance of global warming) and normal short-term shortages.

■ Low maintenance

This is a self-explanatory advantage in any form of shelter, since it encourages a cost-effective upkeep, a reduction in the use of fossil fuels for heating and cooling, and the development of building technologies adapted to regional climates.

■ Recycling of buildings

In the battle against rampant new construction and the delusion of an endless supply of raw materials, a commitment to salvaging existing structures and sponsoring adaptive re-use may define the most innovative area of architectural practice in the future. This approach also maintains the regional texture and scale of cities, helps keep history alive, and preserves a unique civic identity.

■ Reduction of ozone-depleting chemicals

As the greatest threat to human survival, the search for a solution to this problem goes to the heart of every consumer-based economy. It also refers back to all questions of material choices, recycling, and finding alternative energy sources.

■ Preservation of the natural environment

The voracious encroachment on existing landscape is at the top of the list of ecological concerns. Essentially, the presence of one tree means four people can breathe, and the absence of adequate green space in most urban centers is at the root of massive health costs and mental stress. Real estate development is the prime enemy of nature preservation and should be held in check by every possible means of legislation.

■ Energy efficiency

This refers to an increased use of diverse sources of energy (passive solar, wind power, water power, etc.), a reduction of the dependence on fossil fuels, and the construction of architecture in response to regional climates and existing contextual influences.

■ Solar orientation

This is an extension of energy efficiency and prescribes that all buildings should be situated to take full seasonal advantage of the sun's position and its energy-generating potential.

■ Access to public transportation

While not a direct architectural design issue, the reduction of private vehicle transportation in favor of buses and trains is one of the bottom-line opportunities for energy savings and the improvement of air quality. The architect can effectively impact on public transport facilities by designing buildings and spaces that include easy access to these systems.

It should be noted again that, however commendable, these conservation measures represent various forms of expedient action – much of it too little, too late – and are put into practice only infrequently by those societies with the worst environmental track records. These depressing scenarios aside, increasing numbers of exceptionally talented architects internationally are exploring a range of approaches and definitions for a new ecological architecture. For certain designers, the latest advances in engineering and environmental technology are central to their objectives; while, for others, it is important to return to the lessons of history and the use of indigenous methods and materials. For another group, the resources of topography, vegetation, solar energy and the earth itself are the means to achieve an expanded vision of organic buildings. In the interests of organizing information and establishing some categorical areas of design activity, the architects included in this discussion are examined from the standpoint of the most distinctive features of their buildings and their own stated objectives in the larger environmental cause.

These general categories include:
- The integration of architecture and landscape, the fusion of buildings with context, and using the elements of earth and vegetation in such a way that they seem to be part of the raw material of construction
- The combination of shelter and garden space, created as microcosms of real or imagined environments (like the Japanese concept of "borrowed scenery"), which produce symbolic tableaux of other situations
- The use of nature-related symbolism as a means of connecting architecture to its cultural context and to an earth-centered imagery
- A translation of the most advanced environmental and construction technology and their related materials and processes into aesthetic terms
- Green design research and environmental technology innovations that provide the foundations of sustainable and ecologically responsible architecture
- Bridge-building environmental design ideas and construction techniques that have encouraged a new acceptance of green architecture and the fusion of buildings with their contexts
- Environmental attitudes that, while not strictly ecological, have implications for the

architectural profession in terms of conceptual thinking
- Visionary and conceptual ideas in architecture and urban planning that offer prophetic visions for the future, based on changes in global communications and social and political (as well as design) influences that may affect the building arts and environmental policies

Only a relatively small number of the designers included in this survey have made a concerted effort to satisfy the primary challenges of environmental architecture – these are, the integration of buildings with context,

House
Malcolm Wells
Brewster, Massachusetts, USA
1980

Rocky Mountain Institute
Aspen Design Group
Aspen, Colorado, USA
1984

the conversion of environmental technology into aesthetic terms, and the development of a persuasive theoretical context for their ideas. Certain architects have constructed or conceptualized buildings which represent impressive models of ecological principles, yet in many ways remain as remote in appearance from the image of nature as their non-environmental counterparts. Certainly all of the work illustrated here includes admirable contributions to eco-friendly design and a very high level of aesthetic invention. At the same time, instead of capturing a true sense of connectedness, or visually reflecting a broad-based earth-centric philosophy, a number of these examples of environmental architecture demonstrate a rather didactic and showcase-like approach. This goes back to the issue of what constitutes "green" in architecture and the tendency of the design profession to restrict this term to

checklists of moral responsibility and remedial action. Only rarely is it expanded to include artistic experience and social or psychological references. Another problem is that some examples of buildings with a green commitment can seem awkward and out of place when compared to the mainstream of derivative style, ubiquitous clichés, and faceless anonymity that characterizes so much of architecture today. This is to be expected. A new movement in art, literature, philosophy, or science invariably stumbles through a certain period of self-conscious gestures and discouraging dead-ends, while the language of discovery is being tested. It is simply the natural path of creativity and experiment. In the end, this process invariably generates art that is far more vital than anything produced by continuing to work in well-traveled territory.

The work of Emilio Ambasz is central to any discussion of environmental architecture, and he has played a seminal role in the integration of vegetation and terrain into buildings since the 1970s. Born in Argentina, he was educated at Princeton University, served as a former curator at the Museum of Modern Art, and has been a major innovator in industrial design, as well as in architecture and theoretical writing. Ambasz's multi-disciplinary professional experience has uniquely prepared him to feel at home with the concept of connectedness in nature. In the fullest sense of the word, his work is pivotal to the green architecture movement, and he is among the very few practitioners whose ideas embrace the full range of ecological, urbanistic, philosophical, poetic, and aesthetic components that this book has advocated from the beginning.

Ambasz, like any architect today who would dare to promote visions of Arcadia in a dominantly high-tech profession, has taken his share of rejections and critical brickbats from the mainstream design scene. Also, he has had to endure client and community indifference to the ecological cause, resign himself to numerous canceled projects, and confront a wall of resistance from commerce and government to any ideas that question the supremacy of technocentrism. Thankfully, as a result of the general increasing interest in environmental issues, he is now winning on most levels. In the past few years he has emerged as an international figure of considerable stature in terms of architecture's critical future. Progressive young design students, who are increasingly hostile to the wasteful technology, pretentious theory, and derivative design conventions of

**Integration
of Architecture
and Landscape**

**Schlumberger Research
Laboratories**
Emilio Ambasz
Austin, Texas, USA
Project, 1983

Page 70 and 71
Lucille Halsell Conservatory
Emilio Ambasz
San Antonio, Texas, USA
1981–83

the academic establishment, are rallying to his ideas and establishing Ambasz as a new messiah of environmental architecture.

Emilio Ambasz's conceptual direction fits most of the admirable characteristics of green architecture – the fusion with context, innovative uses of landscape, symbolism, environmental technology, and visionary theory – but, perhaps his work is most comfortably associated with the idea of landscape as an intrinsic part of buildings. Like all architects who have explored the interactive relationships between nature and shelter, his work owes a great debt to Frank Lloyd Wright. However, while Wright tended to see trees and plants as compositional accents in or around his buildings and habitat as an extension of its adjacent terrain, Ambasz sees landscape as a ritual experience. Like a combination of the Zen notion of "borrowed scenery" and the Celtic celebration of cosmology, he uses topography and vegetation as narrative microcosms of an imaginary utopia. His actual elements of architectural structure are often reduced to minimal geometry, functioning as coded directionals to frame the presence of landscape.

In his Schlumberger Research Laboratories in Austin, Texas, Ambasz designed a computer research center that responded to the client's demand for flexible space to accommodate an expanding and contracting staff. At the same time, he utilized the impressive landscape of the site by giving it a massive ceremonial presence. The buildings are distributed throughout the area as if expressing the flow

of information through a computer. All facilities are integrated into the land by means of a series of earth berms which assure the laboratories and recreational facilities fit into their surroundings. Clearly they accomplish this objective and include the additional feature of earth-covered shelter, with its decided advantages in maintaining comfortable interior temperatures in all seasons. The Schlumberger Laboratories also appear to have a cosmological relationship to ancient Celtic monuments and elevate the fusion of communications technology and earth art in the computer age to a similar level of ritual-like experience. These intentions have been confirmed by Ambasz, who speaks of his work as "myth making acts. In my architecture I am interested in the rituals and ceremonies of the 24-hour day. ... My work is a search for primal things: being born, being in love, and dying."

Extending these aspects of surrealism and ritual to the Lucille Halsell Conservatory in San Antonio, Texas, Ambasz again used earth berms and a fusion with landscape to give the total complex its combined impression of Babylonian garden and space-age celebration. In this case, since there was a necessity for greenhouses to shelter botanical displays, he designed these features as assertive, pyramidal forms (totemic in themselves), which are embraced by ground surface incisions and sculptural mounds. The Halsell Conservatory produces the effect of a living monument that pays homage to both the visible manifesta-

tions of plant life and their invisible sources of nourishment from the sky and earth.

In April 1995 Ambasz's most ambitious urban project to date opened in Fukuoka, Japan. The ACROS Building – a center for international culture and information – is a 15-story structure offering facilities for exhibitions, conferences, musical and theatrical events, offices, and commercial enterprises. Its most distinguishing feature is a massive terraced wall of vegetation, functioning as the extension of a series of public gardens that service the surrounding complex of buildings.

Oddly, although this impressive structure is acclaimed in Japan, it has not yet received due attention in the Western design reviews and popular press. It is the peculiar fate of Ambasz's work to generate intense interest in those parts of the world where progressive industrialists, civic leaders, and young designers have understood the importance of greening the cityscape, but then receive only moderate appreciation, indifference, and sometimes even hostility, in places still committed exclusively to technocentric glass and concrete urban centers – or, as Ambasz has observed, cities that continue to make the inhumane choice of "gray over green." The ACROS Building represents one of the most important examples of architecture *as* the garden, versus merely sitting *in* the garden. People who visit or work in the cultural center use its "growing" facade for strolling, jogging, relaxing, and other levels of participation. This unique arcadian ziggurat is thus removed from the category of a mere visual or functional object and achieves a new level of green architecture connecting to and stimulating all of the senses.

For Emilio Ambasz the Fukuoka project anticipated his larger vision of a "Green Town" concept for Japan, based on what he perceives as an emerging new respect for the garden city concept. In general, when the notion of a "return to nature" or living with the natural environment is proposed, most people automatically envision a house in the untouched wilderness. Ambasz points out that for the more densely populated nations of the world, especially small countries like Japan, there is barely a square meter of its land surface that has not been cultivated by humanity; so even those areas that appear to be wild forests and virgin landscapes are almost invariably the product of human intervention at one time or another. As Ambasz suggests, "There is a philosophic question here: we have to redefine what is nature and what is man-made nature. In a situation such as the global one, certainly exacerbated in Japan, where a tree exists either because someone planted it or because someone decided to leave it there, it is imperative that we create a new definition of what we mean by man-made nature. Such a definition would have to incorporate and expand not only the creation of gardens and public spaces but also the creation of architecture which must be seen as one specialized aspect of the making of man-made nature." In this proposal, Ambasz goes to the heart of the issue of green design and civilization's custodial role in maintaining nature. Mankind has always been a fundamental part of ecological structure, and its architecture and commerce (prior to the Machine Age at least) frequently provided essential contexts for the survival of plants and animals. Great varieties of insects, birds, rodents, mosses, algae, flowers, etc. could not have survived in their so-called natural state without the construction of human habitat and the development of agriculture. This concept of the Green Town is not confined to some vision of a picturesque rural village – although, in the face of certain megamall wastelands today, this could be considered a beneficial feature – rather, it suggests the reinstatement of the garden as part of what many scientists predict will be 100 years of environmental restoration needed to salvage the earth from 20th-century industrial damage.

ACROS Building
Emilio Ambasz
Fukuoka, Japan
1989–95

ACROS Building
Emilio Ambasz
Fukuoka, Japan
1989–95

**The Pit
(aerial view)**
Peter Noever
Breitenbrunn, Austria
1971–

Page 75 above
**The Pit
(with blocks of
sandstone and
sandstone stairs)**
Peter Noever
Breitenbrunn, Austria
1971–

Page 75 below
**The Pit
(Wing Stairs)**
Peter Noever
Breitenbrunn, Austria
1971–

Moving from Japan to Europe, The Pit project by Peter Noever in Austria shares the ritual vision of architecture as an extension of landscape in common with the work of Ambasz. Currently the Director of the MAK (Museum for Contemporary Art/Applied Arts) in Vienna, Noever has been periodically working on this major earthwork and underground/overground dwelling since 1971. In the fullest sense of the word, it is a continuously evolving concept paralleling the mutable processes of nature. He recycled a 200-year-old abandoned wine cellar and adjacent quarry in Breitenbrunn and, with the addition of whitewashed cubes as living space (CUBE XXXVII; 1993 and 1989 realisation of the gridded field of 36 concrete cubes). A series of earth berms, and several wing-like concrete slabs, has transformed the entire area into what appears to be the contemporary version of a Neolithic earth shrine. However, rather than see The Pit as a ritual space for cosmological speculations or totemic worship, Noever has shaped this environment as a celebration of simple human interaction and a communion with nature. It is what architect Michael Sorkin has described as "an armature for spectatorship." In this regard, the entire experience of

visiting the project is an orchestrated sequence of participatory events – walking the 164-foot-long quarry passage, arriving at the underground social chambers built into the wine cellar, enjoying the company of friends at a spectacular long table, and contemplating views of the surrounding country that have been articulately framed by doorways and the longitudinal direction of the earth berm.

Reminiscent of the great 18th-century Jantar Mantar astronomical observatories of India, built by Maharajah Jai Singh in Jaipur, The Pit also relates to the earthworks movement of the 1970s, which included artists like Robert Smithson, Michael Heizer, Robert Morris, and Dennis Oppenheim. Yet, unlike the cosmological purposes of the Jantar Mantar or purely sculptural objectives of earthworks, Michael Sorkin points out that "Noever's work tests not the edge of sculpture but the edge of architecture." In this project he has accomplished a hybrid fusion of disciplines, arriving at a unique interaction of habitat, public space, landscape architecture, and ceremonial monument, with provocative implications for ecological dwellings of the future. Beyond conventional earth-sheltered architecture, Noever's Pit suggests the re-examination of troglodytism, as humanity's first form of shelter. It also takes a different perspective on the adaptive re-use of existing space, the creation of a new social orientation based on connections to the earth, and, like ancient Celtic monuments which were built over many centuries, it proposes that the future of architecture can be seen as a continuous evolutionary process.

Continuing to look at those architects whose work has achieved a contextual integration and possible ritual or cosmological implications, Gustav Peichl is another Austrian who has built an extraordinary earthwork-like complex – in this case a Radio Satellite Station in Aflenz. The original concept grew out of protests by the community of Grassnitz against the intrusion of this facility and its potential destruction of the pastoral vistas of a mountainous terrain. The architect responded by designing a series of structures that, in addition to the satellite station, include housing for staff, operations offices, and recreation quarters which are either completely underground or integrate with the landscape by means of earth-sheltered roofs and mounded enclosures.

In terms of space orientation, the Satellite Station design has taken advantage of every opportunity to create an imaginative fusion with the regional environment. The living quarters are connected to the main building by underground passageways, a recessed central court allows light to penetrate the interior spaces, slit windows require the minimum displacement of earth, and the above-ground building elevations are kept to a minimum height. The only vertically assertive statement of the entire complex is a parabolic antenna that takes on the character of a monumental constructivist sculpture, projected in dramatic profile against the distant mountains.

Surreal, functional, and environmentally sensitive, Peichl's brilliant solution for this site, like Noever's Pit and Ambasz's Schlumberger Laboratories, seems to bridge the gap between the earliest principles of troglodytism and a new, computer-connected, habitat for the next century. High-technology communication is

both the premise and subject of the Satellite Station – so it is, in fact, technocentric at its core – yet the resolution is environmental. It demonstrates an aesthetic and functional response to one of the most irreversible global trends today, that is, the opportunity to partici-

**The Pit
(Quarry Passageway
with Wing Stair Element)**
Peter Noever
Breitenbrunn, Austria
1971–

pate in the so-called cybernetic lifestyle as a result of computers. This means that a burgeoning population can now live and work in the same place and communicate to the world by modem, the Internet, and facsimile. While the subject will be discussed later in the context of other green architects, it is to the particular credit of Gustav Peichl's prophetic vision that his communications center was built 30 years ago. In this regard he has pioneered a persuasive early model for an alternative lifestyle.

Peter Noever and Gustav Peichl seem to be rightful heirs to the legacy established by another exceptional Austrian, the Surrealist architect, sculptor, and design theoretician Frederick Kiesler. This extraordinary (but absurdly undervalued) thinker in the arts of this century laid the groundwork 60 years ago for environmental art and organic architecture. He also proposed ideas for anthropomorphic

houses which related more to the evolution of life growing out of the womb and his interest in female imagery than to the aggressive geometry associated with male dominated architectural form. In his seminal book *Inside the Endless House* of 1964, Kiesler observed that "no object, of nature or art, exists without environment. As a matter of fact, the object itself can expand to a degree where it becomes its own environment. ... The traditional art object, be it a painting, a sculpture, a piece of architecture, is no longer seen as an isolated entity, but must be considered within the context of this expanding environment. The environment becomes equally as important as the object, if not more so, because the object breathes into the surroundings and also inhales the realities of the environment, no matter in what space, close or wide apart, open-air or indoor."

EFA, Radio Satellite Station, plans
Gustav Peichl
Aflenz, Austria
1976–79

EFA, Radio Satellite Station
Gustav Peichl
Aflenz, Austria
1976–79

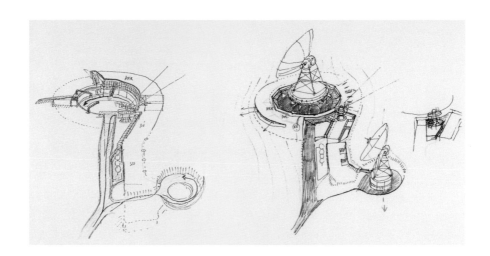

"Borrowed from Nature" – Organic Forms and Cosmic Symbolism

Other heirs to the legacy of Kiesler include architects Jersey Devil, Ushida-Findlay, James Cutler, Arthur Quarmby, Peter Vetsch, and Charles Jencks. In each case their work uses organic form – sometimes directly recalling Kiesler's womb-like imagery – and connects to the surrounding terrain in ways reminiscent of primordial construction techniques and earth-covered shelter. Certain of these designers' buildings and environments seem to suggest elements of ceremony and ritual, especially through the provocative inclusion of "borrowed scenery," as in the houses of Ushida-Findlay, and the calculated cosmic symbolism of the earthworks of Charles Jencks and his wife Maggie Keswick. Generally, their philosophical similarities involve the integration of landscape as

part of the raw material of architecture and the expressive translation of nature's fluid forms into the language of building.

Jersey Devil is an architectural firm of four partners (Steve Badanes, Jim Adamson, and John Ringel), who function as a designer and builder team. Since the 1970s, they have moved around the USA like nomads constructing a remarkable variety of hands-on houses. They met as students at Princeton in the late 1960s, banded together around a mutual interest in combining craft, technology, and green principles, and early on, contributed to a revolution of professional practice in architecture. In an absurd ruling passed by the American Institute of Architects in 1909, it became illegal for designers also to

Snail House
Jersey Devil
Forked River, New Jersey,
USA
1972

function as their own contractors; but, as a result of the persuasive accomplishments and outspoken advocacy of design and build rights voiced by firms like Jersey Devil, the law was ultimately revoked, and an increasing number of architects are now performing as designer and builders.

The peculiar name of the Badanes, Adamson, and Ringel architectural partnership was borrowed from local folklore in the Forked River region of New Jersey where, legend claims, an 18th-century woman presumably bore a devil infant whose curse haunted the region. The female child, who died while young, is said to have possessed cloven hooves, horns, and a deranged behavior. After her death, she was reported to have appeared in the woods on a periodic basis and was blamed for anything that went wrong in the community. During the construction of the group's Snail House, neighbors often commented on this unconventional structure as something the "Jersey Devil might have designed." The architects liked being credited with the devil's work, and they needed a name to start a checking account; so, from this simple origin, their Satanic identity was born.

This maverick team functions like a green architectural "hit-squad," basically camping out on a site to communicate more intimately with its special peculiarities. They then develop their ideas and choices of building technology out of an informed sense of total context. As dedicated advocates of solar energy and land-

scape-related design decisions, the team sees its buildings as extensions of nature and, therefore, renewable by an absorption of the same biomorphic characteristics that nature has already indicated as suitable for a particular situation. "I think of solar as an aperture into being truly in touch with the site," John Ringel explains. "A designer has to be in touch with the site ... you might as well ignore gravity." In this regard, whatever Jersey Devil does with a location architecturally, it is also intended to communicate environmental standards and function as a kind of eco-biography of that place.

Jersey Devil's hands-on approach provides an interesting paradox in today's pervasively high-tech design obsession. Contrary to the architectural profession's increasing immersion in the virtual reality of computers, their preference is for the low-tech reality of an earth-sheltered habitat and the conversion of sunlight to energy. Their seemingly casual, agrarian, attitude toward the environment, coupled with a 1960s Aquarian sensibility and an "outlaw design" hostility towards wasteful building practices, can actually be misleading. Jersey Devil's work is also on the cutting edge of sustainable technology and the use of advanced computer-aided equipment as a reinforcement of their solar commitment. For example, in their unusually large 10,000-square-foot Hoagie House outside of Washington, DC, a computerized mechanism called Roto-Lid is coordinated with a skylight to provide efficient heating, cooling, and lighting on a year-around basis.

From the perspective of an integration with context and the inclusion of regional terrain and vegetation, Badanes, Adamson, and Ringel share many ideas in common with Ambasz and Peichl. The differences lie in their spontaneous, theory-free, and anti-formalist attitude toward building with nature. Their functional and aesthetic decisions, while partly developed through conventional construction documents, are always left open to spontaneous changes and based on an evolutionary set of discoveries. In their famous Hill

House of 1977–79, near San Francisco, they combined what they call "hands-on craftsmanship" with an extraordinary sensitivity to site orientation. The building is carved into the crest of a hill to create a low profile in its natural context, protect it from frequent Pacific wind storms, and still allow light to penetrate. As a result of earth berms and sod roofs, the interior spaces remain at a relatively stable temperature, while a wind-powered pump and gravity-fed delivery system provide water to the house.

For Jersey Devil's 1992 House in the Keys at Islamorada, Florida – commissioned by a potter client – they incorporated a badly deteriorated (but hurricane-proof) concrete structure and supplemented a new addition, oriented around a three-story stair tower. The heating and cooling are passive solar from a radiant roof, ridge vents assure an efficient internal airflow, and a screen armature around the dwelling provides for both sound and sight protection from an intrusive nearby highway. Other environmentally sensitive features include a recycled plastic recreation deck, a thermal mass of concrete for insulation, and an old trailer that has been converted to energy-conserving guest quarters.

By avoiding categorization and what they consider pretentious and creatively restraining design theory, the Jersey Devil team occupies an interesting niche in contemporary green architecture. Their work can be seen as positioned somewhere between idiosyncratic ruralism and highly sophisticated eco-technology. The orchestration of shapes and volumes in Jersey Devil's buildings is clearly informed by their grounding in advanced architectural education; but their sensibility and the actual choice of sculptural shapes and spatial organi-

Hill House
Jersey Devil
La Honda, California, USA
1977–79

Hill House, living room
Jersey Devil
La Honda, California, USA
1977–79

Hill House, terrace
Jersey Devil
La Honda, California, USA
1977–79

zation seems more about animating a pastoral lifestyle than celebrating earth-centered rituals. Unlike the cosmological implications of designers like Frederick Kiesler, Emilio Ambasz and Peter Noever, the architecture of Jersey Devil seems more analogous to the terrain-conscious character of ancient Celtic and Neolithic habitats, but filtered through the influences of Frank Lloyd Wright, Art Nouveau, and the Arts and Crafts movement.

Reflecting a similar interest in earth shelter and biomorphic form, the work of Ushida-Findlay in Japan demonstrates a logical connection to both Jersey Devil and Emilio Ambasz, as well as the much earlier Kiesler. Each architect is identified by an involvement with organic spaces, imagery that reflects a "womb-to-shelter" metaphor, and structures that absorb aspects of their surrounding environment.

The Eisaku Ushida and Kathryn Findlay studio is a husband-and-wife partnership founded in 1988 as a bi-cultural (Japan and Scotland) collaboration and best known for its work dealing with architecture as a reflection of regional topography and the psychological interface between habitat, technology, and nature. Unlike many green architects, who see

House in the Keys
Jersey Devil
Islamorada, Florida, USA
1992

Page 84/85
House in the Keys
Jersey Devil
Islamorada, Florida, USA
1992

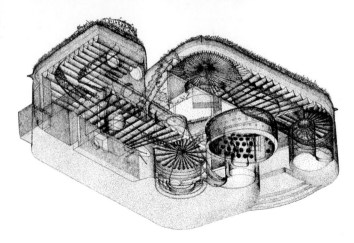

Soft and Hairy House
Ushida-Findlay Partnership
Tsukuba City, Japan
1994

their buildings as structure imposed on the environment – with a certain deference to ecology in terms of energy conservation – Ushida-Findlay's philosophy proposes their work as "the taming of technology, not the taming of nature." They see the combined physical, aesthetic, and scientific role of buildings as a harmony of nature's forces capable of offering a combination of protective retreat from the city and a visual, technical, and atmospheric absorption of the immediate urban context.

Through formal means, theoretical propositions, and an attitude toward garden space reminiscent of the Japanese concept of "borrowed scenery," the partnership has created a vision of the house as a microcosm of the city. By observing that broader social fluc-

tuations outside have an influence on their more compressed counterparts inside, the intimate spaces of residence can be seen as protective capsules, while the more public areas – like the living room and kitchen – can be tied more directly to the cityscape. Conventional urban planners tend to see buildings exclusively from the exterior and as nothing more than physical intrusions conflicting with their ambitions for uninterrupted traffic flow. In opposition to this oppressive type of urbanism, Ushida-Findlay propose that, by acknowledging buildings from the "inside out" and envisioning city planning from a microcosmic-to-macrocosmic perspective, architects can help empower city dwellers to re-shape their own living and working environments. Such ideas are on collision course with most contemporary urban planning procedures, but they lie at the core of the Ushida-Findlay partnership's concept of "re-engagement." They propose a way of looking at the city as an infinitely varied tapestry of corporeal, perceptual, psychological, botanical, and topographical experiences that relate to what they have termed "psycho-geometry." This is a totally integrated cityscape predicated on the ultimate inside/outside experience.

In two of their more famous buildings – the Soft and Hairy House and Truss Wall House – Ushida-Findlay demonstrate their surreal sensibility and notion of infusing elements of the outside urban context. The Soft and Hairy House of 1994 was built for a young couple in Tsukuba City near Tokyo and based on the development of interior spaces as an expression of what the architects have called "orgiastic potency." While perhaps more of a comment on the owners' libido than a therapeutic reality of the architecture, the house does present a sensuous explosion of organic forms that fuse, convolute, and metamorphose into each other to produce a compelling environment of fluid membranes and cradling sanctuaries. The ecologically responsible features of the dwelling include an extensive roof garden, which both enriches quality of life for the residents and provides insulation to maintain a steady inte-

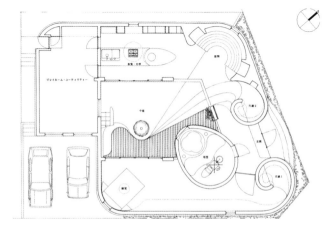

rior temperature. Clearly indebted to Kiesler's Endless House, with its indeterminate flow of ceilings into floors, allusions to pre-natal existence, and feminine metaphors, Ushida-Findlay's interpretation of house-as-living-organism adds an intriguing cross-cultural dimension. It is full of Oriental and cosmic references that suspend this building somewhere between a Zen garden and a communications satellite.

The even more daring and aggressively organic structure Truss Wall House uses curved concrete construction to achieve what is described by the architects as "a fluid continuity of sensuousness and physical imagery which is disseminated with a person's movement through that space." Flanked on all sides by conventional Japanese two- and three-story domestic buildings, this glistening white, dramatically sculptural edifice appears to be an extra-terrestrial satellite that intended to land temporarily, but then decided to stay on in the neighborhood as a prophetic manifestation of future lifestyle. The building functions as a "live-in theatrical event"; it is like a human organ with technological, spatial, and thermodynamic functions. Among its green features, there is a permaculture space between the walls utilizing indigenous planting and offering an agricultural opportunity for the residents to grow their own herbs and vegetables.

While some of Ushida-Findlay's proposed inside/outside relationships in architecture are vividly evident and compelling as formal inventions, their claims for the Truss Wall House as a physical and metaphorical bridge between living space and neighborhood are not as clear. Perhaps if some of the formal vocabulary of this dwelling was to expand into streetscape amenities, adjacent buildings, park lands, and, ultimately, into a larger urban plan, these connections could be made more tangible. However, by choosing such an exotic visual language for the house, the designers have tended to exclude some of the most essential ingredients of communication in an urban environment. This refers to those psychological references that provide the glue of common experience among city dwellers and

Soft and Hairy House
Ushida-Findlay Partnership
Tsukuba City, Japan
1994

the basis of any true fusion with context. These bonding elements are the myriad signs, symbols, icons, and states of reflex identification that shape the "collective unconscious" (in other words, the essential raw materials of recognition which make a city readable). In this respect, an inclusive collage of the familiar is a far more appropriate resource for true integration than an imposition of the unfamiliar.

This question of finding a more integrated urban language – one of the goals sought by Ushida and Findlay – brings up a profound issue in the development of any new environmentally friendly architecture or public space. A major factor in responding to the ecological model of integrated systems is an understanding of nature's capacity to include, rather than exclude. As mentioned earlier, it is still the tendency of most environmentally committed architects today to impose a building on the cityscape and then rationalize its internalized green features as evidence of the designer's awareness of outside natural forces (while the edifice itself is designed as a an insular object). Ushida-Findlay are tactically correct in "wanting to play interior and exterior aspects against each other, by looking for clues in the city which can generate the design." They are also right in seeking guidance through the lessons of natural phenomena and the relationship of city dwellers to their surroundings. But the next stage of architectural development – in fact, the challenge to all green designers – should be the integration of buildings with their contexts as seamless fusions of each other; as syntheses of ecological processes already in place, and as monitors of people's subliminal reactions to environmental signs and signals, which can then be translated into billboards of the collective unconscious. These objectives are the complete opposite of most traditional 20th-century architecture, but they are also the wave of the future.

Whereas Ushida-Findlay seems mostly concerned with the relationship of organic architecture to urban situations, the pioneering work of British architect Arthur Quarmby has concentrated on rural sites and the promotion of a type of earth-sheltered structure he has identified as 'geotecture.' Trained at the Leeds School of Architecture in England, he became a specialist in plastics and tension structures, building the world's largest transparent air-supported dome early in his career. His pioneering work in earth-shelters started more than thirty years ago and, as a result, he has led the way by focusing on the most obvious difficulties involved with underground construction – referring to severe temperature changes, excessive rain or snow, and high humidity – all characteristics of rural England, where he has built most of his structures. In this respect, he is probably the most experienced and technically proficient innovator in the earth-shelter field, since most of his specialized colleagues tend to practise in much more favorable climates. As case in point, the main virtues identified with sod roof structures have been their appeal for insulating houses in desert communities and for energy-efficient cooling systems in sun-drenched environments.

Rather than look to 20th-century technocentric construction for precedents, Quarmby prefers drawing inspiration from such sources as the Tholos Tombs of Mycenae, Nero's trench-like Golden House on the Capitoline Hill, Hindu religious shrines in India, and Bronze Age earth-covered shelters of the Tuatha de Danaan civilization in Britain. By observing the principles of these ancient structures, he embraces one of the most progressive aspects of carving into the land – to create "invisible architecture." The purpose is to develop a complete fusion of habitat with existing topography, so that it becomes difficult to discern where building separates from landscape. "Earth-sheltered architecture is different," Quarmby states. "It is a reverse of the normal situation in which the exterior form of the structure makes the greatest impact." He also understands the revolutionary implications of reducing the physical presence of shelter (as typically synonymous with the art of architecture) and, instead, converting the

Soft and Hairy House
Ushida-Findlay Partnership
Tsukuba City, Japan
1994

emphasis to surface landscape and the use of trees and plants as an extended form of iconography. He sees that "blending into the landscape is by now too limited an aim" and proposes a greater readiness "to use the over-the-top landscaping ... in order to create a striking or even startling feature in the land-scape – but with the use of vegetation."

Arthur Quarmby's vision of earth-shel-tered houses is refreshingly free from any cult and escapist motives associated with a 1960s alternative lifestyle, from the briefly fashion-able phenomenon of suburban troglodytism, or from the urban panic neurosis that drives the agoraphobic city dweller to seek sanctuary in a natural refuge. Even though the popular incentive to build this type of architecture is depressingly low, he still sees himself as part of a mainstream movement and the beneficiary of a reversal of resistance in the near future.

For this reason he has built his structures with consummate attention to technical detail, set up monitoring systems to test results, and committed himself to the personal act of living in an earth-sheltered house. In pursuing his "zero energy – zero land use" goals, he has become a leading innovator in excavation, insulation, prevention of leakage, humidity control, and interior illumination.

When designing Underhill in Yorkshire for his own family, Quarmby cut Britain's first con-temporary earth-shelter into a sloping hillside to a maximum depth of 4.8 meters. By means of skylights and reflections from an internal pool, the interior is flooded with light and, as a result of the deep sod and vegetation covering the roof, the living spaces are comfortable, in spite of the inclement weather of the region. As a result of the large social area at the center of the house, a crowning tetrahedron of glass

Soft and Hairy House
Ushida-Findlay Partnership
Tsukuba City, Japan
1994

Truss Wall House
Ushida-Findlay Partnership
Tsurukawa, Machida-City,
Japan
1991–93

for illumination, and easy access to the well-lit bedroom wings, the building completely defeats the rhetorical complaint among earth-shelter critics that such dwellings are dark, damp, and claustrophobic. By engineering a downhill drainage system that feeds into a porous subsoil of sandstone, and by installing a large capacity extract fan near the pool, Quarmby has kept the interior humidity remarkably low and the temperatures well controlled throughout the year, with a minimum use of fossil fuels. As a final tribute to the ecological intelligence of Underhill, its rooftop has become a microcosmic wildlife reserve and, as Quarmby has observed, "The profit from fattening sheep on the roof should not be discounted."

In a more recent project for the town of Penrith in the English Lake District, Arthur Quarmby has designed the Cumbria Visitor Centre to function as a resource for displaying

the arts and crafts of the region. The main innovation in this project is the architect's intelligent decision to hide what would have been a large and intrusive structure in a beautiful national park by using earth berms and landscaped roofs as natural camouflage. The interior includes some of the largest Gunite vaults ever proposed, and daylight filtered from above supplies ample illumination to the exhibits and shops. The major values of this building to the cause of earth-sheltered architecture are its use of landscape to disguise a large public building, the securing of a commitment from England's Department of the Environment to sponsor a daring technology, and the precedent that has been set for both municipal and commercial involvement in ecological design.

A more exaggerated interpretation of organic form, combined with earth shelter, can be found in Peter Vetsch's series of Nine Houses, built in 1993 in Dietikon, Switzerland. Trained in agriculture, with early career intentions to become a farmer, this Swiss architect shares ideas in common with Kiesler (a fusion of floor planes, walls, and ceilings reminiscent of the Endless House), Jersey Devil (hands-on construction) and Arthur Quarmby (a missionary-like advocacy of earth-sheltered buildings). Vetsch's collection of semi-troglodyte houses are built in concrete sprayed over metal frames, then insulated by a thick layer of foam. These roofs are subsequently covered with fleece filter mats and, finally, a landfill of soil and humus. The architect credits nature itself as the entire source of ideas behind his use of convoluted forms, while the tunnel-like interiors draw inspiration from the habitat of burrowing animals and his deep concern for energy conservation and a more prudent use of land surface. At the same time Vetsch denies historical connections to subterranean architecture and insists his building configurations are entirely a response to the surrounding environment and a rational program of functionalism.

Vetsch's Nine Houses measure from 800 to 2,200 cubic meters per unit, are divided into interior spaces varying from four to seven rooms, and are clustered around a central pond and biotope area. Located within a "U"-shaped hill, each house is enclosed by landscape, with living areas oriented to the south and the bedrooms to the sorth. Light sources for the bathrooms, kitchens, and other centrally located facilities come from skylights. The innovative construction technology consists of a 25-centimeter-thick layer of polymer-bitumen (a foam product made of recycled glass), applied directly to the structural surface of sprayed concrete.

Unfortunately the exaggerated curvilinear forms associated with designers like Peter Vetsch have become illustrative clichés for an earth-centric philosophy – exactly the way rotated grids, skewed I-beams, and exposed duct systems have become stereotypical representations of the technocentric. This is one of the dangers of conceiving architecture as an exaggerated sculptural experience. While Vetsch's environmental intentions are aesthetically reinforced by his choice of flowing volumes, the inhabitants of one of his buildings might well long for the visual relief of a few vertical walls or some reassuring rectangles to serve as formal counterpoint to the relentless use of amoebic shapes. In this respect he might take a few cues from the brilliantly sculptural work of Frank O. Gehry, who has managed to stop short of a perilous plunge into the excessively baroque by maintaining a satisfying tension between his convoluted wave forms and a chunky Cubist geometry. On the other hand, from the perspective of earth-friendly technology, it should go on record here that Gehry's buildings may be organic in appearance, but they are the polar opposite of environmentally responsible architecture. His work is actually a hyperbolic celebration of toxic materials and wasteful technology. For example, his use of massive expanses of titanium and aluminum-clad walls (some of the most lethal materials available in terms of manufacturing technology and industrial pollution) are just the beginning of these offenses. His sculptural virtues aside, Gehry's work is at

Truss Wall House
Ushida-Findlay Partnership
Tsurukawa, Machida-City,
Japan
1991–93

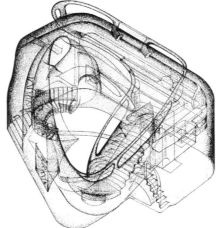

Underhill
Arthur Quarmby
Yorkshire, England
1974

the pinnacle of design-centered architecture today and may also be among the least conscionable from an ecological standpoint. In contrast to this kind of blatant disregard for green principles, Vetsch is at least moving in an admirable direction (his tendency toward a kind of Gaia-fetish organic design notwithstanding) and his targets of research seem destined to make a valuable contribution to future environmental construction.

Like all green architects today, Vetsch's work asks disturbing questions concerning what hope exists for slowing the growth of irresponsible mega-structures that endanger all the principles of the Age of Ecology. The rampant competition for "world's tallest towers" is based on the short-term economics of inflated land values, the profits to be garnered from stacked-up real estate, and is manifesting in record-breaking high-rises in the name of gain. Given these ego-inflating rewards, there seems no way to stop the onslaught. The prospect for any kind of widespread commitment to a technologically

difficult and financially costly earth-shelter, of the kind suggested by architects like Quarmby and Vetsch, seems relatively futile. Furthermore, there are many technical issues to be resolved before the concept can even be totally justified as ecologically favorable. In her 1990 article entitled *Cave Dwellers in the Age of Plastics* Kirsten Fuchs pointed out that Vetsch's iron armatures "deflect natural earth radiation and cause damage to human health due to unnatural bundling or re-direction of such radiations. Also, the polyurethane that was used for insulation has been medically identified as a possible cause of allergies." These criticisms suggest that Vetsch's earth-sheltered architecture must substitute current materials with more natural choices, although this also increases costs and creates a further chasm between the motivations of profit-obsessed real estate development and the acceptance of green architecture.

This evaluation is not intended to single out Vetsch's buildings for a critique of their economic viability or their failure to eliminate all toxic materials – the costs and degree of effectiveness of green technology are problems with virtually all of the work illustrated in this book – but it does bring up the question of how much progress the Western world's profligate consumer culture will realistically sponsor under the circumstances. Messianic designers like Quarmby and Vetsch, with the help of environmental scientists, will undoubtedly come up with the answers to most eco-tech and eco-cost questions over the next decade, although this does not assure a marketplace for their services. Better communications are part of the answer (assuming someone is listening); still, as long as human enterprise is driven by a demand for instant gratification and the acquisition of limitless wealth, there is a profound risk that only a handful of the converted (presently a minuscule percentage of the world's population) will even begin to think about underground architecture as a serious alternative for the new millennium. There are encouraging signs – for example, the fact that huge segments of Tokyo's retail and entertainment industries are now located in the subway system – but the deeper philosophical message of an underground architectural future eludes the majority of architects and their clients.

The work of Vetsch and Quarmby is based on the interpretation of environmental design as a condition of moral resposibility, where decisions about form are driven by an earth-centric conscience and a conservationist view of humanity's role in nature. Their use of serpentine shapes, locally available materials and fusions of structure with topography are as much a reflection of ethical standards as aesthetic choice. As a result, their buildings are purposely rural and linked to regional identity.

Underhill
Arthur Quarmby
Yorkshire, England
1974

Underhill
Arthur Quarmby
Yorkshire, England
1974

The work of Charles Jencks, in association with his late wife Maggie Keswick, is also characterized by convoluted form, partially buried structures and a surreal shaping of landscape; however, their imagery is more about cosmic symbolism and astro-physics than conservation and ecology. In many ways their work can be seen as an example of the ultimate in cosmopolitan cosmology. The Garden of Cosmic Speculation in Scotland is a profound work of landscape architecture designed to demonstrate Jencks' literary theories concerning cosmogenic sources in the building arts. Primarily known as an architectural theoretician and advocate of Postmodernism, he has now proven to be a leading voice in the environmental design movement. Jencks' occasional building renovations, houses, and interior designs have gained him a respectable reputation for the use of complex symbolic imagery (sometimes diluted by a certain decorative excess). His critical texts, on the other hand, have probably influenced the 1980s generation of designers more extensively than any living architectural writer since Robert Venturi unleashed *Complexity and Contradiction in Architecture* during the 1960s. It is always difficult for a prominent figure in literature to jump the fence into the actual practice of the profession of his or her critical

focus. In recent history, one thinks of the perilous decision of certain art and theater critics to exhibit their own paintings and stage their own plays. Jencks' migration into symbolic buildings and landscape architecture has been particularly risky, mainly because he is vulnerable to attack on every level from those disgruntled practitioners he may have trashed, or ignored altogether, during his many years of critical writing.

Fortunately, as a reinforcement of Charles Jencks' already formidable reputation, The Garden of Cosmic Speculation is a compelling and haunting masterpiece. It is also one of the few contemporary environmental works that has been actually drawn from a complex network of cosmological and astrophysical references. Both Jencks and Keswick have studied their subject in depth, and every nuance of the sculptural configurations used in shaping the landscape and the symbolism developed for graphic iconography has been filtered through a carefully researched body of references. Confirming the philosophy expressed in his book on *The Architecture of the Jumping Universe*, he and Maggie Keswick have actually produced a much more persuasive example of cosmological imagery than most of the designers to whom he attributes this achievement in his publication. Jencks has lavished praise on certain contemporary neo-Constructivist architects for their sinuous and labyrinthine formal inventions. In his view, their convoluted forms signify both the organic configurations of nature and the chaotic disorder of the universe. In reality, camouflaged by the artificially progressive conceits associated with computer-aided design, most of this New Age architectural iconography applauded by Jencks is the opposite of advanced environmental design. It is, instead, characterized by an unconscionable use of toxic materials, detachment from ecological values, resolution in forms that lack any true cosmic significance (but seem more like conventional shape-making for its own sake), and a tenacious attach-

ment to formal devices that look suspiciously as if they might have been cribbed from some early Cubist paintings.

The entire Scotland property is filled with symbolic artifacts, and the renovated house includes some masterful uses of wave motifs on ceilings and walls to represent the more recent scientific views of the universe as an endlessly expanding convulsion of chaos and continuity. With the exception of some rather fussily designed artifacts and interior space decor intended to illustrate the cosmic mysteries, the main park areas have been created with a thoughtfully spare design program, composed of interlocking earth mounds, water basins, and plant materials. Jencks' wife was a

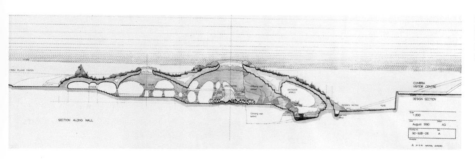

Cumbria Visitor Centre
Arthur Quarmby
Penrith, Lake District,
England
Project, 1990

Page 96 and 97
Nine Houses
Peter Vetsch
Dietikon, Switzerland
1993

space that flows into itself. Their garden also expresses the fractal geometry of nature where (contrary to orderly appearances) everything is irregular. In this way The Garden of Cosmic Speculation is an endeavor to create a terrestrial representation of the jump start surges that have marked the course of evolution, and such non-Euclidean concepts as amorphic, the entropic, and the indeterminate.

On many levels Charles Jencks' literary speculations on phenomenology and architecture seem to parallel the theories on entropy and art generated by the earthwork artist Robert Smithson in the late 1960s. At that time Smithson (later killed in a plane crash in 1973 during aerial photography of one of his projects) was consumed by an interest in the relationships between the human brain, natural processes, and the difficulties of expressing his discoveries in art. As part of an essay entitled Sedimentation of the Mind for *Artforum* magazine in the USA, he wrote: "The earth's surface and the figments of the mind have a way of disintegrating into discrete regions of art. Various agents, both fictional and real, somehow trade places with each other – one cannot avoid muddy thinking when it comes to earth projects, or what I call 'abstract geology.' One's mind and the earth are in a constant state of erosion, mental rivers wear away abstract banks, brain waves undermine cliffs of thought, ideas decompose into stones of unknowing, and conceptual crystallizations break apart into deposits of gritty reason. ... Slump, debris, slides, avalanches all take place within the cracking limits of the brain. The entire body is pulled into the cerebral sediment, where particles and fragments makes themselves known as solid consciousness. A bleached and fractured world surrounds the artist. To organize this mess of corrosion into patterns, grids, and subdivisions is an esthetic process that has scarcely been touched." The poetic power of Smithson's writings and earthworks – combining his vision of brutality, chaos, erosion and a struggle to make sense of natural disorder – relied on a more terrestrial focus than the cosmogenic abstractions in The

leading scholar of Chinese gardens and brought to the project a knowledge of Buddhist meditation environments and the Japanese Zen concept of "borrowed scenery," wherein the terrestrial landscape is only a transitory microcosm representing the paradisiacal archipelagos of an eternal afterlife. Jencks and Keswick combined these traditions with their fascination for the nonlinear dynamics of Chaos Theory and an interest in bridging ideas from ancient cosmology to the latest speculations of astrophysics. Anxious to transcend the mechanistic interpretations of phenomena that have dominated Western culture since the Greeks introduced atomism, their garden represents an endeavor to capture the spirit of cosmogenesis and the endless continuum concept of an outer

Garden of Cosmic Speculation. Although diver-
gent in concept, these artists have explored
environmental symbolism on levels that are
much more consistent with the sensibility of a
post-industrial age than most current green
architecture.

Charles Jencks' and Maggie Keswick's
plan for the estate garden in Scotland incorporated a series of existing hills and the remains
of an old marsh. Then they added a 50-foot-
high spiral mound connected to a series of
snake-like configurations 400 feet long.
Thwarted by the rains of the region, which
tend to aggressively wash away artificial earth
formations, they decided to keep the mound-
ing process fairly primitive and develop the
final earthwork into a composition of site-specific twists and folds. These sculptural features
are both inspired by and submit to regional
terrain, becoming the basis of a formal physics
garden intended to present models of the
atom, the universe, and various other cosmogenic sources of imagery. As Jencks describes
the result: "These were designed with scientists and metalworkers, but they interpret the
truths of the universe metaphorically – they
are not illustrations of contemporary science
and technology so much as reinterpretations
of what these public discourses tell us."

For all their good intentions and their
estimable environmental merits of their work,
architects like Ambasz, Noever, Quarmby,
Vetsch, and Jencks/Keswick are still elitist and
produce work that is exclusively available to
affluent individuals who can afford to clear
their consciences with an occasional gesture in
the direction of ecological design. What the
green cause desperately needs is a universal
commitment by governments to research and
sponsor economically affordable green habitats and a grass-roots movement of hands-on
builders who want to set an example of sane
living at a reasonable price. While hardly representing the start of a global trend, the work of
David Lea in North Wales and Gianni Pettena on
the Island of Elba at least shows what is possible with a low budget, a prudent use of
resources, and a lot of ingenuity.

Page 98–101
**The Garden
of Cosmic Speculation**
Charles Jencks
Scotland
1989–

Forcing yourself to use restricted means is the sort of restraint that liberates inventing. It obliges you to make a kind of progress you can not even imagine in advance.

Pablo Picasso

Architecture in its Cultural Context

David Lea, an architect educated at Cambridge and presently living in Gwynedd, is, like Peter Vetsch, deeply dedicated to buildings as extensions of their contexts, and favors important physical and psychological interactions between the natural environment and the way people relate to all of the various components of a building. Driven by a philosophy that "architecture cannot be divorced from nature," he describes it as a means "to recreate a corner of paradise. By paradise I mean the place where people may experience the fullest possible sense of well-being. The key to paradise is a harmonious relationship between man and nature." This viewpoint sounds almost naive in its earnest simplicity. However, as noted earlier in these pages, his observations are fully supported by psychologist Theodore Roszak and a growing number of his colleagues, who have concluded that nature deprivation is a major cause of mental maladjustment. Lea's convictions are profoundly felt and right on target, given the fact that at least 90 percent of practising architects in the world today could not care less about humanity's connections to nature and seem bent on maintaining this complacent state of detachment.

Although David Lea's central practice has produced impressive housing and educational buildings in North Wales, one of his most intriguing projects is a small rural cottage he built for a London painter with very limited resources. Entitled Studio in the West Country, this tiny thatched-roof structure seems to recall the Arts and Crafts Movement, harken back to Ruskin's and Morris' rejection of the industrial revolution, and resurrect a lost set of values concerning how to live in harmony with the immediate environment. Constructed for a mere £3,300, his house looks like a hybrid cross between a tender for Noah's Ark and an aboriginal mud hut. On closer inspection, however, one understands the brilliant use of minimal technology, the ingenious fusion of materials (bent saplings, chicken wire, cement reinforced with cow hair, straw insulation, and reflective ceramic tiles), and the final aesthetic triumphs of the ensemble.

The dwelling was built by the combined talents of David Lea and his artist client. He worked with her for several weeks on the site, established the basic structural systems of bent wood armature, and then returned periodically to see how she was progressing with the final details. Recalling the hands-on processes used by Jersey Devil – but on an even more elementary and earth-friendly level – Studio West is a mini-triumph of primitive construction and site orientation. It also creates an image that seems to successfully evoke the combination of an ancient Celtic earthwork and a primordial habitat. Every inch of this modest structure leaves the visitor with a peculiar sense of witnessing a prophetic vision for an intelligent alternative to a *Mad Max* future – meaning one ravaged by environmental plunder. Studio West is the alternative to a time when all of the fossil fuels have been exhausted, the rapacious industries have been reduced to archaeological wastelands of twisted steel, humanity has returned to foraging for food in the wilderness, and vengeful forests have reclaimed the world's major cities.

Gianni Pettena's House on Elba is even more primitive and low-budget than Studio West. Pettena, currently a professor at the University of Florence, began his career in the 1970s as a major contributor to an architectural wing of the earthworks movement, at that time being led by artists Robert Smithson, Nancy Holt, Michael Heizer, Dennis Oppenheim, and Walter de Maria. Sometimes credited as the European counterpart of Gordon Matta-Clark (the brilliant French-American pioneer of Deconstruction in art, who utilized existing buildings for a series of surgical cuttings and removals), the work of Pettena pursued a more geomorphic direction. While he shared Matta-Clark's interest in creating interventions with "found buildings," his approach was involved with themes of re-birth through nature, as opposed to seditious attacks on formalist design. As the same time, Pettena's early efforts had guerrilla-like characteristics, using natural phenomena to demonstrate his own subversive tendencies. In three projects, which

Studio in the West Country
David Lea
England
1985

(at least temporarily) uninhabitable; but the result was a trenchant commentary on American lifestyle. Both clay and ice are ecologically favorable construction materials in areas of the globe with severe hot and cold climates; but, in the Minneapolis and Salt Lake City communities, the Pettena projects were interpreted as subversive assaults on the USA's sacred traditions of wasteful resource consumption.

After his 1970s sojourn in America, Pettena returned to Italy and continued to work on a series of politically and environmentally motivated installation and public performance projects. His more recent work has focused on building an ecologically sensitive structure on the Island of Elba. In a location of spectacular natural beauty, his main focus in this personal house has been to intrude on the context as little as possible. The dwelling was developed out of a fisherman's storage shed for nets and assembled mostly out of found objects and materials the architect gathered while scavenging around the island. The effect of the house is like a primordial collage, recalling some beachcomber's cottage in a Somerset Maugham novel – isolated, unpretentious, and improvisational. Similar to David Lea's Studio in the West Country, the Pettena dwelling stands as an example of how more fortunate survivors may live after the impending environmental apocalypse has driven escapees into the wilderness. In many ways this structure is a continuation of the philosophical direction established by Pettena's early projects. It is a concession that, in the final ecological scenario, nature consumes all. In this case, instead of perpetuating the politicized environmental polemic of the 1970s, the House on Elba is an architectural elegy for a more contemplative climate. It strips away the excesses of consumer culture and demonstrates the value of modesty, economy, and a primal sense of an art experience translated into the simplest form of architecture. It expresses the values of a real post-industrial world – not some intellectualized facsimile that celebrates its purported Gaia connections with a kitchen full of ice makers and microwave ovens.

he called "Anarchitecture" – Ice I, Ice II, and Clay House – he developed the concept of using natural phenomena as a metamorphic repossession of architecture. Taking his cues from the importance of building facades in Italy as the "communicative skin of architecture," Pettena operated on a private house and a university administration building in Minneapolis during the winter by spraying water over these structures and freezing them into blocks of ice. In an equally controversial project in Salt Lake City, he covered an entire suburban residence with wet clay in the heat of summer and allowed the sun to bake the dwelling into a kind of "ghost adobe." Once the ice and clay had consumed these structures, they became

Pettena sees his House on Elba as "a place to look at the stars." David Lea believes that the role of architecture is not to "express the age," but instead "to have a resonance which quickens our spirits." As a result, the work of both architects is very low-key, cost effective, and closely aligned with the rhythms and processes of nature. At the polar opposite interpretation of site-specific architecture, Hans Hollein's recent design for a European Center of Volcanism in France is precisely an example of "expressing the age" by means of an aggressive intervention in the landscape.

As Austria's most famous living architect, Hollein has played a role in the forefront of various aesthetic directions over the last few decades – including participation in early 1970s radical architecture, followed by important work in the Postmodernist idiom, a tentative flirtation with deconstructivism in the 1980s, and, more recently, an increasing involvement with the environmental movement. Much of his work has been characterized by a lavish eclecticism, Pop-culture irony, and a tendency toward decorative and sculptural excesses which his razor sharp architectural sensibilities have usually curbed in the nick of time – or, as critic Joseph Rykwert commented on Hollein's risky extremism: "He consciously stands on the brink of kitsch, but never passes the line."

Hollein's 1994 "Vulcania", European Center of Volcanism, designed for the Clermont-Ferand region of France, is a dramatic complex situated at a 1,000-meter altitude and mostly carved out of the basin of an extinct volcano. This boldly profound cultural facility represents a progression in his work that seems to conceptually transcend most of the buildings that have previously defined his career.

The circular configuration of the building, underground exhibit spaces, and a large cone-shaped tower at the surface level symbolize the various elements of terrain associated with volcanoes and are intended to respond to people's curiosity about the violent eruptions that have determined the formation of the earth. Hollein has intentionally given the entire com-

plex a strong ritualistic and cosmological quality, consistent with both the mystical and the scientific aspects of vulcanology. Its surface portions suggest eruptions and incisions in the landscape, while its subterranean sections refer to the layered materials of geological study. By an integration of structure and landscape, the architect has introduced a series of sculptural volumes that metaphorically reflect the existing topography of the region, but which in this case appropriately allude to a Dante-esque or Jules Verne-like descent into the center of the earth.

From an iconographic standpoint, this Center of Volcanism represents a superb fusion of idea, structure, and context. Rather than

House on Elba
Gianni Pettena
Elba, Italy
1982–85

Page 106 and 107
"Vulcania", European
Center of Volcanism
Hans Hollein
St. Ours-les-Roches,
Auvergne, France
1994–2001

Hollein's uses of volcanic materials, incorporation of existing topography, and sensitivity to the total site, place this building in the forefront of environmental imagery; but the next phase of creative development for all eco-oriented architects today is to strike the balance between green science and green art.

Hollein's most acclaimed building to date – and certainly an important experiment with site-specific architecture – is the Museum Abteiberg in Mönchengladbach. The structure is built into an impressive hillside and includes roofs and facades that can be walked upon – very much in the way that pedestrians animate Emilio Ambasz's ACROS-Building in Fukuoka. The concept grew out of an earlier urban plan that Hollein had developed for the city, and this sense of a fragmented hill town on a picturesque promontory informs the entire project. The building cuts, weaves, plunges, and masterfully articulates the site with a sculptural dynamism rarely achieved in the 20th century, save the earlier organic architecture triumphs of Frank Lloyd Wright. This particular structure perfectly reinforces Hollein's belief that "form does not develop from the material demands of use but from the very being of use, from its spiritual meaning, from the sense of all physical reality." He believes that human shelter must be associated with ritual and connected to the sacred and erotic; that buildings speak out (as in *architecture parlante*) appealing to all of the senses through multi-dimensions of participation.

prescribe the building and its study facilities as the final product, Hollein has proposed that the entire region of extinct volcanoes be included as part of the exhibition. From a functional standpoint, he has provided a circular matrix and network of passages that take the visitor through an inside/outside experience, demonstrate how volcanic activity occurs, and allow for the study of strata elements, materials, and other geological information.

While the architect mentions his use of regional materials in the construction of the Center of Volcansim, he has not indicated whether this includes a conscientious program of green technology as part of its realization. If not, this brings up a persistently gnawing question at the core of most environmental architecture, that is, why do so few examples achieve an equilibrium between ecologically favorable building techniques and their translation into a new visual language? Certainly

The work of SITE, an architectural group in New York founded in 1970, has contributed to environmental thinking and the integration of architecture with its context for more than 20 years. Originally identified with the loosely defined movement called "Radical Architecture" in the 1970s – which also included Hans Hollein, Gianni Pettena, Emilio Ambasz, Ettore Sottsass, Alessandro Mendini, and such groups as Archigram, Haus Rucker, Archizoom, and Superstudio, among others – SITE's approach during that period was a critique of Modernist traditions and an exploration of the ambiguous connections between art and architecture.

Page 108 and 109
Municipal Museum
Abteiberg
Hans Hollein
Mönchengladbach,
Germany
1972–82

Among the group's better-known buildings – a series of eight merchandising showrooms for the BEST Products Company – two such structures became prophetic indicators of SITE's future work – the Forest Building in Richmond, Virginia (1980), and the Rainforest Showroom in Hialeah, Florida (1979).

The BEST catalogue and showroom series was sponsored by the company's owners, Sydney and Frances Lewis, who were major American art collectors with an unusually enlightened agenda for bringing art into the public domain. Rather than plunk down monumental sculpture in front of their buildings – a prevalent practice of the 1970s, facetiously labeled by many critics as "plop art" – BEST encouraged SITE to expand the horizons of public art. The corporation's typical stores were formula supermarkets (banal brick boxes sitting on highway strips) which SITE used as a subject matter for art. Given the sanctity of formalist design in the early 1970s, this approach was seen as radical and subversive. From an orthodox Modernist perspective, it undermined the established aesthetic values of "real architecture," which were then (and still are) seen exclusively as a mission of form making, shape making, and space making. Based on an opposite premise, SITE treated the BEST showrooms as existing "readymades" (to borrow a term from Duchamp), and as targets of disruptive interventions for altered meanings. By taking advantage of people's reflex identification with BEST's prosaic commercial imagery, these architectural inversions added an interesting dimension to the idea of "narrative" architecture. They became examples of edifices used as informational sponges, where the absorption of people's subconscious reactions toward certain archetypal buildings was played off against a generally passive view of architecture. For example, the public rarely considers the aesthetic role of buildings in their daily lives, or whether these intrusions have any meaning whatsoever beyond providing shelter. Architecture is usually taken for granted as a generic part of the background, and seldom seen as a notable presence in the foreground.

Also, the rather chilly language of Modern design has only exacerbated this state of indifference. In the case of the BEST showroom, SITE developed the idea of "architecture as a commentary on architecture." This included the use of disorienting elements that tilt, twist, crumble, break apart, and basically question rhetorical definitions by initiating new thresholds of debate concerning the roles of art and architecture in the public domain. As evidence of this, one of the most frequent reactions from first-time viewers of the showrooms has been: "You know, I never thought about a building before I saw this one." These conditions of questioning, bemusement, and ambivalence have become the basis of critical dialogue and a valuable part of these structures' architectural significance.

The original site areas for the Forest Building and the Rainforest Building were each covered with trees and rich ground vegetation. SITE decided that the iconography of these structures should grow out of a conscientious preservation of the natural environment by fusing the context into the buildings. The showrooms' commonplace characteristics were used as a foil to create a new kind of interaction between landscape and architecture. They were designed to seem as though they had been consumed by a portentous role reversal – or as the victims of "nature's revenge." This sense of an intrusion by forest and plant life was achieved in the Virginia showroom by means of a massive incision, splitting the building apart and allowing giant oak trees and ground cover to march through the open chasm. In the Florida Rainforest Building, the existing landscape was extracted and preserved in a nursery during construction. It was then replaced as a garden space between a massive exterior waterwall and a second-layer thermal barrier. In each of these buildings, landscape was interpreted as an integrated and seemingly chaotic extension of the architecture, contrary to its usual role as a peripheral and manicured after-the-fact accessory.

While these early BEST Products showrooms did not contribute to the advancement

Forest Building
SITE
Richmond, Virginia, USA
1980

of green technology, they provided a welcome shade garden environment in Virginia and excellent cooling advantages in Florida. Their main value, however, was to create a communicative iconography based on people's ambivalence concerning architecture's relation to nature. In the Forest Building, for example, the structure was cut into a hillside and, in order to celebrate the connection between the visible surface of the landscape and unseen subterranean levels below, the glass front facade holds back a volume of earth as a geological terrarium. This device carried the inside/outside message of the architecture into a seldom explored "above/below" dialogue with the unseen sections of the earth. The terrarium was composed of multiple strata of regional soil and rock and, over a period of time, became populated by underground life – moles, worms, insects, etc. – that frequently animated the inner surface of the glass. This innovation launched SITE into a series of buildings and parks with terrarium wall features which, unlike the bleak opacity of conventional walls, have resulted in true examples of mutable and evolutionary architecture. Buildings that grow and change with time and acknowledge subterranean life as an integral part of architecture carry a valuable message for the green revolution, without proclaiming it through the usual channels of political propaganda.

In 1992, SITE completed a major structure, combining public space and a series of green buildings, for the Seville World Exposition in Spain. The Avenue Five was one of the main pedestrian arteries providing visitors with access to the national pavilions and event areas. Designed as a celebration of the Guadalquivir River that divides the city and of the Expo theme "discovery," this project was also a commemoration of the site where the great explorers' ships were built. After the closing of the exposition, this project has become the centerpiece of a Columbus Park.

The design challenge of Avenue Five was to treat the entire length (nearly half a kilometer) of a grand pedestrian space as a unified experience. The result is based on a fusion of references to the adjacent river and the need to join a series of disparate facilities, including a monorail train, a central station, several leisure gardens, three restaurants, and two information kiosks. In plan, the building is dominated by the straight line of the monorail. This train track is intersected by an undulating glass waterwall that functions as a skin-like membrane to enclose the restaurants and as a metaphorical microcosm of the topography of the Guadalquivir area. The waterwall creates one side of a grand processional, while ivy-encrusted columns and pergolas define the opposite elevation. The surrounding paving is terraced downward to create a riverbed effect along the base of the waterwall and, at the West end of the processional, the source of this canal is contained within a mountain-like earth shelter covering the information booth.

In response to the hot and arid climate of Seville, all of the restaurants in Avenue Five are enclosed by the heat-filtering waterwall and covered by the cooling elements of either an earth-sheltered roof or a vine-covered pergola. These overhead gardens – or "lifted landscapes" – provide a maximum of shade and demonstrate a successful example of aesthetic decisions that grow directly out of incorporating nature's own green technology. Even the low-energy irrigation system servicing the elevated gardens is powered by the static electricity generated through the flow of water over glass. In addition to creating a building that users can hear, smell, touch, and experience

atmospherically, the visual effect (especially with the benefit of time that has elapsed since its completion in 1992) is a building totally constructed out of water and vegetation. In this respect, Avenue Five stands as an excellent example of SITE's continuous endeavor to interpret "art as a condition of climate control."

In a 1997 project for the Museum of Islamic Arts in Doha, Qatar, SITE developed a total fusion of architecture, exhibition spaces, communications technology, and landscape. Confirming the group's belief that architecture should reflect the integrated systems governing nature, the project was the result of a tight collaboration among designers, artists, and technicians. The lead team of SITE, Tourbier and Walmsley (landscape architecture), and Land Design Studio in London (exhibition design) started with the premise that this museum should express the spiritual unity of Islam by means of very simple organizing features. These include: a 12-meter grid plan that "de-materializes" on the exterior to define a public garden, a series of lateral walls that pass from inside to outside becoming an intrinsic part of the exhibition experience, and a sequence of undulating roof planes that create dramatically sculptural interiors with varied ceiling heights. Viewed in context from the adjacent neighborhood, the museum is intended to appear as though "the building is the garden and the garden is the building."

From an environmental technology standpoint, this museum design had to deal with the extreme summer heat and humidity of Qatar, particularly the issue of how to de-humidify the interior spaces in order to accommodate priceless Islamic manuscripts and other historical artifacts. Solutions for these issues include honeycomb insulation and special heat resistant materials for the roof planes, the use of deflected daylight on the interiors, radiant cooling for large spaces, and passive solar cooling for the offices and park areas. In addition, there are shade walls with overhanging pergolas, heavily vegetated courtyards, the use of light-reflecting colors on walls, and the latest advances in green air-handling and de-humidification technology for all galleries and storage areas. To further the cause of green technology, the museum design proposes such innovations as using the nearby ocean as a receptacle for evacuated heat, interior thermal storage to retain cooler night air for daytime use, and a natural ventilation system that reduces heat build-up during the warmest hours.

The architectural imagery of the Museum of Islamic Arts is a response to sources associated with Doha – including Islamic culture, the rolling desert, the sea, nautical commerce, regional vegetation, and the specific topography of the site area. In this sense the choice of configuration is "biomorphic"; meaning that

Avenue Five
SITE
World Expo, Seville, Spain
1992

Page 115–117
Avenue Five
SITE
World Expo, Seville, Spain
1992

**Mary, Star of
the Sea Church**
David Arkin
Gualala, California, USA
1995

lized physical volumes, grid structures, and a sequence of partitions in space which translate this legacy into sculptural form. These layers, starting with the main facade facing south, are a processional colonnade wall, a massive glass waterwall that filters light and cools the lobby area, a grid structure showcasing fragments of Islamic architecture, followed by a succession of exhibition walls in various materials and degrees of opacity, perforation, and transparency. The centerpiece of the museum is a dome-capped building-within-a-building, based on classic Islamic architectural proportions and dedicated to exhibiting religious history.

The interior exhibitions, in addition to showing historical art works, include the latest video equipment to help explain the origins of the artifacts on display and computer technology as part of a global outreach program to access Islamic cultural institutions internationally through a website and the Internet. Most of the showcase facilities are designed as an intrinsic part of the wall system, which also emphasizes SITE's fundamental approach to the integration of architecture and its context – in this case, an endeavor to combine the symbolic presence of the wall, climate-related architectural elements, and cybernetic communications systems to embrace global culture.

In many ways the Museum of Islamic Arts consolidates SITE's belief that the future of architecture will increasingly combine environmental principles with communications technology. It has provided an opportunity to explore these principles within the framework of exhibiting a religion-based history of art, educating people about Islamic culture, and housing these functions in an edifice that weaves together a network of structure, information, and regional imagery. This project also represents a comfortable bridge to the next category of environmental architecture – ritual and symbolic devices that connect buildings to their cultural context.

Although it is rare to find ideal examples of the marriage between green science and green art, the work of California designer Sim Van der Ryn has contributed substantial

both form and content are intended as a visual reflection of the evolutionary processes of nature. It is also "geomorphic"; proposing the building as a metaphorical microcosm of the surrounding area, with references to the wider geographical hemisphere that includes Qatar. From a compositional perspective, the museum has been developed as a system of passages – walls that pass from interior to exterior and slice through dune-like roof vaults – giving visitors the impression of a vast desert landscape, punctuated with architectural features and an occasional oasis of greenery. The design also reflects the traditions of geometric pattern in Islamic art; in this case, rather than limit this choice to wall decoration, SITE uti-

groundwork to both symbolic content and innovative ecological design for more than two decades. As founder and president of the Ecological Design Institute in Sausalito, California, he has continuously served as a leading pioneer in green construction technology (coordinated with aesthetic approaches) that reduces water consumption, utilizes grey water, converts organic wastes into humus for the enrichment of soil, and expands the uses of solar energy. In pursuing his goals he has taught, written books, lectured globally, and developed architectural projects to demonstrate his theories. Unfortunately, as with most revolutionary voices, he has been resisted by the politically threatened, marginalized by the establishment, and frequently denied a rightful access to design commissions. In fact, only

within the past few years has he started to build on a consistent basis.

In association with David Arkin, Sim Van der Ryn has led the Ecological Design Institute's basic missions: to interpret every building as a teaching tool, to think of architecture as an extension of natural processes, to treat ecological responsibility as a pact with the environment, and to make nature visible through design. Whereas a great percentage of their work is directed toward pure environmental research, the construction of a simple chapel by David Arkin – Mary, Star of the Sea – at Gualala Point, California, 120 miles north of San Francisco, provided an opportunity to create a symbolic religious building in fusion with climate, atmosphere, and site. The building, seating about 175 people, is located on a

Mary, Star of the Sea Church
David Arkin
Gualala, California, USA
1995

appears to be a fluid extension of its surroundings. Metaphorically, it seems like both a forest and clearing, a web of branches and an open meadow. The structure communicates an immediate impression of spiritual purpose – although not an obvious church in terms of conventional imagery – and uses its green technology merits to connect the terrestrial to the transcendental.

Two churches in Arkansas, the Thorncrown Chapel in Eureka Springs and the Cooper Memorial Chapel in Bella Vista by the American architect Fay Jones, share David Arkins's concept of translating an earth-centered philosophy into sacred iconography. In the case of the Jones buildings, there is a conscious use of the Gothic style traditionally associated with early Christian churches. However, unlike those weighty medieval predecessors, his religious structures have been ingeniously woven out of a network of web-like timbers that metaphorically connect to surrounding forests. These imaginative edifices actually invert the Gothic construction traditions of massive stone elements in compression; instead, Jones' chapels have been assembled by linear wooden members in tension. The results are distinctly contemporary and lyrical embodiments of Industrial Age technology, expressed through a visual language that evokes a timeless sense of nature and cosmology.

Fay Jones is sometimes condescendingly referred to as a regionalist. In today's cutting-edge critical circles, this marginal category usually refers to any architect who is not located in Los Angeles or New York and whose work doesn't display some overt manifestations of late-version Constructivism. To his great credit, Jones is simply a courageous independent. He is a teacher at the University of Arkansas – with a practice in Fayetteville – who studied with and worked for long periods under the shadow of Frank Lloyd Wright in the 1950s. He finally emerged with a body of environmentally inspired original work in the 1980s and was awarded the American Institute of Architects' highest honor (the A.I.A. Gold

windswept crest overlooking the sea and includes certain physical features that take full advantage of the prevailing air currents. Deflected by an obliquely slanted roof on the west elevation, the wind passing over the east facade clerestory creates a Bernoulli effect (a controlled zone of low pressure) under the roof plane. In combination with temperature-sensitive hydraulic arms that open the windows and prevent overheating, the warm air is thus drawn outward toward the low-pressure zone. In the colder season the heat from the sun is stored in the concrete floor. Arkin's final achievement is a chapel with a consistently comfortable interior temperature in all seasons, side walls that open up completely and allow parishioners to experience services in the open air, and a site orientation that enhances its combined environmental and religious experience.

Mary, Star of the Sea is designed to accommodate a notch in the natural rock formation of the hillside and also relate to a nearby cluster of pine trees. As a result of the atmosphere-responsive technology, of the choice of Douglas Fir as the basic building material, and of an ingenious construction system composed of many short diagonal trusses and split ring joints, the building

Page 122 and 123
Real Goods
Solar Living Center
(see also page 148 and 151)
Van der Ryn Architects
Hopland, California, USA
1996

Medal) in 1990. Since then, he has finally been given a long-overdue important place in the history of American architecture.

The similarities between the Fay Jones and David Arkin ecclesiastical structures derive from a shared American sensibility. Both Jones and Arkin have drawn inspiration from Frank Lloyd Wright's vision of organic architecture, they have had a major influence on the work of students and young professionals, and have demonstrated a profound dedication to green values and a respect for context. Admittedly, from the standpoint of formal choices and a failure to break through into new aesthetic territory, the work of Jones and Arkin is locked into certain residuals of traditional design; but in terms of environmental commitment, their motivations make them assertively part of the future. This paradoxical situation again brings up that nagging question concerning the green movement: when is it going to develop a visual language that is sufficiently radical and con-

tent-driven to aggressively dislodge the dominant Modernist or Constructivist orthodoxy?
In a peculiar way, creativity across the board
in contemporary architecture suffers from
a polarity that is equally regressive at both
ends of the ideological and stylistic spectrum.

By comparison to the rural American spiri-
tualism of Jones' and David Arkins's churches,
or the aggressively cosmogenic symbolism of
Jencks' and Keswick's Scotland park, the ecological and cosmological factors in Antoine Predock's buildings are, by his own admission,
neither conscientiously green, nor particularly
symbolic in origin or intent. His work invariably
demonstrates a brilliant use of sculptural mass
and sensitivity to context. Describing his work
as "abstract landscapes," he is one of the few
architects who proudly sees himself as a regionalist – interpreting this status as the essence of
a new sense of contextualism. His buildings are
distinguished for ideas that emerge out of what
he calls a "naturalistic cosmology."

Educated at Columbia University and
the University of New Mexico, Predock has

designed buildings that have been characterized as south-western since the beginning of
his professional practice in 1967. This identity
has usually referred to an imagery drawn heavily from sources in the adobe construction of
the desert regions and the New Mexican pueb-
los. At its best, Predock's work is brilliantly
fused with landscape in the organic architecture tradition of Wright, or the timeless monumental legacies of Luis Barragán and Louis
Kahn. His less successful examples can be dangerously close to the ubiquitous Taliesin West
chic and the rather cloying "puebloesque"
styles pervading communities like Santa Fe
and Taos. Transcending such problems in his
La Luz Townhouses of 1970, a resident community in Albuquerque, Predock designed a
series of dwellings along the top of a ridge,
thus preserving the ecological balance of a
fragile riverbed. Built of sun-dried adobe
extracted from the site, these houses are especially effective in resisting the desert heat by
reason of the architect's intelligent use of a
time-tested approach to construction technol-

ogy for a warm and dry climate. He also engaged passive solar heating and cooling, and his well integrated, stepped-form imagery for the buildings is distinctly regional in every respect, reflecting what Predock calls the three souls of the south-west: "the Indian, the Spanish, and the Anglo."

He describes his work as "an adventure, a discovery." One of the best examples is the Rio Grande Nature Center of 1982, where Predock built a small educational institution in the middle of a natural wetland and delicate ecosystem. Adjacent to the Rio Grande River as its major watershed, the site is located in the flood plain, and the building had to impose a minimum intrusion on a waterway essential for the sustenance of both the natural and man-made systems of the region. Breaking away from his earlier "puebloid modern," the archi-

tect has retained his loyalty to classic Modernism. For the Nature Center project he has added strong elements of expressed engineering and a primal, fortress-like, imagery that somehow contributes a counterpoint to the soft marshland environment. The building is successfully environmental on several levels. It is symbolic of the local eco-system, provides a tunnel that delights young people who visit the site, and the interior water tubes, which demonstrate how wetlands function, also serve as a passive solar storage facility.

In some respects, Predock's architecture – usually enclosed and inward looking – resembles aspects of Islamic buildings, where walls are designed to enhance the canons of faith, keep out intruders, and deflect the sunlight. To Western eyes, the visual effect of this type of structure can sometimes be perceived as

Page 126 and 127
Cooper Memorial Chapel
Fay Jones and
Maurice Jennings
Bella Vista, Arkansas, USA
1987–88

Originally catapulted to fame as the co-designer (with Richard Rogers) of the Centre Pompidou in Paris and as a progenitor of the so-called "high-tech" movement in architecture, Piano was selected to design the Tjibaou Center through an international competition in 1991. By responding to the wisdom of native advisors within the local Kanak culture, he created a consummate integration of regional materials, traditional construction methods, contemporary technology and ecological design. His conceptual decision to resolve the plan as a series of beehive-like pavilions – reflecting a long legacy of conical architecture in the South Pacific – becomes a sensitive counterpoint to contemporary formal strategies and the existence of topography and vegetation, uniquely identified with the New Caledonian landscape.

From a green design and climate control perspective, Piano has utilized weatherproofed bamboo – the world's most easily erected and rapidly regenerated raw material – as vertical elements that capture and control wind through adjustable ventilators. The use of bamboo also renders the building infinitely renewable and establishes a consensus imagery that fits comfortably into the culture. This motivation toward iconic familiarity is further confirmed by the architect's decision to connect his series of pavilions along a "backbone" ridge, which recalls the linear patterns of typical rural village development.

With the completion of the Tjibaou Center, Piano has achieved the seemingly impossible in contemporary architecture. He has created an inhabitable bridge to the 21st century that embodies past, present and future. Our present Age of Information and Ecology suggests an architecture of less substance and more information, less intrusion and more inclusion, less objectification and more fragmentation, less Euro-centrism and more cultural diversity. Renzo Piano is nearly alone in combining all of these progressive elements in one building.

In many ways the concept of a high art manifestation of green architecture, growing

uninviting and autocratic. On the other hand, like Predock's work, its visual appeal derives from the use of rich earthen materials, a profound sense of context, and a comfortable human scale. While exhibiting a less environmentally sensitized fluidity than the work of architects like Quarmby, Vetsch, and David Lea, Predock maintains a formalistic majesty that seems naturally responsive to each situation – precisely the way desert towns in Arabia impose an assertive geometry that melts seductively into the surrounding rocks and dunes.

From the standpoint of symbolic devices that connect buildings to their cultural context and the achievement of sheer visual poetry in architecture, nothing in recent memory surpasses Genovese architect Renzo Piano's Jean-Marie Tjibaou Cultural Center in New Caledonia. This structure is located in the French territory of Oceania, approximately 1,000 miles east of Sydney, Australia. As a tribute to Piano's sensitivity to the regional environment, it celebrates the multiple layers of Melanesian culture. As the architect observed in developing his vision, "it was not feasible to offer a standard product of Western architecture, with a layer of camouflage on top: it would have looked like an armored car covered with palm fronds."

Above and left
La Luz Townhouses
Antoine Predock
Albuquerque,
New Mexico, USA
1967–74

Right and below
Rio Grande Nature Center
Antoine Predock
Albuquerque, New Mexico, USA
1982

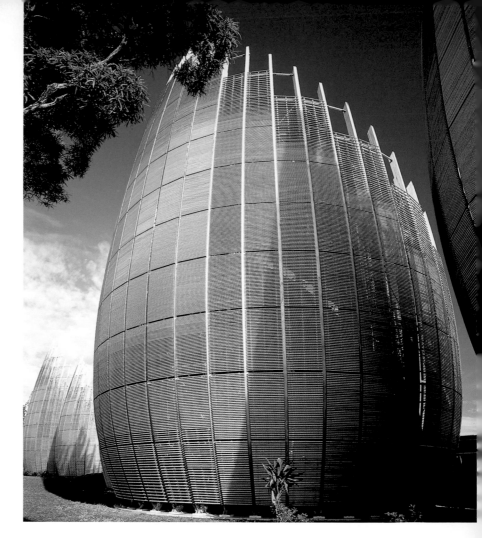

Jean-Marie Tjibaou Cultural Center
Renzo Piano
Nouméa, New Caledonia
1992–98

out of "advanced technology translated into aesthetic terms," can be seen as a contradiction in terms. One primary mission of this text from the beginning has been to identify evidence of a new eco-centric imagery in the building arts that may ultimately dislodge the prevailing clichés of techno-centrism. The most obvious indication, manifested in the work of architects like Ambasz, Noever, Quarmby, Predock, and Piano has been a greater sensitivity to site and the increased use of terrestrial materials and vegetation. This is admirable as part of a public health and artistic choice rationale. At the same time, the

results still fall short of transforming the manufactured metal, chemical, and digital products of environmental technology into a communicative iconography. On the most basic level, very few factory-built artifacts are popularly regarded as humanistic or nature-connected in appearance. For example, if one agrees that the earth art of Robert Smithson is a profoundly humanized representation of his ideas about de-materialization and entropy, then most of today's high-tech environmental architecture – no matter how earnest its ecological and symbolic intentions – tends to look slick, decorous, and glacial by comparison.

The physician can bury his mistakes, but the architect can only advise his clients to plant vines.

Frank Lloyd Wright

Translating Technology into Art

Some dedicated architects are trying to address this issue of eco-tech as art, but their means of expression are often locked into Modernist conventions. In a few cases the results have been convincingly adapted to environmental experimentation, without falling into the trap of an overly cultivated stylistic orthodoxy. The architecture of Thomas Herzog fits this description. Since the 1970s he has been a thoughtful and consistent pioneer in combining a rationalist economy of means with ecological concerns. A professor of design at the Munich Technical University, a believer in interdisciplinary teamwork and research, he would also have to be included on any respectable list of the "world's greatest Modern architects." He maintains this role with a dignity and power that makes it easy to discern the difference between his inventive formal means, imbued with content, and the derivative, vacuous, shape-making associated with academic Modernism. In fact, he now finds himself at the cutting edge of the "new minimalism" which is rapidly gaining ground

as an alternative to the excesses of a declining neo-Constructivism. Compared to an international architecture scene now suffocating from baroque extravagances, Herzog's thoughtful focus on what he terms "constructional physics" is a breath of fresh air. Rather than dwell on the dead-end pursuit of high-tech style, he interprets technology as a response to such issues as zoning, natural infrastructure, economics, site restraints, solar energy, and the thermal value of different materials. He is guided by the laws of physics and the mutable conditions of nature that are destined to be an intrinsic part of all progressive architecture. Lamenting today's superficial flamboyance, he states that: "I am not interested in being provocative; but in view of the all too familiar picture one has of the built environment – with the wretched structures of the past few decades – I don't feel obligated to conform." Herzog believes in "less exhibitionism" and views architecture as "large, expensive objects with long term effects; for short term impressions they are the wrong objects, the wrong medium. They must possess a neutrality that will allow life to develop." His call for restraint in the midst of so much pretentious current grandstanding is a point well taken; but this argument is flawed by the fact that some of the most grandiloquent "exhibitionist" buildings in history have also been among the most enduring (for example, the immortal excesses of the Italian Baroque), and even a few extravagant indulgences planned for the short term (the Eiffel Tower and the Barcelona Pavilion) have a secure place in today's world. Additionally, these monuments have certainly "allowed life to develop."

Thomas Herzog's 1977 House in Regensburg is a simple diamond-shaped structure with a sloping glass roof that allows extra light to penetrate the interior. Indicative of the designer's view that environmental architecture should "make necessary technical features visible ... detailing them in an aesthetically effective form," he created a passive solar dwelling using a layered house-within-a-house integration of an intermediate temperature zone

House in Regensburg
Thomas Herzog
Regensburg, Germany
1977–79

Page 132
House in Waldmohr
Thomas Herzog
Waldmohr, Germany
1982–84

wrapped around an inner core. The visual appearance of the house from some directions is that of a greenhouse (which is actually the case in the lower prismatic sections facing south), locked into a neighborhood of nonde-script high-rise housing and its own cluster of beech trees. The image is certainly high-tech, but it is also comfortably integrated as a result of the use of lean-to timber beams and the feeling that it grows (plant-like) out of its sur-roundings. All of the technology is visible. It has a glazed southern face, sloping roof for passive solar heat gains, natural limestone floor tiles for radiant heating, stilts to raise the edifice above the high ground water level and protect the beech trees, and the general light-weight construction materials that blend with nature, rather than assert the building's impor-tance.

For the plan of a House in Waldmohr, Her-zog used the "thermal onion" plan, involving another interpretation of the building within a building. The basic principle is to place the rooms requiring the highest indoor tempera-tures – bathrooms, for example – in the center of the house, surrounded by rooms where the temperatures decrease proportionally as they

get nearer the exterior. In Waldmohr, Herzog placed a cube in a square on the diagonal of a south-facing site to create both an external and internal glass facade. A conservatory between these membrane walls functions as a temperature control buffer zone, and heating comes from hot water under the floors. Each of the environmentally favorable features of the house is clearly visible and part of its aesthetic statement, inclusive of the surrounding trees, laminated timber construction, mylar foil sun screens on the interior, planted roof, and ver-dant trellis structure shading the east and west elevations.

In 1988 Herzog won a competition for a new congress and exhibition complex in the city of Linz, the state capital of Upper Austria. Designed as a low-sweeping arch, this 204 x 80-meter structure composed of 34 flat-arched steel girders provides the maximum covered space for exhibits and conference events with a minimum of column intrusions. One of the most resourceful innovations was built into the roof as a way of benefiting from diffused daylight to illuminate the interior. This idea also provided a maximum resistance to the penetration of heat and cold. In this sense, the roof becomes an intelligent skin, where even the changing angles of the sun are compensated for by retro-reflecting grids inserted between the double-glazed sections of the surface. This exhibition center offered Herzog an unusual opportunity to research the entire spectrum of climate control within a single building – including air circulation, air quality, lighting, and tempera-ture control – and demonstrate his basic belief that truly bionomic buildings also have a corre-sponding resolution in aesthetic form.

If the buildings of Herzog can be described as "cerebral cool" high-tech, the architecture of Jourda and Perraudin might be described as "humanistic cool." While each of these architects' buildings can be character-ized as lyrical interpretations of construction technology and rooted in classic Modernism, they have managed to stay on the positive side of a rather perilous fine line between brilliant innovation and a fashionable retro-vision.

Unlike their less inventive colleagues who cling to the technocentric mainstream, they have embraced the environmental dimension as an open avenue of exploration that has liberated their design sensibilities and helped avoid that anti-ecological plethora of curtain-wall turgidity prevalent everywhere. For Jourda and Perraudin this has been no small achievement – especially in France during the past decade, where the nation has been identified since the early 1980s with a glut of techno-slick and Po-mo bombast.

Françoise-Hélène Jourda studied at the School of Architecture in Lyon during the late 1970s and joined with Gilles Perraudin, also educated in Lyon, after leaving college to form a professional practice with an emphasis on environmental issues. Although critically acclaimed at the forefront of French high-tech

in their early work, Perraudin ultimately drew on his experience gained while doing research at the Institute for Sahara Studies in Algeria. He became heavily influenced by the notion of regional construction technology that respects the availability of local materials. Perraudin responded enthusiastically to the intelligence of traditional mud-brick building techniques for a hot desert community and embarked on a mission in architecture to incorporate sustainability, a symbiosis with site, and the valuable lessons of nomadic cultures.

Jourda and Perraudin adapted the Algerian experience to their philosophy of design, developing the concept of "reactive" buildings that "transform themselves according to exterior data and modify their envelope to fit climatic movements ... the first step to the design of 'living buildings'." With regard to

Page 134 and 135
House in Regensburg
Thomas Herzog
Regensburg, Germany
1977–79

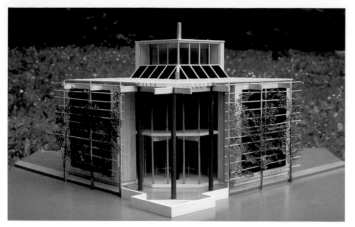

the archetype of flexible habitats that can breathe, adapt, grow, and easily accommodate new behavior patterns at very short notice. Jourda and Perraudin's main case is for flexible living and working spaces, based on a belief that Western cultures will ultimately embrace nomadic societies' environmental wisdom and adaptability.

A few of Jourda and Perraudin's private houses are notable for the imaginative use of physical site to determine creative choices. In the case of their Experimental Houses in Stuttgart, the buildings were designed as part of a large garden exhibition in 1993 and intended to serve as models for a new lifestyle closely aligned with the environment. Three related dwellings were linked by a metallic roof shell and supported by tree structures. The first provided a minimalist enclosure, the second a more rustic stone dwelling, and the third a glass house opening onto a garden. The nomadic aspect was suggested by an opportunity for the inhabitant to have a selection of three environments to choose from – all distinctly different ambient experiences – each based on climate conditions related to seasonal change.

For their 1987 Private House in Lyon-St. Just, the architects developed an inside/ouside situation similar to Herzog's House in Regensburg by creating a canvas cover that shelters the building, a micro climate between the layers of structure, and both exterior and interior vegetation. The shed-like structure has a 21-meter-long glazed facade and can be completely opened to expand the living space into the garden. Taking cues from the superb cross-ventilation techniques learned by studying desert dwellings, the Lyon structure has been designed with a capacity to breathe and offer a compatible environment for both plants and people.

Jourda and Perraudin's most impressive building is the 1990 Cité Scolaire Internationale de Lyon, where they designed a massive, snake-like, glass wall with sun screens that are both functional and iconographic. This classroom building is situated along the Rhone River – reflecting the undulations of its natural

nomadism they feel that, even though our Western societies enforce stationary lifestyle (for example, gypsies are outcasts as a result of their migratory habits), there is much to learn from the nomads' remarkable ability to live in a give-and-take relationship with the environment. As reviewed in the second chapter of this book, aboriginal cultures share the same capacity to interweave Man and nature; but the rich world commitment to technocentric dementia and ecological aberration is so advanced that reversal seems unthinkable. In any case, these persistent young architects hold to their optimism by interpreting the nomadic experience not so much as a state of physical mobility, but rather as providing

course – and includes an 8,000-square-meter, tent-like roof, suspended from poles and covering the primary, intermediate, and upper school classrooms. This assembly of services under one large umbrella space, called the "Center of Life," has the feeling of several symbiotic villages, connected by a green canopy of plant life. The most interesting aspect of this building is the fact that, even though its general appearance seems to be late Modernist, its actual effect is topographical. The visitor has the feeling that, if this structure was not made of steel and glass, it could be interpreted as a technological Arcadia, where the machine-made ensemble becomes both a support mechanism and a metaphor for nature.

One of Jourda and Perraudin's most original projects is their design for a metro station at Gerland. The design calls for a linear parallelpiping of the train platforms and a series of three cone-shaped light wells, creating a surreal interface between above and below-ground relationships. On the surface level, these cones suggest an imagery suspended somewhere between geomorphic observatories and dormant volcanoes. On the tunnel level, they resemble troglodyte pocket parks and a total inversion of the typical subway train experience. In an intriguing reversal of the Tokyo metro's endless subterranean metropolis, the Gerland station suggests a future world where surface civilization becomes too congested and escapes to more peaceful and arboreal sanctuaries underground. In spirit, this project parallels those science fiction film sagas where space nomads transport verdant replicas of terrestrial life to other planets because the ravaged earth has become uninhabitable. Whatever its implications as environmental commentary, this subway project opens up a compelling above/below dialogue. It also fulfills one of the primary objectives for a new earth-centered iconography, that is, it demonstrates the capacity of architecture to use terrestrial references to influence the direction of urbanistic development.

The work of Jourda and Perraudin is frequently linked to the architecture of Jean Nouvel, probably the best known of the new wave French architects who participated in the Mitterand era's "Les Grands Projects." This was an architecturally flamboyant decade during the 1980s, when France's President sponsored competitions for a series of ambitious – and for many critics, vainglorious – civic works in and around Paris. Reflecting Mitterand's distinctly Modernist tastes, a few of the resulting structures were worthy masterworks. Nouvel's

Private House in Lyon-St. Just
Jourda and Perraudin
Lyon, France
1984

Page 138 and 139
Cité Scolaire Internationale de Lyon
Jourda and Perraudin
Lyon, France
1989–92

Métro Station Gerland
Jourda and Perraudin
Lyon, France
Project

Institut du Monde Arabe was in this esteemed category, while other structures were simply ostentatious baubles in the cityscape. The banal new Paris Opera building stands out as one of these offensive reminders of a rather pretentious epoch.

Jean Nouvel's career hit meteoric heights after the construction of his impressive Arab center, and he became one of the most influential gurus of the French high-tech movement. While most of the work of his colleagues fell into the abyss of slick pastiche, Nouvel has demonstrated a special genius for side-stepping the minefields of "techno-glitter" and for coming up with a substantial body of thoughtful and imagistically compelling buildings in the Modernist idiom. None of them could be credited as ecologically motivated, but several of his structures possess a contextual awareness and a billboard-like presence that demonstrate the architect's intelligent absorption of site-specific feedback and his ability to give this information an urban scale.

The Fondation Cartier of 1994 on Boulevard Raspail in Paris is a superb example of Nouvel's use of the architectural facade as a chronicler of environmental information. It is built on the site of an esplanade of cedar trees, planted by Chateaubriand. The architect set back the major volume of the building and allowed the trees and ground cover to remain in the gap between a free-standing glass partition and the actual curtain wall of the exhibition center. Recalling SITE's 1979 Rainforest Building in Hialeah (without the waterwall element), this use of facade as an independent membrane in front of the actual thermal barrier creates a layering of space that frees architecture from the restraints of traditional enclosure. The Fondation Cartier contributes to the concept of "passages" mentioned earlier – referring to the use of walls as filtering diaphragms for regional data. Like the Florida Rainforest Building by SITE, Nouvel's sequential glass partitions draw their informational significance from the ambiguous relationship

Institut du Monde Arabe
Jean Nouvel
Paris, France
1981–87

between exterior and interior, the stratification of vertical transparencies, and a condition of kinetic scenography provided by the interactive reflections of sky, vegetation, street life, and the surrounding buildings.

The architecture of Jourda and Perraudin and Jean Nouvel is held in high esteem primarily as a result of their ability to balance artistic mission with technological wizardry. The fact that they also manage to embrace certain aspects of environmental design is further evidence of their prescience in ecological matters; nevertheless, it is not the primary message communicated by their work. They show a tacit commitment to the earth-centric cause, although, by contrast, the primary shakers and movers in green technology use earth science research as the motivational center of their architecture. This leads to the next area for review – green design research and technological innovations.

Page 144 and 145
Fondation Cartier
Jean Nouvel
Paris, France
1991–94

Green Design Research and Technological Innovations

Among the architectural teams most directly associated with progressive research is the German firm LOG ID. This interdisciplinary group (with a name that sounds like an astronaut role-call for the next *Alien* film) is uniquely composed of architects, engineers, medical doctors, botanists, physicists, and communications technologists. Founded by Dieter Schempp, the firm has become a world-class contributor to solar energy research and the economics of green technology. While the work of LOG ID is primarily science-oriented, their use of functional coordinates translates into buildings that have a convincing artistic profile – very much the way pragmatic demands in aerodynamic design have spun off consummate examples of minimalist sculpture.

Dieter Schempp was born in Stuttgart in 1944, and studied at the Technical College of Detmold, with an internship spent in the Lizero office in Cannes, France. He opened LOG ID in 1972 in association with Dieter Wolter, based on the development of innovative solar construction systems for architecture. Approaching climate control technology in a way similar

to Thomas Herzog's 'thermal onion' theory, the Schempp and Wolter team created a series of building-within-a-building constructions using layers of walls that collect the sun's rays efficiently, allow for a flow of controlled air temperature throughout the interior, and make it possible to incorporate vegetation for air cleansing. The principles guiding this green solar system are based on the symbiotic relationship between Man and nature. Like Herzog's House in Regensburg, the exterior glass enclosure covers a well insulated core structure capable of storing the sun's heat in winter. Through a diathermic heat transfer, warmth flows from the outer transparent partitions through the walls of the interior building and, to enhance this process, special doors are opened and fans are engaged to accelerate the flow of air currents. In summer, the trees and plants between the thermal and opaque walls offer welcome shade and vegetal transpiration, while the ventilators reverse their winter role to provide cool air circulation.

Schempp and Wolter have focused most of their research on the office interior, since it has traditionally been the most culpable villain in terms of its obscene violations of air quality and resource conservation in the working environment. LOG ID's emphasis on solar answers to these problems goes back to the most essential source of energy since the dawn of human civilization, where the sun was rightfully seen as the only true source of energy. They also understand the equation between the presence of light and its conversion to human energy – an ideal model where the maximum productive return is generated for the minimum of energy input.

LOG ID's 1989 Research Laboratory for Experimental Traumatology in Ulm is one of their prime examples of green solar architecture based on the right of inhabitants to breathe clean air and enjoy a sense of well-being in the work place, as well as the client's right to lower fuel costs and build economically. This structure includes a complex range of services – offices for doctors, educational classrooms, laboratories, X-ray facilities, a computer center, and a library. It offered an ideal situation to put into practice LOG ID's theory of an "experiential" as well as functional green environment, since the interior had to accommodate research and the examination of patients who have suffered some form of traumatic accident or disease. For anyone who has been subjected to the grim standards of medical building design these days – where every service space seems inspired by the interior of a urinal – the entire mission of clinical architecture appears predicated on creating the discomforting impression that any wall surface can be hastily hosed down to remove the unsavory evidence of surgery. In admirable contrast, the medical center in Ulm is a fusion of light, fresh air, vegetation, and spaces that inspire the researchers and laboratory technicians. In this sense the final aesthetic accomplishment of the building is its psychologically reinforcing ambience, based on an ecologically sensitive design program.

The 1990 Medium GmbH printing factory in Lahr, Germany is another example of the environmentally favorable layering of wall membranes. This company specializes in the production of catalogues, magazines, newspaper supplements, and advertisements with a daily capacity to 14,000,000 pages. The enlightened client, Alfred Schütz, specifically requested a building that would protect employees from harmful manufacturing substances, reflect sound ecological planning, and demonstrate to the public that Medium was willing to do its share in protecting the natural environment.

The LOG ID office built a divided structure (designed by Fred Möllring) – one half for production and the other part for administrative offices. The centerpiece is a glass greenhouse, with an interior garden, that bridges the two sections and provides solar benefits in all seasons. The fan-like plan seems to have been chosen as a subtle metaphor for the rays of the sun, while the general effect of the building – with its curved walls and dramatically visible interior vegetation – suggests a living organism in the regional landscape. The interior space is heated by utilizing the rays of winter sun collected under the glass atrium and guiding this warm air into the offices. The

Page 146 and 147
Research Laboratory for Experimental Traumatology
LOG ID/Dieter Schempp, Fred Möllring
Ulm, Germany
1989

Medium GmbH
LOG ID/Dieter Schempp,
Fred Möllring
Lahr, Germany
1991

ing the summer. The vegetation is composed mainly of subtropical plants, which function as both an air cleanser and a restful sanctuary for employees and visitors.

Returning to the work of America's venerable environmental architect, Sim Van der Ryn, his work – in association with David Arkin – on the Real Goods Solar Living Center in Hopland, California has been one of the most celebrated examples of green design research in action. This progressive store, catering to an ecologically enlightened clientele, was created primarily as a showcase to demonstrate the philosophy of energy independence and how a shopping center could be realized in deference to nature. As in the climate-conscious and solar-adaptive structures of LOG ID, Van der Ryn's Ecological Design Associates have loaded this retail enterprise with a profusion of energy-saving and cost-conscious innovations that have consolidated its milestone status. For example, as a result of the use of photovoltaics in energy production, the building actually sells back electricity to local power companies. Also, a destroyed region of the Feliz Creek flood plain surrounding Real Goods has been restored through stream-bed reclamation and a landscape plan favoring regional ecology. This has established the store as a major tourist attraction and, at the same time, totally justified the extra investment in green initiatives.

The Real Goods construction technology includes straw bale insulation (covered with several inches of a pneumatically applied earth and cement mixture), a glu-lam support structure, cement columns, a sprayed-on membrane roof made out of recycled automobile tires, and a re-used redwood trellis. The final cost per square foot was $90 – a figure confirming that ecological design can compete favorably with conventional building budgets.

The aesthetic and green design ensemble of Real Goods has successfully achieved the client's objectives. In an early program he stated: "The site plan should maximize elements of beauty, serenity, and spirituality; this should be a sanctuary and a testament to

machine hall is climate controlled by heat waste recovery. Employing an intelligent (and seldom considered) feature in contemporary architecture, the walkways and parking areas surrounding the printing plant are constructed with perforated paving, which allows for rain penetration into the earth and the natural process of transpiration to take place – a commendable alternative to the usual obscene loss of water through gutter run-off.

LOG ID's Glasshouse in Herten, a library and cultural center in the city of Herten near the Ruhr Basin, is a third structure built around the principle of a centerpiece garden. Like the Medium GmbH, an atrium solar collector distributes warm air in the winter and releases the sun's heat through ceiling ventilation dur-

Glasshouse
LOG ID/Dieter Schempp,
Fred Möllring
Herten, Germany
1994

sustainable building practices, energy systems, living, agriculture, and community. When folks pull off the Highway 101 and proceed through the entry way, they must be overwhelmed with a sense that they have crossed into another world, into a green, cool, comfortable parallel universe." The finished building and its adjacent landscape communicate a free-flowing, collage-like, appearance which, in spite of its exacting eco-technology and energy-saving features, seems totally uncontrived. The curvilinear, shell-like, roof planes integrate with the wooded surroundings, the plan acknowledges regional typography, and the fundamental premises for this project have set new standards for a shopping experience in deference to the environment. In comparison with the mega-malls that blight American suburbia and increasingly lay waste to vast areas of wetlands and forests, the Green Goods store is a new and optimistic paradigm of eco-centric intelligence – and proof that commerce and nature do not have to be mutually exclusive.

Sim Van der Ryn's accomplishments have been centered around a site-specific and regionally oriented commitment to green design research. The work of the Center for Maximum Potential Building Systems (CMPBS) in Laredo, Texas has, on the other hand, taken a more universalist approach. This organization, under the leadership of Pliny Fisk and Gail Vittori, studies the patterns of habitat around the world with the intention of understanding the correlation between living conditions, climate, botanical life, and topography as drawn from a variety of geographical locations. While more utopian in its objectives than Van der Ryn's down-to-earth Ecological Design Associates, CMPBS remains very similar in its hands-on, design and build approach and its translation of regional design solutions into archetypal models for other situations.

Laredo is actually an ideal township to conduct such research. It is connected to early Southwestern cultural traditions, characterized by a legacy of adobe construction, situated next to a former US Army wind-research

energy laboratory (complete with creaking windmills), located in a hot desert climate, and faces the looming potential of a severe local water shortage. In general, the community is very similar to locations in South America, Africa, and South-East Australia. The focus of CMPBS's research is on the problem of global urbanism and the failure of most commerce to base its operations on the integrated systems of nature for the protection of its own continued profits and sustainability. As part of recent showcase projects, the group has monitored the construction and performance of each environment.

Page 150 and 151
Glasshouse
LOG ID/Dieter Schempp,
Fred Möllring
Herten, Germany
1994

The Advanced Green Builder Demonstration
CMPBS
Austin, Texas, USA
1994–97

CMPBS's centerpiece ensemble is the Laredo Demonstration Blueprint Farm, started in 1987. It is the prototype for a new farming technology in the Southwest and potential model of an integrated regional community with a global perspective. This self-sustaining design takes into account its regional climate and surrounding landscape, with an emphasis on food production, the recycling of wastes, water conservation, and the creation of an alternative to suburban sprawl, with its usual absence of urban agriculture. This advocacy of a fusion of farming, manufacturing, and habitat is one of CMPBS's most important contributions to contemporary community planning. In support of this idea, ecologists unanimously

agree that the major key to environmental success in ancient cities like Cairo and Jericho was their capacity to balance the diverse activities of agriculture, service professions, and commodities exchange within an urban situation. It is an accepted fact that nature thrives on diversity and deplores regional concentrations of specialized industries and crops – or, for that matter, any kind of excessive demands related to single-purpose human enterprise. As a case in point, there is the classic absurdity of vast one-crop agricultural communities in the Midwestern USA. They are besieged by equally specialized plant diseases and insects – but deprived of these pests' natural enemies because the predators are overwhelmingly outnumbered – so the crops must be drenched with chemical insecticides, which destroys the taste of the produce and poisons the consumers. The Blueprint Farm offers an alternative to this kind of one-crop operation and has the additional advantage of setting the stage for diversified farming, which could reduce the need for energy-consuming long-distance transportation in bringing food to supermarkets.

Pliny Fisk has designed the two-acre farm prototype in Laredo as a flexible building system that can adapt to different natural conditions and human requirements. For this reason its operations are broken down into various component parts, each serving like a demonstration unit that functions as an plug and play part of an integral whole. For example, there is a need to save water at the Laredo site, so the project depends completely on rainfall collected in reservoirs located adjacent to rooftops. All water is then purified in polishing beds of gravel and aquatic vegetation. Mesquite, a local hardwood species, is used as a flooring material because it grows rapidly like a weed and produces a wood product even harder than mahogany. Its building characteristics were discovered in Argentina and Africa, but since it grows readily in Texas, its advantages have translated successfully into the CMPBS project. In another globally useful contribution to eco-technology, the Blueprint

Farm buildings are equipped with down draft evaporative cooling towers. This system is based on an ancient Iranian cooling technique for circulating air through a building by means of natural drafts that exit warm air out the top and let cool air sink into the living and working spaces.

All of the Blueprint Farm shelters are built from salvaged oil rig drilling stems as armatures that hold shade support, infill walls, green houses, or cooling tower roofs. The cools hade increases annual production by 30 percent. Considering the small size of the two-acre site, this contribution has major profit implications for the local farm community. Additional inventions under development include underground cisterns, wastewater treatment areas, and the establishment of a major regional marketplace for selling local produce. The CMPBS team is also working on two proposals for refrigeration. One idea incorporates a natural mineral called zeolite, originally used by Sioux Indians. It is a material that absorbs and desorbs moisture and can be used as the basis of a refrigeration system. In a second cooling experiment, Fisk and his team

worked on a nocturnal reradition technique that cools water to below the freezing point during low humidity periods.

Fisk proposes that the CMPBS philosophy is a reflection of the "New Science." He believes that green architecture is controlled by the principles of indeterminacy lying at the root of modern physics. Reports from science tell us that "no sub-atomic event is independent of another and no sequence of such events is strictly predictable." To Fisk, this suggests that being part of an ecological system means "engagement from within." Since all of nature is subject to the laws of chaos, he supports a "bottom-up" theory that takes this element of chance into account and postulates that every human enterprise is precariously situated between disaster and evolution, with the result that every detail of natural phenomena is answerable to operations within a larger matrix. This concept reaffirms an ancient Islamic architectural principle, whereby, simply described, the interior space of a dwelling is seen as a microcosm within the macrocosm of the house. The house can then be interpreted as another microcosm, relative to the macro-

The Advanced Green Builder Demonstration
CMPBS
Austin, Texas, USA
1994–97

153

Laredo Demonstration Blueprint Farm
CMPBS
Laredo, Texas, USA
1987–

materials, and craft skills. The industrial products include photovoltaics, a sheet metal cistern, pv's, and recycled rubber products.

From an aesthetic standpoint, the work of CMPBS is another example, like the work of Sim Van der Ryn, where the architectural imagery of a building is a direct reflection of its environmental commitment. CMPBS and Ecological Design Associates both demonstrate a search for post-industrial paradigms that acknowledge the need for an iconography which reflects a use of solar energy, a sensitivity to land and water preservation, and a desire to connect to the surrounding context.

Pliny Fisk was educated at the Graduate School of Fine Arts at the University of Pennsylvania under the pioneering environmental theoretician, Ian McHarg, and informally with the great architect Louis Kahn. As a result, his green mission and future choice of design language was profoundly influenced by these creative giants. He was also exposed to the controversial and sociologically oriented work of Robert Venturi, another influential alumnus of the G.S.F.A. In fact, quite visibly in a number of Fisk's recent structures, there is a strong connection to his inspirational origins at Penn. The fundamental principle that human intervention in nature should be an obligatory extension of ecology came from McHarg's teachings and seminal book *Design with Nature*. At Blueprint Farm, the imagery of certain buildings shows evidence of a fusion between Kahn's eloquent geometry and the brash, pop-Americana of Venturi's early house designs. The oversized iconic chimneys of the Venturi dwellings have become, in Fisk's hands, a witty and environmentally appropriate adaptation of Middle Eastern cooling towers. In the Green Building Demonstration, its collage of industrial elements speak to an entire range of cross-cultural references, which would be equally at home in the desert regions of Africa, an oasis in Arabia, or a suburban town in Texas. In this case, the industrial framing and mixture of materials communicates an impression of architecture in the process of flux and change. Even CMPBS's use of steel

cosm of the city. The city, in turn, is viewed as a microcosmic part of the macrocosmic nation – and so forth until the concept of habitat relates to the ultimate macrocosm of the worldwide condition.

In a project entitled The Advanced Green Builder Demonstration in Austin, Texas, CMPBS has organized another "life-cycle" prototype for international applications. Similar to the Blueprint Farm, this structure is also based on readily available materials and technologies which have been orchestrated as a showcase of symbiotic relationships. The checklist includes earth block and straw construction, a selection of plants, caliche block and stucco, etc. – each based on easily accessible byproducts, raw

and concrete seems to imply a symbiotic relationship with the growing processes of plants and trees.

The ecological design research of both Sim Van der Ryn and Pliny Fisk, while philosophically committed to redefining humanity's relationship to nature, is primarily focused on low-tech green solutions for contemporary urban and suburban architecture. Motivated by a more psychologically oriented and Gaia-inspired set of objectives, Association Sens Espace was organized in the Paris studio of Hervé Baley in 1969 with the purpose of reconnecting people to their origins in the natural environment. The group is composed of architects, artists, and engineers who support the currently held view of most environmental psychologists that nature deprivation is at the root of an increasing number of mental disorders today. Reflecting certain aboriginal cultures' beliefs in the value of spiritual transference to achieve a more profound level of earth-centric identity, this experimental design organization from France seeks a better understanding of biomorphic relationships in the search for a coherence with nature.

Under the direction of Jean Pierre Campredon, Association Sens Espace has taken the position that most contemporary architecture asserts its presence in the environment using a litany of technical systems and aesthetic choices that only increases people's alienation from nature. The group further points out that buildings can actually impose psychological barriers through design choices, destroying any hope of coherence. Sens Espace members feel that this problem is infinitely more complex than the partial solutions provided by energy conservation and sustainable construction technology; rather, they see a new role for architecture in the realm of spiritual leadership. In this respect they propose the idea that architecture be landscape and deal with new levels of plasticity that simulate the way nature stitches together its fabric of organic and inorganic life. Sens Espace is interested in a soft, flexible, morphogenic architecture that takes advantage of the lessons learned from past

nomadic lifestyles and the mutable characteristics of nature.

The Sens Espace-designed Cantercel Project, begun in 1988 in association with the Ecole Supérieure d'Architecture in Paris, is a training center founded with the purpose of promoting a sense of harmony with the environment. While the architectural features include familiar components of green construction – for example, rammed earth, raw wood support systems, fabric coverings, passive solar energy, etc. – there is also a conceptual motivation which the group defines as an evolutionist sensibility. The principles behind this approach and its built manifestations in Cantercel are to create an ensemble of demonstra-

Laredo Demonstration Blueprint Farm
CMPBS
Laredo, Texas, USA
1987–

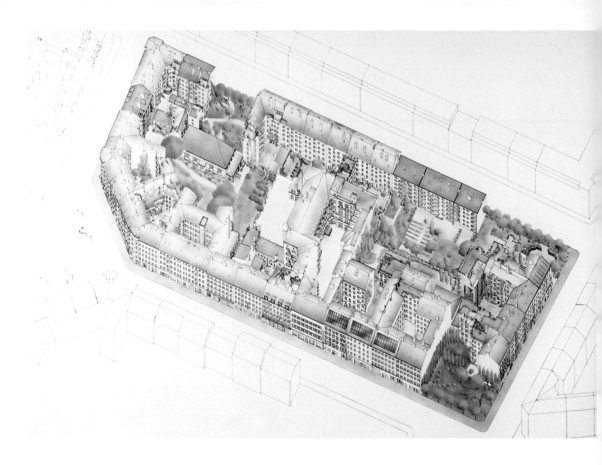

Block 103
STERN
Berlin, Germany
1980s

tion buildings, agricultural areas, natural land-scape, and outdoor/indoor seminar spaces. From an educational standpoint, the objective is to simulate the interactive processes of nature, so that building technology and occupants' behavior become a logical extension of the eco-system. With this in mind, many of the physical features of Cantercel were chosen for their sympathetic equations in nature, including a lozenge-like central building with a textile roof and a structural pattern of wood columns that mirror the rhythms of the surrounding pine trees (as though the building is bending to the force of the wind). The main innovation was provided by team member Michael Flach who developed a free-flowing and lightweight support system that, rather than concede to the rigid column grids associated with heavy roof planes, achieved his view of architecture as part of a spontaneous con-

textual flow. His success was made physically possible by an extremely economical canvas covering that is held firm in wooden grooves by a series of rods. The fabric is stretched with a rope, forming a diagonal arc and creating a double curvature for strength. At the same time, it forms a union with its surroundings and a spare, contextually respectful, visual presence.

The Cantercel project is a model of inter-action that encourages students, professors, community members, and professional designers to develop a living environment where, in the words of Campredon, "Architecture can become the science of relationship and communication, rather than that of protection." In spite of these rather utopian ambitions (reminiscent of 1960s Drop City idealism), Cantercel has become a viable and productive testing ground for eco-sociology and a demonstration

of the wisdom of constructing shelter that behaves like a living organism. The most valuable lessons of this educational center propose that, by trying to find operational parallels in ecology for each element of structure, the builder-as-inhabitant can ultimately recover that lost sense of earth-centric coherence.

The Berlin contractor for urban reconstruction, STERN, founded as an outcome of the 1978 International Building Exhibition (IBA) in Berlin is dedicated to the principle of sensitive urban reconstructions. They design and coordinate alternative planning concepts for the redevelopment of inner-city areas. By looking at the city as a form of biotope (a clustering of people for mutual social and economic benefit), they envision successful urban design as an organized response to certain bioclimatic imperatives. In the process of researching

and developing municipal projects, they share Sens Espace's belief in the "science of relationships." STERN practises a policy of working with community leaders in an effort to bring the integrated forces of nature into civic life. The firm's work is dedicated to finding solutions for typical urban design problems. These include the lack of adequate vegetation in cities, the destruction of salvageable properties in favor of totally new development, and the construction of buildings without regard for climatic considerations.

For Block 103, a housing project in Berlin, STERN worked closely with the community to help determine their space needs and quality-of-life expectations. Based on their response, the architects included a series of interventions to humanize the environment with green technology and landscape. Among those features most appreciated by the tenants is a

Buildings at Fraenkelufer
Hinrich Baller
(in association with STERN)
Berlin, Germany

communal garden, the opening up of light shafts and skylights to bring illumination to the interiors, the use of photovoltaic roof panels to capture solar energy, and an innovation which they call "vertical swamp" to capture grey water for recycling.

This housing project addresses two of the most important objectives in ecological design: the recycling of an existing structure and the use of a public project as a major resource for environmental education. In addition to a series of aesthetic decisions that retain the old factory elements as part of the conversion, Block 103 includes an interweaving of industrial fragments with landscape which demonstrate the designers' sensitivity to the elements that join together Machine Age imagery, ecological design, and garden space.

The work of LOG ID, Sim Van der Ryn, CMPBS, Association Sens Espace, and STERN has pioneered the fusion of the technological side of green design with aesthetically related imagery. For the average architectural patron, however, their work is identified with experimentation and, in some cases, includes a controversial visual interpretation that only fuels client suspicions about newness and risk. In contrast, there is a group of designers with a generally more traditional approach in terms of form and imagery, who can be extremely persuasive in client acceptance of green design. The value of these architects to the environmental cause is their tendency to construct highly appealing buildings that make the ecologically favorable features of their work seem quite natural and somehow less threatening to conventional tastes. Unfortunately the term "experimental" is frequently interpreted as a code word for cost overruns and a positioning of the client in the psychologically uncomfortable role of seeming like a test case. In reality, part of the game of selling ecological design lies in the ability of the architect to generate feelings of confidence. This marketing process usually means camouflaging the riskier aspects of green technology and its inevitable increased costs. Within the larger picture, this client resistance to experimentation has been the principle road block in the development of a new environmental design language to match the progressive achievements of green technology.

Block 103, "vertical swamp"
STERN
Berlin, Germany
1980s

The Seattle, Washington, architectural firm of Olson/Sundberg has been at the forefront among those architectural practices leading the way among designers who have had an influence on the acceptance of green design. In terms of professional profile, this practice is the opposite of STERN, with its focus on the issues of urban decay and rebirth. The Olson/Sundberg partnership works mainly for a wealthy clientele with an environmental conscience. While their buildings are usually conservative from a design perspective and firmly rooted in the influences of Frank Lloyd Wright and European Modernism, the value of their accomplishments has been to demonstrate the advantages of an ecologically aware lifestyle.

An important part of Olson/Sundberg practice is residential, so they engage client input on a highly personal level – even providing illustrative collages to determine image preferences – in the interests of making connections between architecture, nature, and the residents' preferred lifestyles. This attention to detail has resulted in a series of consummately

designed and ecologically programmed buildings in the Pacific Northwest. The firm's outstanding legacy of structures has included an admirable checklist of environmental features that include a total fusion with surroundings, sod roofs, recycled materials, and solar-oriented construction.

The Olson/Sundberg office was formed in 1985, but both architects had worked independently on ecologically favorable projects starting in the late 1960s. Jim Olson and Rick Sundberg are graduates of the University of Washington, started practice in the 1960s, and currently represent one of the most highly regarded Northwest architectural studios internationally. The firm's best-known emblematic project is the Filucy Bay Residence in Longbranch, Washington. It was designed by Olson in 1968 for the former Ambassador to Iceland as a structure that would reflect the client's memories of the sod roof houses that surround Reykjavik. Since the owner suffered from various allergies, the house had to be built out of non-toxic materials. For this reason, the archi-

Building a Bridge to the Common Client

Filucy Bay Residence
Olson/Sundberg
Longbranch, Washington, USA
1968

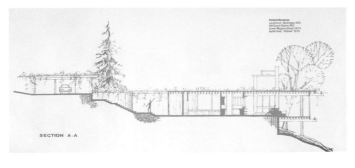

SECTION A·A

Left and below
Filucy Bay Residence
Olson/Sundberg
Longbranch,
Washington, USA
1968

Above and right
One Carillon Point
Olson/Sundberg
Kirkland, Washington, USA
1992

tects chose concrete block, wood, and a careful fusion of the structure with the surrounding landscape. The building is cut into the hillside so that the roof plane supports grass and vegetation and seamlessly joins the building to the surrounding landscape, making the entire dwelling seem like an excavated sanctuary in the natural environment, rather than an imposed structure. In addition to its admirable green design features, Olson wanted the structure to be symbolic of the fact that "our culture is at the turning point as we begin to shift our roles from consumers of limited resources to stewards of the planet." Given its time frame of the late 1960s, the Filucy Bay Residence is a remarkably visionary building that predicted the gradually increasing awareness of environmental responsibility that has reached a crescendo today. Although the house owes a great deal to the influence of Wright's cave-like interiors, overhanging eaves, and Japanese-inspired use of materials and partitions, it also demonstrates great originality in its site-specific design features and attention to climate control. For example, the cedar wood used for construction has weathered well and enhances the feeling of the building as an extension of nature. From an energy efficiency standpoint, the aggregate concrete block walls store heat from the sun and release it into the house.

In terms of providing an inviting interior environment, the Filucy Bay Residence offers a variety of rooms that vary the living experience. The upper living room is cave-like and protective, while the lower social area takes advantage of the panoramic view of Mount Rainier and the bay below. For the pleasure of the inhabitant, this creates the impression of standing in space at the point where sky meets earth.

In a second major environmental project – One Carillon Point – in Kirkland, Washington, Olson/Sundberg brought their green sensibility to a luxury condominium. The project is a 31-acre mixed-use development structure on Lake Washington, including 14 residential units. In addition to a series of esplanades for panoramic views, there are shops, restaurants, a private marina, and a public park. The housing complex uses its garden setting to isolate the dwellings spaces from the noise of the street, and two bridges provide access to the residences, each with its own private garden.

Drawing upon lessons learned in accommodating the allergy-plagued resident of the Filucy Bay Residence, the condominium project is built with a minimum use of toxic materials and, particularly for one dwelling, the owner was so severely afflicted with allergies that all interiors had to be free of any toxins resulting from building materials, paint, upholstery, and manufactured artifacts. The client suffered fainting, blurred vision, and headaches from automobile exhaust fumes, off-gas emissions caused by carpeting, and even the most common chemicals used in household cleansers. Rising to the challenge, Olson/Sundberg created an environment that was totally free of artificial pollutants by favoring an entire range of special products – unpainted wood, water-based colors, concrete block construction, non-toxic grout, natural stone, special glues, wall insulation with two sets of vapor barriers, and a charcoal-filtered air-conditioning system to free the air of dust particles and formaldehyde residues. While this extreme case of a toxin-free environment did not translate directly into the building's artistic statement, the extensive use of natural materials produced an atmosphere that is visually and physically superior – especially as compared to the claustrophobic oppression and lethal toxicity characteristic of most contemporary apartments and offices.

The environmental design value of Olson/Sundberg's work is the product of a subtle and visually appealing invasion of conventional architecture with ideas that seem both organic and functional. Since the Filucy Bay Residence and One Carillon Point projects have been conceived for luxury living, their green demonstrations tend to get lost on the general public. While they tactically qualify as showcase situations, their actual communicative appeal is limited by the price tag. From this perspective,

the work of the Jones Studio in Phoenix, Arizona, founded by the brothers Eddie and Neal Jones in 1979, represents an intentionally populist level of communication on the subject of ecological design. Following a credo of the three R's of green advocacy – "reduce, reuse, and recycle" – the firm is specifically concern-ed with outreach programs in the development of environmental sensitivity and making green technology available to a larger marketplace. These concerns include the promotion of pas-sive and active solar energy, preserving virgin landscape, encouraging a more productive and economical use of water, and demonstrat-ing the options for low-maintenance architec-ture.

As a student of Frank Lloyd Wright's architecture, Eddie Jones spent his student years looking at the special characteristics of desert architecture and following the example of Wright by using context and climate as the premises for design decisions. In association with Neal, the firm has taken on a mission in Arizona to generate a truly regional architec-

ture that addresses the problems of living in a desert environment.

The Jones Studio's most prominent green project, from a public demonstration perspec-tive, has been the 1992 Arizona Public Service Environmental Showcase Home in Phoenix. In the words of the architects, it has been devel-oped as a "shopping center of green ideas," with more than 150 available technologies, strategies, and materials that can be readily used by the average home builder. Sponsored collectively by the A.P.S., the Federal Environ-mental Protection Agency, and the Arizona Department of Environmental Quality, the Ari-zona Department of Commerce, Arizona State University, and the Home Builders Association of Central Arizona, the entire purpose of the structure has been to increase public aware-ness of the value of thinking environmentally and explaining the social, economic, and qual-ity-of-life advantages of green architecture. The unique contribution of this project is that it has represented the first successful partner-ship in the USA. that has joined together the

Arizona Public Service Environmental Showcase Home
Jones Studio
Phoenix, Arizona, USA
1992

resources of private, federal, and state regulatory agencies for the purpose of environmental stewardship. In addition, as a tribute to the design talents of Jones Studio, the building translates its instructive content into a successful aesthetic result, which has helped communicate the green messages and has encouraged the public to see the environmental revolution as part of a viable change in home-building paradigms.

In addition to using innumerable recycled elements in its construction, the Environmental Showcase Home uses 60 percent less fossil fuel and water than a normal regional dwelling. This translates over a 30-year period into a reduction of 540,000 pounds of air pollution and a saving of 2.3 million gallons of water. Among the outstanding innovations of the experimental house from a recycling standpoint are its insulation fabricated out of compressed newspapers, a carpeting made of soft drink bottles, floor and wall tiles using 70 percent recycled glass, cement blocks made with flyash aggregate (a residual of burned coal, usually regarded as waste), and virtually all interior furnishings constructed out of harvested pinewood. From an energy conservation standpoint, the thermal envelope is based on principles that were used in historic desert architecture. There are eight-inch-thick concrete walls, shaded windows for heat deflection, thermal glass, passive solar energy using reflected daylight to illuminate interiors, and a solar heating system for water that uses no electricity or gas. The solar collector panels are filled with non-toxic liquids and mounted flush to the roof to avoid the typically unsightly appearance of such devices, which frequently discourages high design architects from utilizing the sun's benefits. In addition, about one half of the home's electricity is derived from photovoltaic cells with a southern exposure on the roof.

A superior air quality in the Environmental Showcase Home is assured by the absence of pollutants normally used in carpets and fur-

niture, and a minimum of covered floor surface that collects allergy-activating dust and pollen. Additionally, all of the house's clerestory windows are mechanically operable to open and close according to weather conditions and serve as sources of natural drafts.

The main purpose of the water-management system is to eliminate the use of potable water for regular irrigation and conventional home uses. The special features include a desert plant landscaping plan, sub-surface irrigation using grey water and rain run-off, low-flow faucets and showerheads, and various water-conservative appliances. By another ingenious system of recycling, the water used in dish washing and bathing is converted to flushing toilets before passing into the grey recycling system. The collective effect of these innovations reduces household consumption of water by more than half of standard American living demands.

From an aesthetic perspective, the Environmental Showcase Home offers a convincing diagram for the combination of green lifestyle and design features that reflect its functions. Even though several aspects of the original concept were modified by a conservative local administration to curb its "radical appearance" (for fear it might scare away potential converts to environmental reform), the basic idea remained intact. It lost an innovative butterfly roof to accommodate photovoltaic panels and a sunken garden with water which would have provided a convectional air current to cool the house in summer. While somewhat disappointing to the architects, Eddie Jones' reaction was to look at the situation from a broader viewpoint: "If the fundamental concept is strong and sincerely prototypical, then it can respond to variations." While heavily influenced by Wright's tilted roof planes, shadowing eaves, and earth-hugging architectural profiles, this demonstration dwelling brings a series of important messages to a public that would normally never think about green issues.

One inherent problem with the Environmental Showcase Home is the impression that it demonstrates too little home and too much technology. In this sense it seems removed from the realities of everyday life and could potentially fall prey to the dissipating effects of today's information overkill. This kind of self-conscious presentation tends to be seen as part of an all-consuming techno-pastiche that gets drained of substantive content by the nature of exposure – like the squandering of ideas through mass media. Still, this project represents a viable beginning in the stimulation of public awareness and a credit to its originators' courage and conviction. Its success, where mass media usually fails, is in its impressive physical presence and its capacity to offer the audience a hands-on demonstration experience.

With informational purposes similar to the Jones Studio Environmental Showcase Home, the American architect Kimberly Ackert constructed a 1992 competition-winning Aus-tralian House of the Future project for the Monier Corporation in Perth, Australia. Constrained by a tight budget of $300,000 and a 4-acre site in the Swan Valley region, the dwelling features both passive and active solar energy. It is located in a lush section of Australian bush country and is composed of two split-level rectangular volumes which conform to a steep slope in the landscape. Consistent with Australia's geography, the south-facing side of the dwelling is the cooler elevation and protected by a rammed-earth wall composed of an iron-rich soil mixed with 4 percent cement.

The innovative environmental features include an interior courtyard that functions as a kind of exhaust flue, drawing cooler air from the floor surface and exiting hot air out through a series of louvers. Expansive eaves shade a series of glass doors, while soffits and

Page 170 and 171
Australian House of the Future
Kimberly Ackert and Robert Dawson-Browne Swan Valley, Australia 1992

Page 172 and 173
Spring Lake Park Visitors Center
Obie Bowman
Sonoma County,
California, USA
1992

a ceiling clad in corrugated iron reflect natural light into the interiors. A steel energy tower contains an electric wind turbine, solar hot water panels, and water tanks to activate sprinklers to protect against the bush fires which frequently plague the hot and arid community.

One of the most convincing aspects of this experimental house is the way it seems to comfortably nestle into its bush country surroundings and express a message of urgency and usefulness as an intrinsic part of its aesthetic resolution. The collage-like uses of iron, timber, glass, and the tools of environmental technology suggest the transient look of garbage housing built by certain Aboriginal communities. These humble dwellings – composed of tin siding, packing cartons, old fabric, and other discarded materials – represent a sad commentary on the continuing abuse and deprivation imposed on native Australians; but the shacks are also evidence of tenacity, spirit, and creativity in the face of adversity. Once their natural habitats had been usurped by the European invaders, the Aboriginal cultures were forced to fabricate shelter out of the refuse of the conquerors. The results have always been far more interesting, livable, and environmentally instructive in their use of recycled materials than the government-sponsored, pre-fabricated home units that have been their replacement. In point, many Aboriginals refuse to live in these sterile industrialized products, preferring instead houses of their own invention.

Kimberly Ackert's Australian House of the Future offers a type of structure that seems to grow logically out of the garbage housing tradition and, at the same time, reflects the Aboriginal civilization's acute awareness of nature as an extension of the body and the need to use the earth's resources wisely. Although conceived as a self-conscious environmental showcase, her green project captures some important aspects of the native Australian spirit with a great economy of means. In this respect, its relevance to the future is rooted in its absorption of the past.

Like the Jones brothers and Kim Ackert, Obie Bowman is another architect whose best work is identified with a regionalist situation and the promotion of a popular acceptance of green technology. His office is at the Sea Ranch, and in many ways, his work is an extension of the contextualized Western sensibility, but he has contributed a distinctly progressive attitude toward environmental issues.

The experience that moulded Bowman's commitment to environmental reform in architecture started with a childhood spent in the San Fernando Valley region of California, where he affectionately recalls a 1950s agrarian com-

munity. After returning from his education 15 years later, he was horrified to witness the suburbanization of the area and the typical onslaught of dreary housing projects and relentless destruction of the natural landscape. Reflecting the philosophy of the noted ecopsychologist Alan Thein – who admonishes the perpetrators of industrialized greed as totally reprehensible in their disregard for the environmental inheritance of future generations – Bowman's guiding principles match those of certain earth-centric civilizations that understood that classic equation – by destroying a part of nature, one destroys a part of oneself.

Also, in concert with observations voiced earlier in this book, Bowman expresses great suspicion of the current popularity of green architecture as nothing more than another chapter in architectural vogue – deploring the similarity between the frenzied rhetoric of sustainability advocates and the now deflated discourse that once heralded Postmodernism and Deconstruction only a few years ago. He describes his work as being concerned with

such issues as "concentrating on what buildings do, rather than what they look like," "fulfilling the potential of each site by connecting the architecture to the uniqueness of setting," or "recognizing that each project has impact on the earth's resources and trying to celebrate this fact in a memorable way."

Obie Bowman was selected in 1990 to design the Spring Lake Park Visitors Center in Sonoma County, California. The principle purpose of the building is to provide an information resource on the natural environment, Native American history, and the regional water system. The project brief indicated that the building should reflect its functions by means of a physical harmony with the surrounding landscape. Spring Lake is a flood control reservoir for the community, and the terrain has been formed out of an ancient lava flow, with a plant life reminiscent of volcanic regions in Sicily. In order to bring the various natural elements together and establish an appropriate image for the building, Bowman designed a pyramidal structure as the most

Page 174 and 175
Brunsell Residence
Obie Bowman
Sea Ranch, California, USA
1987

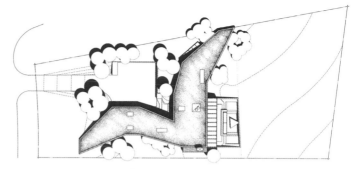

SITE PLAN

logical and serviceable approach for the fragile context. While he makes no claims that this unusual shape has been influenced by memories of a volcanic mountain or the surrounding hills, in the final analysis it has proven to be an ideal choice of image from both symbolic and functional standpoints.

By means of an ingenious site orientation to make sure the tourist facility did not negatively affect the landscape, the architect isolated the forested areas with low walls to protect the botanical life and segregate the intrusive processes of construction from potential tree damage. To Bowman's credit, only three trees were uprooted in constructing the 2,000-square-foot edifice.

The pyramidal shape of the Visitors Center is made of steel framing with redwood louvers, set on a concrete base. For interior temperature control the south-east elevation is clad in solar collectors, made more efficient by the slope of the walls. For cooling in summer, the north side of the building has suction ducts which draw cooler air inside, while a ceiling fan blows out any accumulated warmth through attic vents. The complex also includes a below-grade storage room and a sod-covered office and workroom to help maintain a constant temperature within these service areas. While metaphorical references are not acknowledged by the architect, one of the unique aesthetic strengths of this structure is the iconographic presence of the pyramid. It appears to be both a logical expression of its own genesis as part of the landscape, as well as a

reflection of the path of the air flow system within. It is a rare example of the environmental message compressed into a simple, but highly communicative and ceremonial-like, configuration.

For the 2,800-square-foot Brunsell Residence at Sea Ranch, Bowman has absorbed some of the wood siding and moviescape Western vernacular that has become a trademark of this Pacific Coast Highway architectural monument. With a respectful acknowledgement of the compound's stylistic origins (referring to Charles Moore's 1960s Venturi-influenced affection for American regional imagery), Bowman has assimilated aspects of this pop iconography while still creating a significant environmental house. Fortunately his building emerges as a lot more interesting than its clapboard counterparts at Sea Ranch – primarily because of the architect's strong sense of how to fuse structure and landscape.

By creating a casual and sprawling plan that respects both climate and panoramic vistas, Bowman accommodates the gourmet chef owners' requirement for a large kitchen with an adjacent social area and accommodations for a large number of weekend guests. With his decision to allow a surrounding meadow to cover the roof planes, he has saved the building from unfavorable comparison to the mock-shantytown imagery characteristic of most earlier structures in Sea Ranch.

Although the Brunsell Residence has only portions of its structure 4 feet underground, Bowman cleverly used an earth berm to create the impression that the dwelling is mostly buried in the earth. In addition to providing a stable climate control for the interior, this innovation gives the house a rather primitive image, recalling the architecture of certain troglodyte cultures. He also uses site orientation to protect the house from strong prevailing winds, to capture heat through solar collectors for hot water, and provide winter sanctuary in a south-facing solarium.

There are strong conceptual and programmatic links joining the work of Olson/Sundberg, the Jones Studio, Obie Bowman, and the West Coast architect James Cutler, in terms of their gently persuasive approach to green education through demonstrative design. Each designer has been profoundly influenced by the work of Frank Lloyd Wright – absorbing his theories of organic architecture in personalized ways – and each has focused on the social and psychological implications of cooperating with nature, as an extension of environmental technology. Cutler, like Olson and Sundberg, is another Pacific Northwest architect from the Seattle area who has had the advantage of being surrounded by a unique verdant landscape and the support of an admirable level of politically endorsed green advocates.

In connecting the architecture of James Cutler to Wright, it should be seen as a very positive feature in his architecture, since so few contemporary designers have ever really grasped the environmental importance of this American titan. While certain Wrightian stylistic devices can be found in the work of Cutler, his main contribution has been to grasp the far-reaching ecological implications of organic architecture and put them into a distinctly contemporary context. He has recognized their value in the face of a catastrophic environmental crisis in a way that Wright could only prophesy, but never actually witness. There has been a tendency to dismiss the buildings of architects like Cutler (or any structures integrated with landscape) as part of a residual school of Wright-derived clichés (mostly generated by Taliesin West and its depressingly moribund interpretations of the master's teachings), which has been justifiably dismissed by the current architectural forefront as picturesque and outdated. At the same time, it is paradoxical that certain architects dismiss the Wrightian legacy as regressive, while their own catalogue of Industrial Age imagery is seldom more than a computer-aided rehash of the 1920s.

James Cutler has described his work as wanting to "express the ambiguity as to whether the building was applied into nature or whether nature is reapplying itself over the building." He believes that the entire act of construction should be approached in cautious def-

erence to landscape because "architecture is always an insult to the environment" and, therefore, any building should expand upon and pay homage to the ecological demands, physical features, and even the unseen processes that already exist in a natural situation. He sees the role of architecture as an extension and celebration of biomorphic phenomena.

In one of his better known houses, the 3,000-square-foot Houdek/Pope Residence (1998) in Seabeck, Washington, Cutler was able to ideally express his "nature first, architecture second" philosophy, since the structure

was part of an existing forest and had to bridge over a wide depression in the terrain without disturbing the landscape. By the simple innovation of reflecting the vertical rhythms of the trees with the supporting wood pillars of the house, he created a highly successful wedding of architecture to its surroundings. In this sense, the dwelling seems as organic and changeable as the forest itself.

In a similar site-specific 2,200-square-foot structure of 1987, located on Bainbridge Island and titled Bridge House, Cutler dealt with the problems of a difficult site, which was bisected by a ravine and mountain stream. His solution preserved all of the existing trees and ground cover by spanning over the stream and using hand-excavated foundations to avoid excessive damage. As special environmental features, he included a solar-responsive south elevation overlooking a small bay on Puget Sound. He built the entire structure out of non-toxic materials, including solid pine and cedar shingles. Taking some cues from the forest-enclosed 1974 Tucker House in Westchester, New York by Robert Venturi and the spiritually

inspired geometry of Louis Kahn (his teacher at the University of Pennsylvania), Cutler has created this residence as an unusual juxtaposition between nature's evolutionary growth, the wit of pop culture Americana, and the simple formalism of a ritual monument.

The 1999 Gates Residence in Medina, Washington, designed as a joint venture by Cutler and Peter Bohlin for the Chairman of Microsoft Corporation, is one of those projects that apparently started idealistically and, through various client interventions, finally came out as something different. Although shrouded in military-like secrecy – with only an occasional leak of photos to the press when Bill Gates deemed it expedient for public relations purposes – the home was originally intended as an environmental milestone. Conceived as a showcase for Cutler's green innovations – recycled lumber, non-toxic materials, solar collectors, partially buried rooms, sod roofs, and Wrightian terraces saturated with cascading vegetation – the seemingly never-ending structure has become more or less a shadow of Cutler's actual intentions. The interiors have been changed according to the clients tastes and equipped with a level of high-tech paraphernalia that would shame the Pentagon. It has been proposed that when the Gates family wakes up in the morning the electrical overload triggers a blip in the Seattle power grid. After weathering a sort of "ecology be damned" reversal of the original design brief, Cutler and Bohlin have still managed to retain some evidence in the Gates Residence of their artistic intentions, including a series of fragmented walls, the use of a variety of admirable eco-conscious materials, and a successful fusion of the structure with its topographical setting.

As an anecdotal footnote to the Gates Residence saga, two years ago the research team for this book tried in vain to get illustrations of the house and its interiors from the Microsoft Public Relations Department. At the directive of Mr Gates, the researchers were informed that, for security reasons, no pictures could be released for publication. Given the

insurance implications, this rejection seemed logical enough ... until, several months later, a double-page spread showing the Gates Residence appeared in *Time Magazine*. With encyclopedic detail, the illustrations described the floor plan of the building, including a complete checklist of its technological features. For any potential invader of the Gates' privacy, here was a cat burglar's dream diagram revealing access to every room and the operational advantages of each electronic gadget (short of how to switch off the alarm system). One can only surmise that, in Mr Gates' peculiar notion of security, inclusion in an architectural book is seen as a liability, while exposure in *Time* is somehow perceived as low risk.

In contrast to the mainly rural and organically landscaped work of James Cutler, Alain Peskine of ED Architectes in Paris, France, is an environmentally oriented urbanist who works with existing situations. His buildings are generally an intriguing mix of referential sources. On the one hand, his imagery seems to grow out of Le Corbusier and traditional Modernism, and on the other one senses that he is using the familiarity of this idiom by inverting and twisting its conventional relationships as part of an architectural commentary. In some projects, he confronts the limitations of constrained urban sites by treating them as collages of odd shapes and materials. For other situations, he introduces decorative devices that appear to be borrowed from Art Nouveau and Art Deco, but then extends the references to nature by introducing lush pockets of vegetation that seem to have migrated to Paris from a Frank Lloyd Wright prairie house. This rather perverse hybridism is thoughtfully calculated and creates an architecture of wit and irony, with a comfortable sense of human scale as a counterpoint to the current Parisian craze for sleek and bleak high-tech megastructures.

Peskine's 1983 15 Rue de Vanves Apartments in Paris face an 18th-century park, and each of the living units has a planted terrace reminiscent of the Japanese concept of "borrowed scenery" – in this case, seemingly extracted from the adjacent public gardens.

The collage of architectural vocabularies in the building plays with references from the neighborhood (as well as Modernist history), resulting in an ensemble effect where the entire structure appears to have been shaped by the individuality of its tenants, rather than the typical imposition of an architect's rigorous autonomy. This gives the apartments a sense of personal identity that plays off well against the profuse planting of the terraces and atrium garden.

In dealing with a very compressed site surrounding a visually eccentric tower house in Paris, Peskine (as partner in charge) designed four small condominiums that frame this odd centerpiece and play spatial games with its architectural idiosyncrasies. Completed in 1989, the La Tour de Clamart Apartments can only be appreciated by physically participating in its complex weave of Lilliputian spaces. For this reason, the Peskine interventions are almost impossible to photograph

with any degree of justice to their aesthetic merits. The visitor experiences a labyrinth of intimate gardens, terraces, stairways, and visually intriguing collisions between old and new stylistic fragments that give the ensemble a feeling that one has stepped into a surreal folly; but it is a fantasy environment that plays amusing games of commentary with its urban surroundings. Consistent with all of ED Architectes work, the vegetation is completely fused with the building and, even though structure and garden are distinctly separate, there is a comfortable sense that vegetation, dwelling space, and the cityscape have evolved together in a compatible dialogue.

Like Alain Peskine, the American architect James Polshek is committed to designing new architecture for the existing city by treating his structures as part of an integrated tapestry. Unlike the stylistically animated work of ED Architectes, his interpretation of urban and suburban contextualism is more focused on a

Page 180 and 181
**15 Rue de Vanves
Apartments**
ED Architectes/Alain
Peskine
Issy les Moulineaux,
Paris, France
1983

the equivalent of a classical Italian garden. Even though the actual recycling facility is a metal-clad industrial plant, it is skillfully hidden in such a way that it seems like a gracious public institution. In addition to the functional buildings, the project includes an exhibit center to educate the public about waste management, a viewing gallery, and a small auditorium.

The 70,000-square-foot Plant Studies Center for the New York Botanical Garden in Bronx is designed by Polshek to gracefully assimilate the neo-classical imagery of an existing institution. The facade of the new section is totally vine-covered to indicate its interior research purposes and collection of plant life. At the same time, this intervention is very contemporary in the way that it both departs from and pays its respects to the 19th-century architectural language of the original building.

As former Dean of the Graduate School of Architecture, Planning, and Preservation at Columbia University and the lead designer of his own practice in New York since 1963, Polshek has always used architecture as an educational force in the community. Whereas most architects equate success to the amount of press their work attracts, he measures his accomplishments by the degree of integration with surrounding structures and the level of ego-concealment his work achieves. In fact, in some of Polshek's buildings, the primary test of architectural quality is reflected in how long it takes the public to notice their presence in the neighborhood. Admirably, he represents a category of environmental thinking that transcends the trivialities of seasonal style wars and media hype by addressing the infinitely more compelling and future-oriented issues of neighborhood preservation, social responsibility, and the application of pluralistic values in architecture.

modest (and sometimes nearly invisible) form of intervention. He describes his objective as a "holistic approach that recognizes the critical social, cultural, and environmental importance of the individual project, founded on the belief that architecture should be more about 'place-making' than 'image making'." This commitment is laudably refreshing in the face of architecture's increasing tendency toward egomaniac excess. While the artistic profile of Polshek's work is low key – in some design circles, seen as too conservative – his legacy of successfully integrated buildings has also become an influential model for a new philosophy of urban design that rejects the ubiquitous "blast and build" pattern of neighborhood renewal.

In designing the North Country Resource Recovery Center in San Marcos, California, Polshek used this structure to demonstrate that a landfill and recycling plant to not have to impose on the environment as industrial eyesores. Constructed on a foundation of wood trusses and masonry piers, the project uses landscape as an effective screen for the facility and transforms state-of-the art technology into

The Sociological Aspects of Green Architecture – Urbanism

The following three architects represent a special category of work that has useful implications for various new directions in environmental thinking, but it is not strictly ecological. Their ideas tend to focus more on a sociological or topographical contextualism than on an orthodox green technology. They address several expanded definitions of environmental reform, for example, using architecture to recapture declining sections of the city, proposing ways to alleviate the alternative (but equally devastating) scourge of rapacious real estate development, and looking at the fusion of buildings with nature as a form of geological symbiosis, rather than a game of formal counterpoint with landscape.

At the grass roots level of a new and context-sensitive urbanism, the work of Troy West holds a leadership position. In contrast to

James Polshek, who tends to work on large municipally sponsored projects, West functions as a neighborhood activist and design entrepreneur who responds to poorer communities that need housing, civic centers, and quality-of-life public spaces. By taking advantage of his role as a professor of architecture at the New Jersey Institute of Technology, he often starts neighborhood recovery projects through the mechanism of class assignments and student intern programs. With his talent for cutting through the labyrinthine resistance of local politics, he has been able to advance environmental education by giving young people a unique opportunity to learn about construction and community values through hands-on experience. At the same time, he has served the cause of green architecture with simple and cost effective innovations.

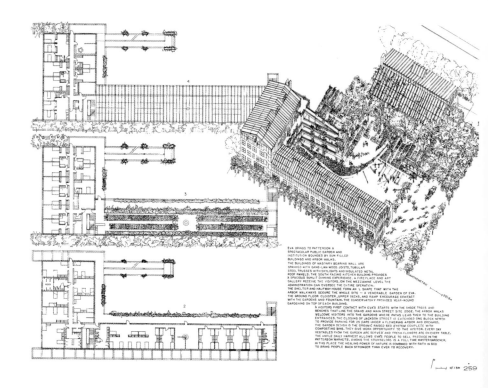

EVA BRINGS TO PATTERSON A SPECTACULAR PUBLIC GARDEN AND INSTITUTION BOUNDED BY SUN FILLED BUILDINGS AND ARBOR WALKS.
THE BUILDINGS OF MASONRY BEARING WALL ARE SPANNED WITH GANG-LAM WOOD JOISTS, TUBULAR STEEL TRUSSES WITH SKYLIGHTS AND INSULATED METAL ROOF PANELS. THE SOUTH FACING KITCHEN BUILDING PROVIDES A SPACIOUS SUNLIT DINING EXPERIENCE, A FIREPLACE AND ART GALLERY RECEIVE THE VISITORS, ON THE MEZZANINE LEVEL THE ADMINISTRATION CAN OVERSEE THE ENTIRE OPERATION.
THE SHELTER AND HALFWAY HOUSE FORM AN L SHAPE THAT WITH THE ARBOR WALKWAYS SECURE THE WHOLE SITE – A VENERABLE GARDEN OF EVA. THE GROUND FLOOR CLOISTER, UPPER DECKS, AND RAMP ENCOURAGE CONTACT WITH THE GARDENS AND FOUNTAIN. THE CONSERVATORY PROVIDES YEAR-ROUND GARDENING ON TOP OF EACH BUILDING.
A VISITORS FIRST CONTACT WITH EVA'S STARTS WITH THE SHADE TREES AND BENCHES THAT LINE THE GRAND AND MAIN STREET SITE EDGE. THE ARBOR WALKS WELCOME VISITORS INTO THE GARDENS WHERE THE PATHS LEAD THEM TO THE BUILDING ENTRANCES. THE CLOSING OF JACKSON STREET IS EXTENDED ONE BLOCK NORTH TO PROVIDE PARKING FOR 25 CARS UNDER A FLOWERING ARBOR AND ORCHARD. THE GARDEN DESIGN IS THE ORGANIC RAISED BED SYSTEM COMPLETE WITH COMPOSTING BINS. THEY GIVE WORK OPPORTUNITY TO THE VISITOR. EVERY DAY VESTABLES FROM THE GARDEN ARE SERVED AND FRESH FLOWERS ARE ON EVERY TABLE. THE AMPLE DAILY HARVEST ALLOWS EVA'S PEOPLE TO SELL PRODUCE IN THE PATTERSON MARKETS. AMONG THE COUNSELORS IS A FULL TIME MASTER GARDENER. IN THIS PLACE THE HEALING POWER OF NATURE IS COMBINED WITH FAITH IN GOD TO BRING PEOPLE BACK STRONGER THAN EVER TO RECOVERY.

259

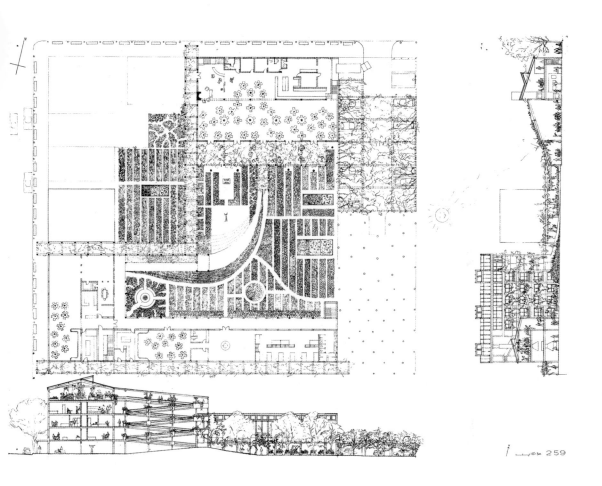

259

Page 184 and 185
Eva's Kitchen
Troy West
Paterson, New Jersey, USA
Project

New American House
Troy West
Wakefield, Rhode Island,
USA
Project, 1984

Kitchen are served in a spacious, sunlit dining room and any overproduction is sold in local Patterson markets. The L-shaped structure also includes arbor walkways, a trellis-shaded parking area, and a passive solar-gain design to conserve energy.

For his prize-winning New American House project in Wakefield, Rhode Island, designed in association with Jacqueline Leavitt, Troy West proposed a series of row houses with gable roofs and gardens, drawn from references to 19th-century English housing, when the British Government declared that every residence was entitled to an attached garden space. Taking cues from this historic tradition, the design team created an assembly of townhouses that relate to the greater community and form an intimate enclave for city living. The primary strength of this project is the masterful way the buildings fuse traditional domestic imagery and lifestyle advantages with a distinctly contemporary feeling and still embrace the larger fabric of the neighborhood.

Troy West's competition entry for an International Center of Communication in Paris, France, represents a masterful endeavor to bring some much-needed evidence of the French capital's scale, garden space, and neoclassical history to the new La Defense commercial development. La Defense changes the Parisian periphery with an imposing glut of super-sleek high-rises that contrast with the rich diversity of the central city. Along with Singapore, Shanghai, and Tokyo, La Defense is just another example of urban development that brings to mind scenes of George Romero's *Night of the Living Dead* horror film sequels. This is probably why an architect of West's gentle urbanistic persuasion decided to undertake the challenge of trying to bring a humanizing vision to this competition.

West's solution for the new center was to create a crescent-shaped building as a graceful culmination for the historic processional axis running from the Arc de Triomphe to La Defense. This terminal enclave includes a facade composed of vegetation-encrusted terraces (recalling the verdant facade of the

For Eva's Kitchen, a 60,000-square-foot shelter and halfway house operated by Catholic nuns in Patterson, New Jersey, Troy West suggested a conversion of several adjoining brick buildings into an appealing social center that is intended to help psychologically elevate the spirits of the inhabitants during their transition back into normal life. For this reason, the facility has an integral greenhouse roof to illuminate the interiors, a ramp system to accommodate the handicapped, and a courtyard filled with flower and vegetable gardens. The fruits and vegetables grown at Eva's

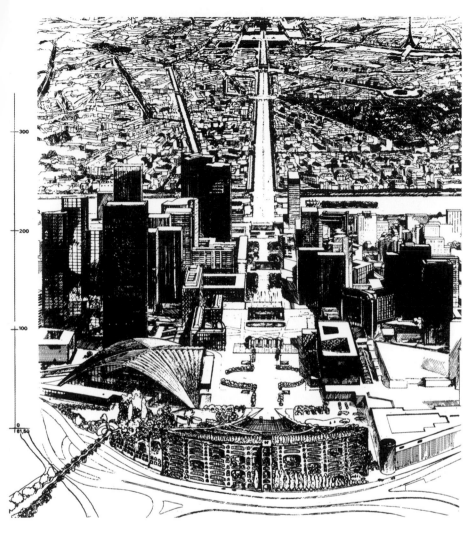

International Center of Communication
Troy West
Paris, France
Project, 1983

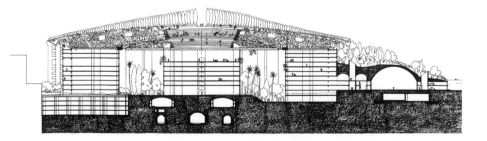

ACROS Building by Emilio Ambasz) and a classical Parisian plaza. The plan also proposed extensive adjacent gardens that visually connect the central city to the formerly verdant suburbs (prior to the intrusion of La Defense), and used natural green features to heat and cool the building. To enhance this purpose, the entire roof structure was conceived as a glazed space-frame covered with vines that function as a passive solar collector in winter and a leafy, ivy-filtered shade in the summer. Pedestrian access within the complex is provided by a system of long ramps and five-meter-square hollow columns that offer both structural support and accommodation for elevators, stairs, and electrical and mechanical systems. Unfortunately, this competition was not realized.

Troy West's International Center of Communication in Paris valiantly confronts the problem of trying to bring environmental sanity to the artificial French megalopolis. In the polar opposite ambiance of the hills surrounding San Francisco, Stanley Saitowitz has carved out a place for his work as part of these Arcadian suburbs. Originally a South African architect (now living permanently in Northern California), he has welcomed the surrounding structure of nature

Cliff House
Stanley Saitowitz
Transvaal, South Africa
Project, 1983

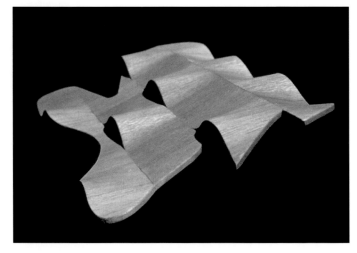

as the primary generator of form. Starting with his first internationally known project for a Cliff House in the Transvaal of South Africa – distinguished by an undulating roof plane that mirrors the configuration of local rock forms – Saitowitz has developed his environmental sensibilities and formal strategies by observing the surfaces and infrastructure of nature. His buildings reflect the rhythms and patterns found in air flow, water surfaces, geological strata, characteristic topography, hydrological cycles, and the seasonal changes of botanical life.

He sees his most successful work as resonating with a site in what he calls "geological architecture." Reflecting a compatible interest in the symbolic references found in the work of such architects as Ambasz, Noever, Ushida and Findlay, Jencks, SITE, and Predock, Stanley Saitowitz has described his buildings as combining biomorphic, geomorphic, and cosmological sources. He writes: "Geography studies natural processes to reveal growth and form as reciprocal: that shape is itself the process of becoming. Human intervention constitutes an abridgement of these natural processes." Saitowitz views architecture as simultaneously earth-centric and cosmos-centric, designing each of his structures as a carefully orchestrated response to these dual forces.

For the Seadrift Lagoon House at Stinson Beach near San Francisco, Saitowitz shaped the building in response to a series of situational references – some actual and some subliminal – including the waves of the bay, a ship cutting through the water, a nearby hillside, and even the sense of an unseen geology. Describing the house as a "cave carved by water," the architect has evoked connections to troglodyte living and other early origins of human habitat. In counterpoint, as a thoroughly contemporary gesture, he has opened up the interior to sunlight by allowing it to pass through large clerestory windows and filter kaleidoscopic reflections of the water's surface on the walls. The horizontal wood paneling of the exterior surfaces and the rolled-back roof plane further enhance the structure's metaphorical connec-

Cliff House
Stanley Saitowitz
Transvaal, South Africa
Project, 1983

tions to nature and reinforce its association with primordial shelter.

In developing his brilliantly sculptural volumes in the Napa Valley Storybook Winery, Saitowitz created a vaulted structure, with cave-like associations, that bridges over a depression in the earth. The entire facility uses the production process of fermenting, bottling, and storage of wine as an architectural analogy to the interdependent flow of energy forces in nature. The building is conceived in the form of a half-buried wine barrel, which is also associated with the shape of a distant hillside. As a way of extending these references to the wine-making function of the structure, there is a pedestrian route that takes visitors from the harvesting of grapes to a tasting of the finished product to an exit that commands a panoramic vista of the Napa Valley landscape.

Seadrift Lagoon House
Stanley Saitowitz
Stinson Beach, near San
Francisco, California, USA
1990

Storybook Winery
Stanley Saitowitz
Napa Valley, California, USA
Project, 1985

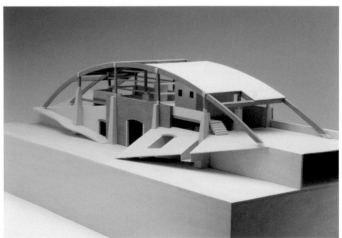

Yumesaki Resort
Matteo Vercelloni
Yumesaki, Japan
Project, 1991

forming two rice-farming water basins into an environment that would evoke the feeling of a classic Zen garden and still qualify as a contemporary recreational center.

The second proposal, a 1993 design for the New Shanghai Club and Hotel in China, is located near a city aqueduct with water tanks and specifically intended to retain the European colonial influence on urban architecture that dominated this metropolis in the 1920s and 30s. Since many of these historic structures still remain and shape the idiomatic consistency of certain neighborhoods, Vercelloni's choice of architectural imagery can be seen as similar in purpose to the work of James Polshek, retaining the stylistic integrity of the cityscape by means of iconographic assimilation. While this approach has also characterized the work of certain Postmodernist designers – Robert Stern and Michael Graves, for example – the Vercelloni interpretation is less about the marketing of style and more about the art of assimilation and inclusion. In addition to a spacious park that recalls Chinese landscaping tradition, there is a roof garden built over the water tanks providing visitors with a panoramic view of the city.

The work of Troy West, Stanley Saitowitz, and Matteo Vercelloni represents three aspects of architecture where the level of accomplishment is measured by how well it fuses with its context and how intelligently it educates the public about the value of conservation. In each case, the merits of their work must also be credited in terms of realistic budget constraints, build ability, and a respect for the indeterminate, fragmented, and uncontrollable elements of nature and the city. Even though the imagery of their architecture can be seen as traditional from the standpoint of form and style, the actual implications of their buildings in an environmentally endangered world are decidedly progressive. The modesty of their intentions and their capacity to understand the green initiative in architecture as a sociological and preservationist issue place their efforts at the cutting edge of ideas and services which are needed in much greater quantity today.

The site-specific work of the Italian architect and journalist Matteo Vercelloni, like Stanley Saitowitz, is rooted in a classically conditioned sensitivity to nature and an ability to incorporate modes of living that have been passed down through the centuries. Born in Milan in 1961, Vercelloni is the son of the distinguished architect and historian, Virgilio Vercelloni. Before his father's death, the two designers collaborated on several history books and environmental design projects for Japan and China. The first of these – the Yumesaki Resort of 1991 – included the development of a master plan and the design of a series of clustered buildings which reflected the characteristics of a traditional Japanese village. This resort was planned for a picturesque valley near Osaka, with the intention of trans-

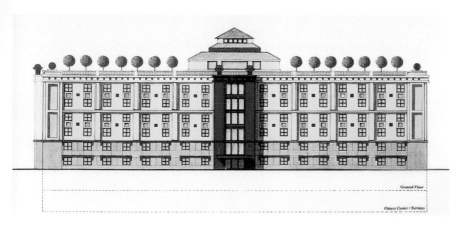

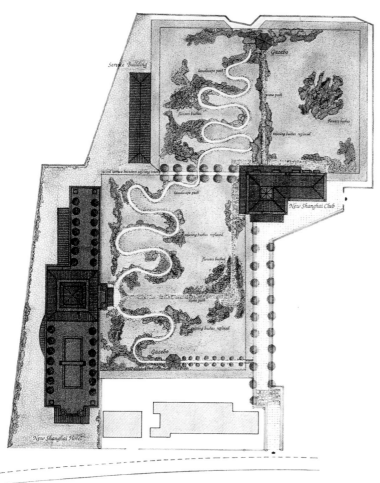

**New Shanghai Club
and Hotel**
Matteo Vercelloni
Shanghai, China
Project, 1993

The architect must be a prophet, a prophet in the true sense of the word; if he can't see at least ten years ahead then don't call him an architect.

Frank Lloyd Wright

Prophetic Visions for the Future

The above defense of "invisible architecture" is intended as a preface to the final section of this review of contemporary architects, which focuses on a selection of aggressively visible and idiosyncratic designers who have made interesting contributions to the green movement. This last group – loosely assembled under the title of "visionaries with ideas that have important implications for the future" – includes innovators whose quantity of built work goes from nothing at all to occasional. The point is that such time-worn terms as "avant garde" and "progressive" are, in themselves, outdated and desperately in need of being redefined. This observation is interposed here in full recognition of the fact that the main lament of this book has been an expressed disappointment that recent green architectural language has not kept up with the dynamic implications of environmental reform, the information revolution and related

advances in technology. Design positions that were once considered peripheral have become, by default and through a shift in priorities, the generators of a new forefront. At the same time, all those overpraised and style-driven architectural pyrotechnics of the past decade are beginning to look hopelessly conservative.

This confusion of terms notwithstanding, the work of American architect Jeffrey Miles demonstrates a high level of futuristic panache and, whether his proposals are feasible or not, he certainly sets the stage for architecture in the next millennium. He is an ecological advocate and Leonardoesque green theoretician who has proposed using design and engineering to attack the problems of pollution. In his extensively researched Ozone-maker, what appears at first glance to be a fantasy out of *Star Wars* is a brilliantly conceived, wind-cleaning series of satellites that repair the ozone layer by removing chlorofluorocarbons and

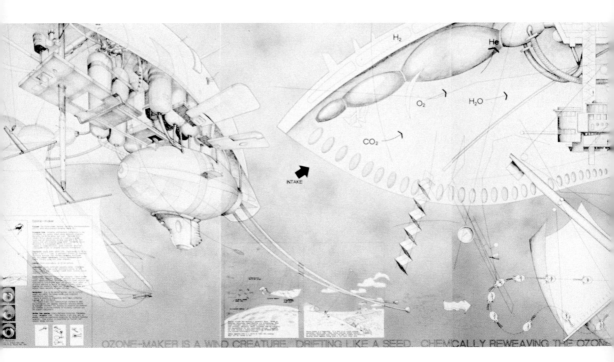

OZONE-MAKER IS A WIND CREATURE, DRIFTING LIKE A SEED, CHEMICALLY REWEAVING THE OZONE

simultaneously excreting beneficial clean air collected from the atmosphere. With a length of 433 meters, a width of 170 meters, and a speed of 5 kilometers per hour, the horseshoe-crab-shaped Ozone-maker circles the earth at 16 kilometers altitude. Miles' project is based on the premise that harmful CFCs from fossil fuel emissions are destroying the ozone layer and threatening life on earth by potentially changing the climate and disrupting the global food chain. Since CFCs remain airborne for more than a century, with catastrophic implications, his green machine concept is designed to help re-establish a balanced atmosphere.

Operated by a crew of twelve "bionauts," the hydrogen-fueled machine is helium-inflated and moves primarily by means of wind power, using sails reminiscent of an 18th-century clipper ship. Supplies are brought aboard from dirigible stations and balloons. Its main service is based on removing CFCs from the ozone

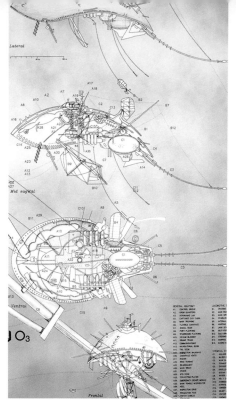

**Ozone-maker
Detail and total plan
(below)**
Jeffrey Miles
Project, 1993

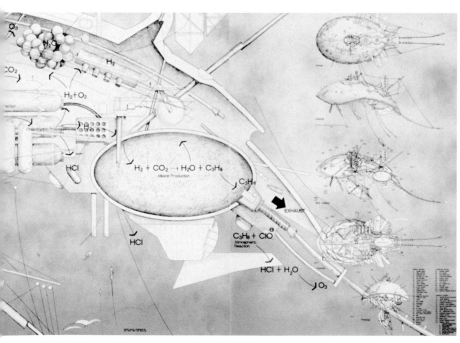

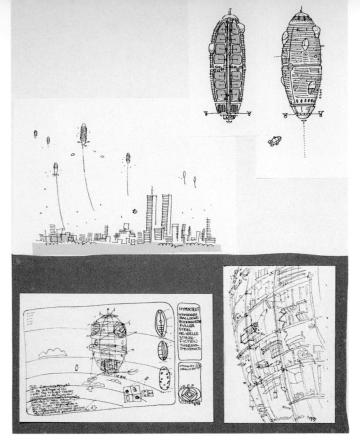

Biotecture, Balloontown
Jeffrey Miles
Project, 1993–95

Page 197
Biotecture, Artificial Island
Jeffrey Miles
Project, 1995

layer. The floating factory uses chemoauto-tropic bacteria to seed the atmosphere with alkanes (chemically removing chlorine as hydrogen chloride). The resulting by-products are collected and oxidized to provide material for extra buoyancy and life-support subsystems.

The Ozone-maker, circling the globe out of human sight, is not exactly an appropriate subject for this book about the art of green architecture; still, its visual features are beautifully articulated in Miles' drawings, and the idea, in itself, is too fascinating to exclude. The function of restoring the ozone layer is such an urgent objective that any architect's work addressing this issue should be treated as the highest form of aesthetic endeavor. This project is, after all, a potential contributor to the art of salvation.

For another science-fiction-like concept, entitled Biotecture, Miles embraced certain aspects of Wright's Broadacre City, with its

idealistic solutions for earth-centric living, and STERN's vision of the urban center as a biotope. By combining similar objectives, Miles has declared that urban centers should be an extension of the integrated structure of nature. He suggests that, by studying ecosystems and the behavior of plants and animals, humanity has the opportunity to enter a productive period of reverse engineering. This idea proposes the future city as a product of total recycling and as a conduit-like structure composed of earth-spanning underground habitat. The purpose is to conserve land surface and develop technologies that can bring the full benefits of sunlight into subterranean living.

Using the potential future benefits of genetic and molecular engineering, Jeffrey Miles envisions an architecture for the new metropolis composed of multiple living organisms (not just plant life) that would function as an intrinsic part of the ecosystem. In Miles' holistic scenario, ecological design is not just a kit of technological remedies for a bad situation. Biotecture should be a subdivision of Gaia and the concept of the whole earth as a living organism. In this way, all human enterprise could become part of an interdependent structure, where the motivational forces are not just products and profits, but, instead, are directed toward shared economies, communications systems, and sources of energy, sustained by a massive, globally-linked system of information feedback.

With a futuristic fervor matching that of Jeffrey Miles, the American architect, Donna Goodman, has been working for more than a decade on a concept she calls the Floating City. She comes from an interdisciplinary background – with studies of art and philosophy at Smith College and architecture at Columbia University – which has contributed to shaping the broad range of her interests in designing this project. Also, she benefited from an opportunity in 1979 to work at a shipyard in Rhode Island and, during this period, became interested in offshore technology produced by the Woods Hole Oceanographic Institute.

Floating City has been conceived in

Habitable program

Shell

Structure

Transport and Processing

Section with thermoregulation

Artificial Island
1995

People love the Caribbean islands so much—
why not build a few more?

197

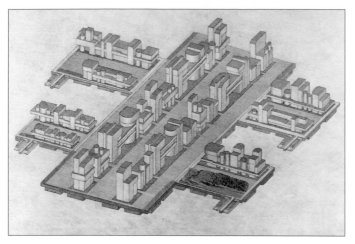

Page 198 and 199
Floating City
Donna Goodman
Project, 1983–95

disruption of underwater ecosystems, Goodman's island would float at 40 feet above water level on large air-filled pontoons. Stabilized by cables anchored to the ocean floor, this buoyant mini-city offers self-sustaining technical and agricultural components that depend on the sea for energy. For additional support, the project has an underwater grid of steel templates that can be adjusted to allow for expansion. Among its economic and environmental advantages, the complex includes clean systems of ocean floor mining of various minerals (iron, tungsten, copper, nickel, and cobalt), aquaculture farming, roof planting to reduce pollution and provide shade, and a state-of-the-art mass transit system.

Services on the artificial island are broken down into various tier levels, including the ocean floor for mining, fishing, oceanographic research, mid-ocean for mechanized farming and industrial production, water level for a shipping port and mechanical and electrical infrastructure, above water platform for light industry and residential communities, and roof terraces for solar collectors and additional infrastructure.

Donna Goodman has given additional attention to sustainable living systems in an ocean-based environment, including its economic and political structures. The government would include a modified Senate, a House of Technicians, with representatives from every sector of the economy, including business, labor, social, cultural, and educational enterprises. The specific ecological features include water-based sources of energy, solar-operated desalination facilities for water supplies, recycling of wastes to generate new energy, and kelp and algae farming for phytoremediation and toxin control.

While Goodman's seductive drawings describe the Floating City as a kind of technological utopia, with an infinite number of computer-driven, convenience-oriented, health-beneficial, and administratively progressive elements, it is not clear from the illustrations how these advantages break down into the personalized fragments that make city life enjoy-

response to future projections of an overwhelming population growth (estimated at almost 8 billion people by 2025) that will overtax land-based resources and threaten human survival. Goodman's proposal is based on the observation that research into the possibilities of over and under sea habitat has been minimal and deserves both a technical and philosophical approach. As precedents, the architect cites land-deprived countries like Japan, where more than 60 artificial islands have been built for housing and general urban expansion during the past decade. Instead of imposing the usual solution of landfill, with its inevitable

able. She describes planting, flexible blocks, and economy of scale, but the drawings seem more about mega systems than mini pleasures. If the gentle inclusionism of architects like Troy West and Stanley Saitowitz can be viewed as too local and modest, then perhaps Goodman's water city can be seen as too sweeping and ambitious. On the other hand, her various texts on the proposal provide a critique of the evils of past utopian plans and their authoritarian prescriptions for community life, so one can only assume that the missing individualized components of Floating City have not yet been visualized. These reservations aside, for all its *Blade Runner*-meets-*Water World* sense of futurism, Donna Goodman's project lays the foundations for an inevitable expansion of human living and working space into the oceans. By analyzing so many aspects of water-based technology and its environmental implications, she has offered viable alternatives to counter a growing fear that great bodies of water may become just another victim of expansionist exploitation. She has understood that the apocalyptic scenarios on land must not be repeated in the seas.

Representing the polar opposite end of the visionary architecture spectrum from Donna Goodman, the Ecstacity project by Nigel Coates in London is primarily based on celebrating all of the chaotic and unpredictable elements of the urban environment. Coates was an early leader in the 1970s narrative architecture movement and once editor of a publication called NATO (*Narrative Architecture Today*). The primary mission of the organization, unlike the Modernists' tendency to proclaim utopian formulas, was to use new buildings as a means of preserving and incorporating all of the imperfections, sensuality, and multifaceted qualities that reinforce civic vitality. As Coates commented about this period of his development: "Our narrative then was not a question of telling stories, but of imposing sensual and illogical fragments of meaning onto reality in order to emphasize it." Since the beginning of his career, he has continued to advocate a complete absorption of

the living, evolving, and disparate fragments of city life as crucial to metropolitan survival. In many ways, his philosophy is the opposite of the green design quest for sustainability. By contrast, Coates states that, in his view, "Real contemporary culture has an inherent ephemerality linked to shifts in taste and the lifespan of information. Architecture, on the other hand, has volunteered to be marginalized by its commitment to lasting forever."

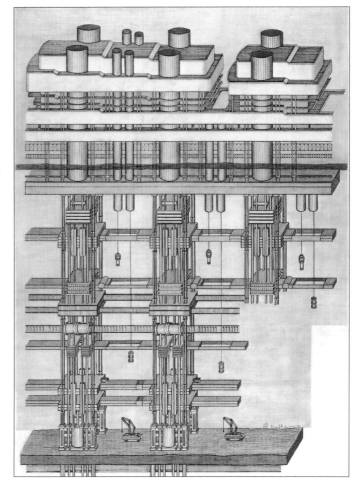

Ecstacity Installation
Nigel Coates
London, England
Project, 1992

Beginning as a student at the famed Architectural Association in London, where he later was involved as a teacher, advisor, and collaborator on special projects, Nigel Coates teamed up with A. A. associates in 1991 to propose his Ecstacity for England's vast millennium celebration. In his pessimism concerning the tendencies of all new city development internationally to take the form of high-rise glut and the destruction of neighborhood identity, he has proposed that London be transformed into a marketplace for what he calls "soft urban interventions." These would include narrative appendages attached to buildings as a way of revealing their origins and purposes, informational artifacts that integrate with the left-over spaces resulting from the ravages of real estate development, art works that erupt out of sidewalks, and continuously changing street works that blend past and future as organically choreographed events. Coates views his collage city as the opposite of James Polshek's and Troy West's unobtrusive inclusionism; rather, he proposes a metropolis

exploding with humor, eroticism, and commentary, a "cyberarchitecture" inspired by mass communications, and an urban plan filled with perverse inversions of the existing cityscape. Although not usually associated with green design, Coates has contributed significantly to theories that have expanded the concept of a social ecology (or the city seen as a biotope) by grasping the value of integrating human diversity, popular imagery, and evidence of the "collective unconscious" into architecture.

With a similar interventionist instinct, but focused on the natural environment, the work of François Roche in France has experimented with that gap suspended somewhere between ritual space and temporary structure. Of all the recent architects now breaking away from the mainstream definitions of "green," Roche has been among the most closely related to aboriginal beliefs in a perishable architecture that returns to nature. He is a confirmed anti-Modernist and rejects the idea that buildings must be permanent and environmentally intrusive, describing his philosophical approach as a

Right and below
Ecstacity (details)
Nigel Coates
London, England
Project, 1992

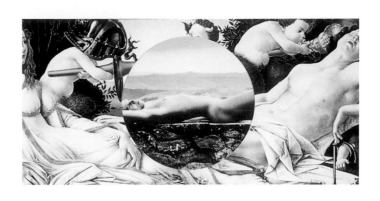

FORET SECHE

FORET HUMIDE

respect for the "chameleon meaning" of architecture. When designing a project, Roche is
guided by what he has termed a "genetic code
of territoriality," where shelter draws sustenance from its immediate surroundings and,
as a result, is in a constant state of renewal.

For a 1993 work called Mimesis, near
Pont del Concorde in Paris, François Roche utilized a site of the former Bain Deligny to create
an intervention by disassembling the swim-
ming pool and sections of the restaurants onto
a series of eight barges located in the Seine,
subjecting them to the movements of the river.

The project uses all of the materials and subliminal images associated with this section of
the Seine and then breaks them down into a
fragmented collage that is both a memory of
their former existence and a suggestion of
their dematerialization into the environment.

For a project entitled Transfert and
another called Camouflage, each dealing with
territoriality and realized in 1993, Roche built
two temporary 10 x 2 meter cabins in the
Forêt de Compiègne. Both were constructed
out of wire netting – one located in a southern
section of the forest with beech trees, and

the other in a northern part surrounded by conifers. These dwellings were covered with moss and built to respond to respective dry and wet environmental conditions. Camouflage extended Roche's interest in exploring the chameleon-like qualities of architecture. In this case, a series of windows is suspended on poles among a cluster of 15 maple trees. As the trees grow and adapt seasonally, the work changes in an evolutionary way.

These structures, intended to disintegrate back into nature, are related to Robert Smithson's Buried Shed at Kent State University in 1973 and his interest in connections between entropy and art. Fascinated by descriptions of the entropy phenomena by astrophysicists and the notion of an entire universe locked into a thermodynamic battle of survival, Smithson felt that art could be interpreted as a metaphor for the degradation of matter and energy.

Bridging art, science, and culture, the work of Roche and Smithson has embraced the implications of entropy, while sharing the Australian Aboriginals' view that a symbiotic relationship with nature means becoming part of its fabric, not resisting its forces.

The site-specific art of François Roche has been included in this section on ideas that have important implications for the future because it functions as a chronicler of topics that architects should be thinking about (but seldom do) – for example, indeterminacy, dematerialization, entropy, mutable and evolutionary process, and territorial feedback – and not because his designs offer a checklist of practical solutions. From a mainstream perspective, his interventions are far too conceptual and ephemeral to have much effect on the more pragmatic initiatives of green technology.

Page 204–207
Maison Zalotay
Elemér Zalotay
Ziegelried, Switzerland
1984

Elemér Zalotay, a Hungarian architect now living in Switzerland, plays a similar maverick role by providing a kaleidoscopic jumble of theory, novelty, and individual expression that can seem peripheral to the cause of environmental design, although in reality he has generated important raw material for change. Zalotay's work is a fascinating mixture of pure eccentricity and serious prescriptions for the Age of Ecology that include everything from vegetation-encrusted skyscrapers, to Broadacre City-inspired urban plans, to the chaotic collage of his own house in Ziegelried, near Berne.

Zalotay was born in Hungary in 1932, where he established himself during his student years as an artistic and political radical and was actually jailed several times during

the Hungarian Revolution. As a consequence of this record of dissent, he was forced to apply 16 times before getting approval for a visa to the West. After moving to Switzerland, he focused his architectural career on promoting a prefabricated panel system for housing that would permit inhabitants to personally construct multi-level buildings. This led to an interest in a wide variety of social and environmental issues, resulting in some theoretical papers published under the title of *Corb Plus*. These manifestos proposed that a viable architecture of the future should combine the urbanism of Le Corbusier with the organic contextualism of Wright – a strange hybrid where Modernism merges with Arcadianism. These speculations were accompanied by plans for cities, suburbs, and buildings that were mostly unbuildable by conventional bureaucratic and economic standards, but which nevertheless revealed Zalotay's masterful sense of assemblage and his uncanny ability to create a kind of collision architecture from patchwork materials.

The Maison Zalotay is a built compendium of the architect's multi-faceted imagination and represents the best example of his liberated sensibilities working in concert with nature. Technically, the dwelling is constructed out of recycled wood, glass, and plastics, grafted around a concrete core and anchored by cables. Visually, it is a hybrid apparition – Robert Rauschenberg meets Frank Lloyd Wright – in the pastoral ambiance of a quiet Swiss village. The Zalotay home fuses with its environment in a way that purposefully celebrates the unpredictable interaction between nature and architecture. It emerges from the landscape like a natural eruption, articulated by a collage choreography that fills the site with a cacophony of anarchic movement. The house is also reminiscent of Clarence Schmidt's famous 1960s House of Mirrors in Woodstock, New York, which scandalized the community with its freely assembled amalgamation of waste materials. Repeating history, Maison Zalotay also provoked the wrath of the surrounding community, and it has even been

Page 208 and 209
Maison Zalotay
Elemér Zalotay
Ziegelried, Switzerland
1984

toned by protesters on several occasions Schmidt's House of Mirrors was subjected to even greater violence when outraged neighbors burned it to the ground in the early 1970s). In terms of public reaction, Zalotay's house has become a local equivalent of Marcel Duchamp's famed "Nude, Descending a Staircase," which inflamed popular opinion during the 1913 Armory Exhibition in New York. Responding to this controversy, he has given a deferential nod to Duchamp's witty accommodation of accident after the breaking of his "Large Glass" assemblage (1915–23). With perspicacious insight, Zalotay has left the bombardments of rocks exactly where they landed on his property as an acknowledgment of the randomness of art.

If Elemér Zalotay's work can be said to represent a regionalist vision of utopia, then Michael Sorkin is clearly an internationalist. In recent years he has become a catalytic figure in urban design, proposing schemes that embrace most of the environmental issues covered in this survey of architects whose ideas have important implications for the future. He is a visionary designer with interests that bridge from the macrocosmic to the microcosmic in rethinking the metropolis of the next century. Like Coates and Zalotay, his intentions range from preserving the serendipitous appeal of an old neighborhood, to the inclusion of green space and ecological design, to programming the organizational matrix of a new city.

Sorkin is an American architect, educated at Harvard and the Massachusetts Institute of Technology, with a dual career as a major writer on architectural subjects and the founder of an influential professional practice in New York City. He has a deep interest in the morphology of the city and those similarities between the mutability of organisms in nature and the growth patterns of urban centers. The configurations of his individual buildings are frequently drawn from sources in the natural environment – usually plants and animals that seem to have migrated into his design schemes as reminders of a community's origins

in some primordial past. This evidence of biomorphism in Sorkin's work is not based on nostalgia for an alluvial glade and, contrary to a movement like Art Nouveau, it is not based on the celebration of flora and fauna as a romantic antidote to the industrial city. For Sorkin, the biomorphic connection is both an avenue of humorous commentary on the traditions of organic architecture and a profoundly intelligent exploration of those connections between the images and functions of the city and their exemplary counterparts found in nature.

Michael Sorkin is also an advocate of the geomorphic city which reflects both local and hemispherical influences. While many of his visually seductive drawings may appear to be descriptions of organizational overkill, the opposite is true; these illustrations must be

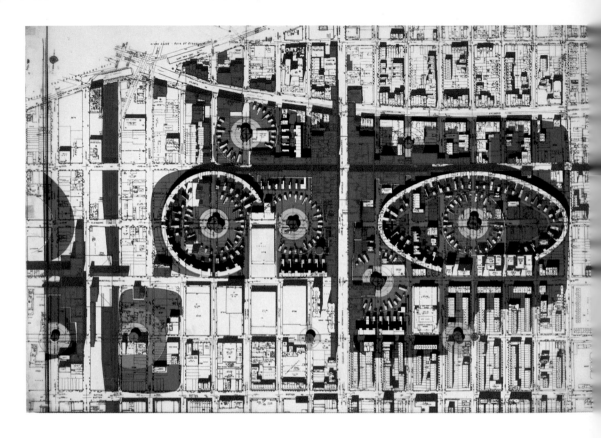

Page 210 and 211
**East New York
development study**
Michael Sorkin Studio
New York, New York, USA
Project, 1996

understood as more diagrammatic than prescriptive. His intention is to graphically understand urban patterns at the macrocosmic level
as a guide for proposing interventions that
flow with existing metropolitan rhythms. In
dealing with the microcosmic level, he accepts
the natural disorder and vitality of street life,
and his architectural role is modulated by the
need to preserve that "complex and contradic-
tory order" in community life advocated by
Venturi. By embracing this duality, Sorkin has
broken away from the authoritarian mold of
Modernist master planning in this century.

As a consequence of Modern and contemporary architects' desire to design the
perfect utopian metropolis, they have often
treated the city as an architectural tabula rasa.
This mission has been based on an assumption
that somehow urban centers are like clean
slates, allowing the designer to ignore the
great wealth of experience already engraved
on the tablet. Thus empowered, they are con-

vinced they bring enlightenment with the
dynamite. Since the days of Le Corbusier's
overweening proposal to flatten Paris as a
receptacle for his (gratefully unrealized) Voisin
Plan, millions of acres of history, identity, and
knowledge have been blasted off the face of
the earth in the name of urban renewal, a scenario that still continues. Many of today's best
designers fall prey to the same delusion, that
somehow the answer lies in leveling the land,
laying down a rigorous grid, and then erecting
a plethora of glass and steel towers. Most of
the urbanistic extravagances are motivated by
that heady fantasy of conceiving utopia as the
product of a single vision.

In designing a project for East New York
in 1996, Sorkin used a pluralistic approach by
resisting what he calls the "homogenizations
of global culture." As an alternative, he favors
looking at the community as a "maximization
of economic, social, cultural, and environmental self-sufficiency" that can still draw on the

collective advantages of greater New York without losing its identity. The area is a poor neighborhood in Brooklyn, where Sorkin took into account all of the region's diverse topography and construction – combining shoreline, wetlands, canals, factories, and some clusters of ugly housing blocks. Avoiding the usual demolitionist tactics, Sorkin's studies evaluated all of the most popular neighborhood characteristics and then proposed a plan to link them together by means of parks, village greens, and various sculptural features that sometimes metamorphose into buildings. The purpose is to help bind the community together through a combination of unifying symbols and surprise interventions. Among what he calls "acupuncture" amenities, Sorkin planted a tree in the middle of an intersection, which created four instant pedestrian arteries (desirably reducing car traffic by reason of inconvenience), thereby setting in motion a program to eliminate harmful emissions and traffic congestion by cutting back on the space available to motor vehicles. Taking his cues from those great pedestrian street models still active and relevant in historic cities, Sorkin uses the human body as "the central measure of urbanity." In summary, his cities are made for walking.

In another East New York plan of 1994, Sorkin proposed a series of souk-like structures (market areas in the Middle East) called Shroom, that would connect the entire neighborhood with a series of pavilions (or "pods"). These units are planned to fill discarded vacant lots or be grafted onto sections of existing buildings as a way of increasing their latent serviceability and adding more gardens and park spaces to the community. The archetype for Shroom is the New York industrial loft, with its inherent flexibility for adaptation to endless uses. This potentially growing necklace of structures in Brooklyn is seen as an alternative to the European concept of large municipal spaces (a universalistic idea that rarely works in the American city). The East New York development is conceived as a chain of public and private facilities that bring people together in more intimate settings for a great variety of services and pleasures. As a visual gesture typical of Michael Sorkin's technique for greening the cityscape, the Shroom project also includes fluid ribbons of vegetation that start at street level and emerge on the roofs of the loft structures. When viewed from above, the entire neighborhood seems linked together with amorphous tentacles of landscape.

Page 212 and 213
Shroom
Michael Sorkin Studio
New York, New York, USA
Project, 1994

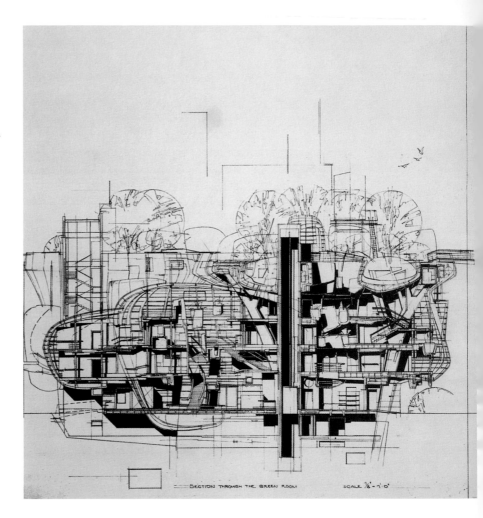

SECTION THROUGH THE GREEN ROOM   SCALE ⅛" = 1'-0"

Michael Sorkin might appropriately be called a visionary with a heart. He has understood that, with all of the buzz about people living in cyberspace and communicating primarily through global wavelengths, this is already a reality and just another convenient tool that will soon be assimilated into the realm of routine. In this respect, computers are just like every other exotic technology that has nourished science fiction hyperbole and ended up in antique auctions. In designing for the future city, Sorkin has taken into account that people are weary of looking at digital screens all day and sitcoms all night, so why on earth would they want their neighborhood to be another "virtual reality"? The fact is that people need and value human interaction more than ever because of computer technology. In the Sorkin city, they walk, talk, sit in doorways, tend their gardens, and breath cleaner air. Preserving this desirable reality is the basic goal of sustainability and the primary urban design challenge of the future.

M Sorkin studio 07.06.1994

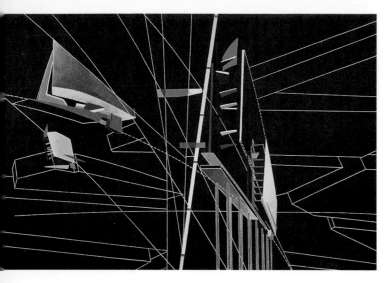

Office on the Kurfürstendamm
Zaha Hadid
Berlin, Germany
Project, 1986

The search for an architectural language to express the complexities of a post-industrial society has been a compelling, but still unresolved, objective of designers during the past two decades. This quest is particularly evident in the work of most green architects reviewed in these pages. It still seems unclear, as in the earliest exploratory stages of Modernism at the turn of the this century, what form this language should take, what residuals from the past should be discarded, and what aspects of societal change should be expressed. At its most authentic and vital level, the original Machine Age aesthetic in architecture embodied everything from a celebration of the way technology functioned to a demonstration of how a 20th-century social utopia might be achieved.

When Modernist ideas had fully matured by the 1930s, their interpretations were imaginatively varied and their theoretical hypotheses were powerfully convincing. In the present slow evolution of post-industrial theory and practice, the opposite is true. Beginning with the late 1960s, when it became fashionable in certain Po-mo circles to trash Modernism as a retrograde and inhuman architectural tradition, the alternatives were frequently far less persuasive than the target of attack. There have been many outstandingly innovative buildings constructed during the past two decades based on the pioneering legacies of Mod-

ernism, Constructivism, and De Stijl – particularly those by Frank O. Gehry, Zaha Hadid, Peter Eisenman, Richard Rogers, Rem Koolhaas, Eric Owen Moss, Morphosis, Jean Nouvel, and some others. But, at the same time, a number of the movements credited as "avant garde" became forums for trendy dissidents, paper architects, and short-lived stylistic tendencies with questionable premises. In the 1970s we witnessed the earnest – and mostly unbuilt – explosion of Radical Architecture, which often became more a mission of social protest and performance art than a premise for viable habitat. During this same period we also saw the nomadic isolationism of Drop City communes, with their green guerrilla dome structures and Gaia-inspired rhetoric, which lost its momentum for a lack of realistic objectives. This was followed by the flamboyance of decorative Postmodernism, the proliferation of pastel-colored pediments and turret-topped skyscrapers, and its ultimate appropriation by the entertainment industries in a grotesque "theme-parkification" of the world. Postmodernism was succeded by a resurrected neo-Constructivism, which unleashed an explosion of sculptural excess in architecture making King Ludwig's Bavarian castles seem sedate by comparison. And even the burgeoning green movement of the 1990s is already in danger of producing a fashionable glut of vine-covered thermal houses with trees on the roof and a climate of environmental elitism seemingly destined to alienate, more than attract, potential friends of the earth. While stylistic idioms and attitudes are an inevitable by-product of epochal identity, the late 1990s appears to be an architectural period of predominantly flamboyant mannerisms, with little evidence of a deeper philosophical grounding.

One contributing factor in this poverty of substantive content is a lack of environmental thinking. This is a conceptual approach to green architecture that goes beyond the conventional elements associated with ecological design. It proposes that a building's most interesting sources of imagery do not derive exclusively from the surrounding elements that

Let the architect be educated. Skillful with the pencil, instructed in geometry, know much history, have followed the philosophers with attention, understand music, have some knowledge of medicine, know the opinions of the jurists, and be acquainted with astronomy and the theory of heavens.

Marcus Vitruvius Pollio

actually exist; rather, they come from thoughts about things that are implied to exist. This is a difficult idea to explain, much less put into practice. What it basically proposes is that a work of architecture, if it is a true product of environmental thinking, cannot be removed from a particular location without sacrificing its essential meaning. There are no clear-cut rules or guidelines that specify which ambient features a building must include to meet these standards of contextual assimilation, although it is probably safe to say that most viewers can tell the difference between a structure designed as an abstract sculptural object with no relation to anything but itself, versus one that responds to its surroundings through symbiotic relationships. Environmental thinking means that walls, facades, interior spaces, and the general materiality of a building – outside of their obvious contributions to architectural function – can be seen as much more than physical components in the manipulation of form and space. They become vehicles for the absorption and communication of contextual information. Within this revised perspective, the new environmentalism is as much a social and psychological condition as it is part of an ecological initiative. Consistent with the information revolution, buildings can enter territories formerly occupied only by conceptual, environmental, and performance art. For example, conceptual art has always emphasized the search for ideas outside of formal relationships and craft-based skills by focusing on the ambiguities surrounding rhetorical definitions in art. Like Michel Foucault's explorations into the equivocal nature of language by demonstrating the blurred edges separating reason and madness, art conceived as a questioning of the definition of art deals with similar levels of ambivalence and a challenge to institutionalized values. Applied to architecture, these areas of indeterminacy can become the basis for using buildings as both a source of psychic inquiry and the means to achieve an expanded awareness of context.

The classic precursor for this challenge to definitions in art is Marcel Duchamp's famous "Fountain" (a standard urinal, signed R. Mutt; 1917/1964), which when it was first shown in the New York Independents Exhibiton forced viewers to confront issues of categorical legitimacy. "The Fountain" was obviously not hand-carved sculpture and did not reinforce the showcase expectations of an art gallery; it was, instead, the heretic act of selection and placement of a manufactured object that shattered the conventions of exhibition space. It acquired its meaning from an inversion of situation. Applying this attitudinal game to architecture, the suggestion is that a building's presence in a landscape or an urban center embodies a subliminal set of associations that can be used to invert its meaning. In other words, the conventional design criteria for site planning and the archetypal identity of certain categories of buildings can become the raw material of inversion. The communicative content of architecture is then based not on pure sculptural form, but, rather, on its capacity to absorb and transmit ideas by other means. The exploration of these other means is one of the main challenges for a new level of environmental thinking.

While the works of a number of the architects included in the present survey reflect certain aspects of this search for an expanded environmental language, some designers' capacity to embrace new conceptual territory seems inhibited by the self-imposed restrictions of style, taste, and orthodox design ideologies. Unfortunately this has been a habitual constraint throughout the century, a limitation which has thwarted architects' access to alternative means of communication. The commitment to expressive freedom and ground-breaking innovation in the arts seems to have excluded most architecture after the 1930s. For whatever reason, once Modernist and Constructivist influences had supplanted the traditions of iconographic content, decorated surfaces, hand-crafted detail, and earth-centric construction methods in favor of the impersonal language of industrial production, there seemed to be no hope of recovering these humanizing elements. At the same time, archi-

Piazza d'Italia
Charles Moore
New Orleans,
Louisiana, USA
1975–78

Public Service Building
Michael Graves,
Portland, Oregon, USA
1980–83

tecture became conceptually inert, locked into formulaic guidelines for good and bad design, and based on a rather limited kit of formal and tactical premises. In contrast, the visual arts have been a vigorous dialectical battleground of abstraction versus realism, conceptualism versus expressionism, and minimalism versus maximalism. With the exception of certain contributors to radical architecture in the 1970s and Venturi's advocacy of an imagery drawn from "the everyday world, vulgar and disdained," the dominant stylistic commitments in the building arts have remained depressingly consistent. Most architects have strenuously

resisted any potentially threatening assaults on their beliefs, continuing to describe design values in such constipated terms as "rigorous," "disciplined" and "formally consistent," while the built manifestations of this orthodoxy have been glacial and uncommunicative. There is an insular and coded litany of theoretical premises, materials choices, compositional mannerisms, and formalist conventions that determine an architect's 'in or out' status in the mainstream today. The building arts seem to be in desperate need of a critical voice with a Duchampian sensibility – an iconoclastic figure who, like Duchamp, could describe his own questioning process as "I taught myself to contradict myself in order to avoid conforming to my own taste."

The most blatant evidence of this conservative drift in the architecture of the 1990s is the ascendancy of the art museum as a preeminent cultural icon. It has replaced the religious edifice, public park, and civic center as the most coveted category of architectural commission. As a design challenge, its purposes represent the polar opposite of an inclusionist sensibility. The art museum is hermetic, elitist, accessible only by paid admission, obscenely expensive to build, and its primary mission is to isolate art objects from public life. Also, while architects pursue museum jobs with an unprecedented fervor, rarely do the sponsors of art institutions demonstrate even a shred of environmental conscience. The pattern of recent museum construction sometimes seemed to be an administrative decision to resist anything even remotely earth-friendly. Oddly, these indulgences appear to be increasing in proportion to a curatorial preference to maintain the primacy of the traditional art showcase.

The economically audacious and resource-wasteful tendencies of recent art museums notwithstanding, this is not the main point here. Their negative significance has been to serve as the opposite of environmental thinking; in fact, they are the optimum models of object thinking. The art museum today is an anachronism, primarily identified with the growth of private art collections in the 19th century, when the monarchies (as the principal sponsors of civic works) began to collapse. As a result, its main purpose ever since has been to function as a reinforcement of ego-centric indulgences. When artists began to lose their sources of public patronage, after the 1850s, their work became more introspective, reflecting a withdrawal into the privacy of the studio. By the turn of the century, "private art" became synonymous with "real art," and the exhibition gallery replaced the public domain as the showcase of choice. Even the identification of what could be deemed "avant-garde" was predicated on challenges to the art museum context (translating, naturally, into a consensus acceptance of its protective sanctuary). No matter how outrageous and iconoclastic the manifestations of art, the main credential that it was art in the first place has been dependent on an institutional seal of approval, which has also functioned as the qualifying barometer for public acceptance. One courageous alternative was offered by the environmental art movement of the 1970s. With the exception of the pioneering achievements of such museum-resistant artists as Vito Acconci, Robert Smithson, Nancy Holt, Mary Miss, Christo and Jeanne-Claude, Gordon Matta-Clark, Alice Aycock, Richard Long, and a few others, the "object on display" conventions have prevailed as a criterion for the recognition and evaluation of visual art.

Museum enthusiasts counter such criticism by pointing out that the unprecedented attendance in art institutions today is proof of a valuable community function – although clearly not from an environmental perspective. In reality, museums seem to be a kind of culturally enlightening alternative to the enclosed shopping mall. Art is obviously deemed better for people's intellectual health than a glut of chain stores. But, like the regional mall, the museum has become big business, it is designed to attract selective (meaning affluent) customers, it encourages people to see art works as commodities, and demonstrates an absence of green awareness. To cite some

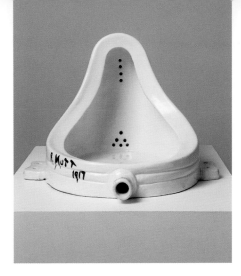

Fountain
Marcel Duchamp
Dimitris Daskalopoulos
Collection, Greece
1917/1964

examples, institutions like the Soho branch of the Guggenheim Museum, Metropolitan Museum and Museum of Modern Art in New York and the Louvre in Paris now include shopping center-like museum stores to strengthen their financial revenues (and probably, from a sociological standpoint, to accommodate people who do not visit museums on a regular basis with multiplex attractions that help them feel more at ease with art). Whatever the perceived cultural and economic merits of the art museum may be, as a conceptual and philosophical statement it is the ultimate confirmation of precious object celebration and a failure to connect with the integrated systems and multi-dimensional sense of purpose associated with the Age of Ecology. As environmental artist Vito Acconci appropriately observed in a recent lecture: "A museum is a public space, but only for those who choose to be a museum public. A museum is a 'simulated' public space; it is auto-directional and uni-functional, whereas a 'real' public space is multi-directional and omni-functional. ... In order to go to a museum, you have to be a museum-goer; you go to the museum in order to continue to be a museum-goer."

The search for conceptually liberating horizons in architecture – leading to the inclusion and transformation of environmental content – would certainly have to start with a questioning of architects' insular ideologies and xenophobic tendencies to resist new ideas. The first of these questionable shibboleths would have to be the assumption that architecture is an obligatory orchestration of massive sculptural volumes. Obviously any building is a composition of physical elements, but this does not have to be seen as an interpretive bias. More often than not, Industrial Age design conventions fail to address issues of human scale and the pedestrians' psychological need for the reduction of large vertical surfaces into a readable level of detail and communicative content. Certainly the primary lesson of medieval and Renaissance architecture in Europe is the powerful artistic value of light and shadow-capturing sculptural features and iconographic legibility of buildings and public spaces. The fundamental urban design flaw of the 20th century was the tendency of architects to assume that abstract formal exercises, shrunken to table-top models – however seductive as Lilliputian artifacts – would automatically convert to a comprehensible scale when actually built. The relentless bleakness and oppressive gigantism of the contemporary cityscape is ample testimony to these misguided indulgences. In contrast, the profusion of evocative subject matter associated with nature, its comfortable scale relationships to the human body, the complexity of its structure, and the science of describing its processes offers a vast reservoir of ideas and imagery for infusing architecture with a more relevant visual content.

Taking a further look at the question of table-top design – especially now that it is reinforced by computer-aided technology – opens up architecture to an aesthetically revealing evaluation that might be described as "the pedestal test." This means of critique has multiple functions. It confronts that endless 20th-century debate concerning the differences between "art" and "design" and helps to sort out "object" versus "contextual" sensibilities when applied to buildings. The pedestal test confirms that works by certain architects with strong sculptural characteristics – Le Corbusier, for example – can be equally impressive as built structures and as models on a base. On the other hand, this test also targets buildings for criticism which only look good as

table-top artifacts and others that are nothing more than bad design at any scale. The exhibition base points out the fact that a great deal of current architecture is derived from Cubist and Constructivist sculptural forms, which are usually dismissed as stylistically old-fashioned when analyzed from an art perspective, but enthusiastically embraced by various contemporary architects as a source of cutting-edge emancipation. The pedestal criterion proposes that good buildings in model form – particularly those with proclaimed environmental ambitions – can be weeded out from the bad examples, based on whether they look more convincing installed on their intended sites, or mounted on exhibition plinths.

The pedestal test can throw new light on the "art versus design" debate. For example, when applied to the seminal work of important sculptors like Vladimir Tatlin, Julio Gonzales, Constantin Brancusi, Alberto Giacometti, David Smith, Richard Serra, Robert Smithson, and Vito Acconci, a major aspect of their art can be evaluated by the degree of innovation with, or liberation from, the confines of the base. Particularly in the work of Smithson and Acconci, their major objective was to free sculpture from gallery restraints altogether and make it conceptually environmental. It is important here to focus on the fact that, unlike architecture with its functional responsibilities and subjugation to commerce, the notion of "use" doesn't exist in pure art; therefore its aesthetic merits are based on how creatively the artist has taken advantage of this implicit freedom. Two fundamental standards for the appreciation of art are its effect on other art and the absence of practical applications (although political and religious propaganda might be considered a certified function). Since the central purpose of architecture is serviceable shelter, its "art quality" is usually assessed in terms of its degree of submission to – or escape from – functional restraints. The pedestal test can help expose buildings of questionable quality and distinguish whether they are mediocre sculptures or contextually insensitive objects – or both.

Guggenheim Museum Bilbao
Frank O. Gehry
Bilbao, Spain
1991–97

Getty Center
Richard Meier
Los Angeles, California, USA
1984–97

Relative to the exhibition of traditional sculpture, obviously a Henry Moore bronze is most appropriately viewed on a standard base. Conversely, Robert Smithson's "Spiral Jetty" in Salt Lake City is an art work conceived as an intrinsic part of its context and would be absurdly awkward and meaningless, even in maquette form, sitting on a pedestal. Returning to the architectural model, Le Corbusier's Villa Savoie, for example, is a great structure as built in the French countryside, yet its sculptural innovations are also persuasive when reduced to miniature scale for exhibition in a museum. On the other hand, Wright's "Falling Water" in Bear Run, Pennsylvania, looks ridiculous when separated from its heavily forested environment (even when, as in the Museum of Modern Art model, sections of the topography and landscape have been faithfully simulated for table-top viewing). In summary, the pedestal test becomes a provocative (and usually reliable) source of assessment in distinguishing whether or not the aesthetic content of a building is dependent on the inclusion of contextual information, mutable phenomena in nature, and social and psychological connections (referring to those "thoughts about things that are implied to exist" discussed earlier). It could be postulated that any artifact which can be visually improved by being presented on a pedestal simply reinforces its limited state of objectness. One exception, already noted, would be Duchamp's urinal Fountain, where the viewer's reflexive acceptance of art-on-a-base conventions were used

to draw new meaning from an inversion of the gallery context. In architecture, the pedestal test seems to indicate that if a building looks better as a model on a base, there is a good chance it should probably stay there.

The questions raised by this critical process open up a potentially fertile chapter in the development of a new environmental architecture. This challenge is conceptually complex. It means continuing to offer the essential standards of usefulness in buildings, preserving the most familiar characteristics of an archetypal imagery (as a way of maintaining the communicative power of consensus symbolism), embracing the concepts of indeterminacy and chance that dominate today's philosophical discourse, and still creating architecture that qualifies as ecologically responsible art. By abandoning the subliminal power of recognition in buildings, the designer forfeits an opportunity to play with subtle levels of signification, commentary, and a layering of meanings. These compelling goals in the building arts are already being threatened by a prevailing tendency toward facile shape-making for its own sake (with the inevitable intrusions these conceits impose on functional space), and – as confirmation of pedestal test usefulness – by the risk that all buildings may end up looking more like regressive sculpture than progressive architecture.

From the standpoint of developing a new "pedestal-resistant" architectural imagery based on connections to the environment, it is clearly a question of seeking the opposite of a

Spiral Jetty
Robert Smithson
Great Salt Lake, Utah, USA
1970

Splitting
Gordon Matta-Clark
Engelwood, New Jersey,
USA
1974

Public Art Project
Vito Acconci
MAK (Museum for
Contemporary Art/
Applied Arts),
Vienna, Austria
1993

and have come to regard language as a rather inadequate mechanism to search for any ultimate revelations. Derrida took this situation to mean that there is no absolute truth, and has frequently returned to such dialecticians as Hegel and Heidegger in order to read their ideas in this revised context. In doing so it became apparent that the ambiguities of language matched those of philosophy and science, thus requiring an entirely new system of reading that might embrace the concept of universal chaos and its absent center. In pursuing his objective – and to demonstrate that literature is just another manifestation of indeterminacy – Derrida has proposed that life itself is a text and that there is no meaning outside of this text.

The process of deconstruction usually starts out with the premise that most literature contains traditional narrative structure, prompting a reflex response to certain uses of language. What Derrida has called "archetexts" form a pattern of operative meanings to be deconstructed. It stands to reason that a similar methodology applied to architecture would call for the identification of archetypes to serve as the equivalent of archetexts. In the absence of words as critical tools, a comparable means of access would have to be substituted to

Portlandia Sculpture
Raymond Kaskey
Portland, Oregon, USA
1985

Draped Reclining Figure
Henry Moore
Museum Ludwig,
Cologne, Germany
1952/53

determinate technocentrism. In some ways this unraveling of rhetorical assumptions in design, by filtering them through our perceptions of chaos in nature, might be compared to the investigations of deconstruction during the 1980s (meaning its contributions to literary criticism, not the appropriation of Jacques Derrida's theories as justification for a stylish neo-Constructivist fragmentation in architecture). In a broader context, deconstruction becomes a useful model of critical methodology. It can be seen as an inversion of language – or language as the critique of language – used for questioning people's habitual acceptance of form, syntax, structure, and meaning in literature. It is a way of liberating the reader from traditional structuralist formulas, interpretive bias, and ritualized reading habits, which can inhibit a deeper understanding of written and verbal communications.

Inspired by new observations in physics, which have increasingly abandoned an orderly model of the universe for one conceived in disorder, Derrida has taken his cues from science because it no longer depends on a traditional center as its axiomatic point of departure for theoretical ideas. Scientists and philosophers have recognized that the human brain is merely a fragment of infinite disorder (and a rather crude instrument for speculations about the complex phenomena of which it is made),

Rue Larrey Door
Marcel Duchamp
Paris, France
1927

Max Reinhardt House
Peter Eisenman
Berlin, Germany
Project, 1994

uncover an equivalent level of deeper readings in architecture. In dealing with buildings, this language would most logically derive from conventional component parts and standard construction processes – or, in other words, a set of archetypal objects, methods, and materials that trigger associative meanings in the viewer's mind.

For example, one classic demonstration of this inversion process that could be seen as relating to deconstruction in architecture is Duchamp's 1927 Rue Larrey Door in Paris. Simply described, the artist installed a conventional wooden door at the corner of a room where two adjacent entryways met at right angles and provided access to the kitchen and the toilet. The single door unit was hinged at a point where it served both rooms. If the door was closed on the bathroom, it was open to the kitchen and, conversely, if it was closed on the kitchen it was open to the bathroom. With this delightfully perverse gesture, Duchamp questioned the entire nature of "doorness," the way we unconsciously accept its practical functions, and the word-versus-object relationships of a commonplace architectural element. The Rue Larrey Door was not conventionally open *or* closed, since it was always simultaneously open *and* closed. By interpreting the rhetorical notion of "use" as the subject matter of art, Duchamp prophetically set the stage for

a much more complex and interesting application of deconstruction in architecture than its appropriation as a rationale for certain 1990s revisionist versions of constructivist design.

Unlike the cerebral and intangible qualities of literature, where deconstruction represents a naturally fertile means of exploration, the physical mass, cumbersome elements of fabrication, and environmentally intrusive handicaps of architecture appear resistant to this kind of critical approach. On the other hand, if applied to architecture and its relation to the environment, deconstruction can be seen as offering a way to incorporate the inconsistencies and contradictions of nature as a language of access in the search for new relationships between buildings and their surroundings. These "de-architecturizing" forces provide a subversive tactical means to question the methodical practices of construction technology and their influence on choices of imagery.

This being said, most post-Structuralist philosophy in architecture today is turning away from references to deconstruction and chaos theory, in favor of ideas that could be considered more in concert with both the information highway and the ecology movement. One recent direction, referred to as "folding," is being described with such terms as "pliancy," "continuous and heterogeneous systems," "fluid transformations," and "smooth mixtures of disparate elements." While much of this dialogue seems to suggest a renewed sympathy for the organic architecture of Frank Lloyd Wright, the actual manifestations in built and model form (unlike Wright) tend to treat the surrounding environment – especially landscape – as an alien territory, typically populated by random grids of lollipop trees bearing little or no reference to the centerpiece building. Folding in architecture is generally characterized by formal exercises in the use of warped planar surfaces to alter conventional relationships between exterior and interior. Whatever its claims for "pliancy and fluidity," the folded building still remains a familiar hermetic object based on abstract art principles and can usually be photographed apart from its context without a loss of meaning.

While some of the propositions of folding in architecture appear to be in accord with the new eco-sensibility, there is no real earth awareness or intent to fuse structure with context implied in its objectives. Also, there are no references to even the most elementary responsibilities of conservation technology and sustainable design. Instead, like the appropriation of the word "deconstruction" as a camouflaged way of describing simple neo-constructivist design, the general interpretation of folding seems to be just one more extension of 20th-century orthodox formalism. Its representative examples are still very much a part of the notion that a building must always be some form of abstract sculpture – in this case, comparable to a kind of architectural origami.

One interesting linguistic contribution of folding in architecture is an expansion of the meaning of "information" to "in-formation," which implies a fusion of both the transmission of data and the developmental process of shaping ideas. This thought leads directly to the interpretation of architecture as a system of "passages" (a design approach used in SITE's Qatar Museum of Islamic Arts). It is a concept that links buildings, landscape, and elements of social, contextual, and environmental communication. Edifices designed on strictly formal terms and then plunked down to await a

patch of peripheral vegetation tend to remain static and insular. Buildings conceived as integrations of structure and landscape create a biomorphic ambiguity that encourages a dialogue between the inert and the mutable, the technological and botanic, the architectural and the topographical. It provides new levels of communication by opening up a wealth of connections to both the information and ecology revolutions.

A potentially productive way of looking at the integration of architecture and landscape relates to an observation about television. The TV set in one's living room is seldom regarded as anything more than a generic artifact for receiving and disseminating electronically generated images. The TV viewer usually does not even notice the physical receptacle as an example of good or bad design, nor as an important object of furniture (although it can obviously be both). Instead, the significance of the ubiquitous box is its capacity to process information. By drawing an analogy to buildings and their relation to the environment, this communications role suggests shifting the aesthetic focus of architecture from sculptural object to its capacity to absorb and transmit messages. This suggests that walls, instead of

American television
USA
1970s

223

being seen mainly as barriers of enclosure or compositional elements, can serve as information-filtering membranes (or points of passage) that fuse and dissolve traditional inside/outside relationships and incorporate narrative commentary. There is nothing new about the idea of walls delivering messages – all of the historic churches and civic buildings of medieval and Renaissance Europe were based on this objective – but its radical appeal today derives from an opposition to conventional architectural geometry and a rich potential to establish the fusion of buildings and environ-

Passages diagrams
James Wines
1996

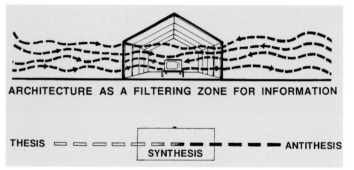

ARCHITECTURE AS A FILTERING ZONE FOR INFORMATION

THESIS ▭ ▭ ▭ ▭ ▭ ▭ ▭ ▭ ▭ ▬ ▬ ▬ ▬ ANTITHESIS
SYNTHESIS

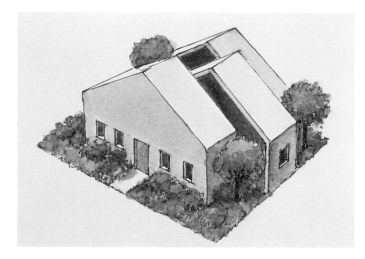

mental awareness as the raw material for a new and relevant iconography.

The interpretation of passages is infinitely variable and should not be considered as any kind of design formula. Basically, the concept proposes that walls and floor planes in a building should be seen as fluid and contextually responsive elements, converting the measure of aesthetic quality in architecture from formal design to how well a structure reflects and engages various aspects of landscape, regional identity, topography, and cultural references. In most contemporary architecture walls are viewed as vertical partitions, used mainly to divide up interior space and define the outside limitations of a floor plan. Walls as passages can defy the plan and perform a range of communicative and functional purposes. These include: reaching out into surrounding territories, veering off casually as indeterminate ribbons of transition in space, and functioning as monitors of changing attitudes in environmental thinking.

In terms of architectural construction, the concept of passages proposes that trees, vegetation, water, and other combinations of atmospheric and terrestrial elements should be as much a part of the physical substance of shelter as conventional building materials. From an aesthetic standpoint, the objective is to look at the fusion of structure and landscape as a kind of interactive dialogue visually describing their mutual origins in nature. This entire direction in design suggests the development of new paradigms in the building arts, based on ecological models.

There are also obstacles to this approach. Since our society has no collectively shared cosmology or religious associations with nature – of the kind, for example, that built the Celtic monuments of Wiltshire or rock-cut temples of Ajanta – designers of today's environment cannot rely on any consensus iconography for communication. The global awareness of ecology has become a motivating sociological and psychological force in the development of a post-industrial version of C. G. Jung's collective unconscious.

Highrise of Homes
James Wines
Concept drawing, 1981

Whereas the term "folding" in architecture seems to suggest a design process of methodial, geometry-driven, formal strategies, the notion of passages is intended to describe an organic and informal set of connections between buildings and landscape. For example, this concept might take the form of a series of informational walls that can be distributed randomly over a land parcel, allowing roof structures and the surrounding context to casually bridge and/or penetrate the separations between the vertical partitions. This system creates great flexibility in the orientation of sheltered spaces and can completely break down the established definition of where architecture begins and landscape leaves off.

Some practical and conceptual problems occur in trying to apply the theory of passages to a standard formula for high-rise architecture. When the cost of real estate becomes the determining factor in ecological and aesthetic decision-making, the vision of an office tower as an example of "indeterminate and disparate elements" or as the product of "an absorption of its own context" is difficult to sell. On the other hand, there is the possibility of interpreting large urban structures as multiple tiers of terraced gardens and as vegetated microcosms of their regions. Taking cues from the Japanese Zen notion of "borrowed scenery," tall structures can be seen as tableaux of other places, or as contemporary equivalents of the Gardens of Babylon. As a footnote to this issue of high-rise buildings, there is a now a fundamental question concerning their continued viability, especially since skyscrapers are increasingly conceded to be ecologically problematic as a result of their unreasonable demands on resources and questionable choices of construction technology. In fact, environmental protection laws in the future may ultimately prohibit all high-rise development in favor of low-height and clustered buildings, or of mostly underground architecture, as land surface becomes more precious and the need for urban agriculture increases.

Hopefully, by using the idea of passages as a critical tool and as a premise for revised thinking about architectural enclosure itself, this process will serve to reverse today's anti-ecological and unproductive conventions in the building arts.

The Age of Ecology is a critical point of transition and connection. It has arrived for some architects like a plague on the conscience, threatening their beliefs, stylistic preferences, and habitual work methods. For others, it has become the revolutionary and resource-saving opportunity to develop a new technology. For more contemplative architects, it has been seen as the beginning of a deeper awareness of the earth and a cause for re-thinking the foundations of architecture by blending art, philosophy, technology, and nature's integrated systems. While this third group is potentially the most productive, the challenges it faces are daunting. It means confronting, questioning, and probably having to ultimately embrace concepts that endanger various institutional frameworks, not to mention most things the building arts have been about since the advent of the Industrial Revolution.

If we re-enact earth as living connectedness, then we are called to see our place (being placed) in/on the earth in a transformed, enlarged way. We need, then, to re-inhabit our place. ... To re-inhabit is to relearn dwelling.

Martin Heidegger

'I also know,' said Candide, 'that we must go and work in the garden.' 'You are quite right,' said Pangloss. 'When man was placed in the Garden of Eden, he was put there to dress it and keep it, to work, in fact; which proves that man was not born to an easy life.'

Voltaire

Conclusion – Turning over a New Leaf

Aboriginal lean-to habitat
Northern Territories, Australia

Most of the works by contemporary architects presented in this overview of environmental architecture would not be considered legitimate examples of "true green" within the strict definition of conservation technology today. However, before the ecologically correct forces begin attacking the art and philosophy focus of this book, it must be emphasized that virtually no form of shelter constructed today (with the exception of habitat built by a few remaining aboriginal cultures) can be credited as authentically green. Everything that technologically dependent societies assume is essential for survival – including the remedial solutions offered by the greenest of green architects – is plugged into the same diminishing sources of power. Every absorber plate and foil insulator required to build a solar collector, every chemical detergent used in a waste-composting plant, every ream of paper needed to spread the ecological message, and every drop of jet fuel consumed in transporting environmentalists to international conferences places an additional drain on these sources. In the larger picture, green architecture is still nothing more than band-aid treatment where major surgery is required. On the other hand, that "every little bit counts" aphorism is still valid; but it does need to be activated on all levels of human enterprise. In architecture this includes changing the profession's basic philosophical and aesthetic values, as well as taking a mercilessly critical look at its technology, politics, and economics. The primary message of this book always goes back to that call for a more profound commitment to the concept of integrated systems.

In a majority of recent ecological buildings, green orthodoxy is measured primarily by the degree of investment in energy-saving systems, the durability of construction materials, and the number of recycled products used in fabrication. The more obsessive supporters of technological solutions disdain aesthetic considerations as merely frivolous. In fact, throughout the USA and Europe today there are exclusive clubs composed of finger-wagging, eco-moralist architects who, in spite of noble intentions, have been excluded from this book because their message is too shrill and the artistic aspects of their work are too dismally deficient. Dangerously (because it negatively impacts on the green movement's credibility), environmental architecture has become a camouflage to justify the work of some vociferously righteous, but very bad, designers.

This tendency toward dogmatism represents a growing divisiveness among other categories of environmental advocacy as well. It is a form of ecological factionalism that is based, like most religious faiths, on tribal trust in some ordained answer. This absolutist mentality sees all other interpretations as insufficiently rigorous to merit the blessings of a proprietary "Green God." In their more extreme versions, these divisive groups can be outright messianic and confrontational. For example, there is a lingering 1960s nostalgia wing committed to geodesic minimal-tech, agrarian communes, and a slogan-weary political war against the dreaded atrocities of an industrial or military conspiracy. Rejecting such tactics as antiquated, there are the eco-universal synthesizers who envision salvation as a worldwide network of equitably shared resources. Unhappy with this emphasis on economics over nature, the Gaia globalists believe the earth itself is a living organism and that humanity's role is to function as a custodial gardener. Disdainful of Gaia's arguable hypotheses, the radical deep ecologists propose extreme cutbacks in high-tech living that could return civilizations to foraging for food in the wilderness – or, this failing, they would con-

cede the earth to the earthworm. Finding deep ecology too pathological, there are the eco-psychologists who believe that the real doom is festering in people's minds and we will perish not from global warming, but from earth-deprivation neurosis. Unwilling to be persuaded by the vagaries of psychology, there are the cutting-edge "techies" who look at the whole environmental movement as nothing more than a quest for better clean-up machines, deeper waste dumps, and bigger databases. And finally, critical of all the above groups as cultural philistines, there is the aesthetically committed salvation-through-art camp that sees the earth as a vast horticultural Sistine Chapel, desperately in need of restoration. Each of these alienated factions can be found on one level or another in green architecture today. While all activist positions in the environmental movement have much to offer, there is only one reasonable mission – to organize as a unified cause and condition all response to fit nature's model of connectedness.

The danger now is too much reliance on those illusory visions of a technological salvation, in the face of a vastly more complex problem of psychological distress caused by an alienation from nature and the lack of an earth-centered philosophy. Rarely do the healing measures of environmental technology address the metaphysical, phenomenological, or symbolic dimensions that shape people's collective unconscious. In our high-tech world, environmental commitments are mostly based on repair, not cosmology – on salvage, not philosophy. They represent neither a significant change of priorities in consumer culture, nor any new revelations about our connections to the earth. When evaluating ecologically favorable actions in Western societies, we are forced to see them as mainly defensive, curatorial,

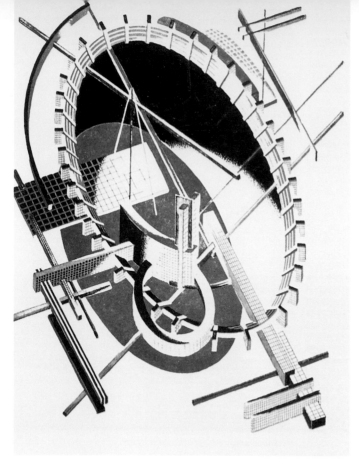

City of the Future
Iakov Georgievich
Chernikhov
Project, 1931

and expedient. They are also the reflection of a fatalistic melancholy that Thomas Lovejoy blames on the growing magnitude of global warming. He observes: "I fail to see that there's any conclusion to draw from all of this other than that there will be massive extinction no matter what we do in the way of conservation. Therefore, the only logical conclusion is to prevent as much of the climate change as possible." This prospect of a collective sense of hopelessness reinforces the view of major segments in the scientific community that warn of a very real doomsday in the not too distant future. The specific villain in this final scenario is still speculative – global drought, massive crop failures, nuclear waste pollution, atomic explosion, lethal viruses – but some unprecedented catastrophic event is deemed inevitable. Depending on the causes and extent of this damage, humanity will either

resign itself to extinction or learn from the experience and take constructive charge of its own destiny through a heightened level of union with nature. Science also suggests that, psychologically, the magnitude of our tools of destruction and the extreme measures of change needed for survival may be too much for people to mentally and physically accept. In this respect, Martin Heidegger has proposed that the potential for mass annihilation (like atom bombs that can eliminate millions in a second) has profoundly influenced the universal psyche and produced a phenomenon he refers to as a "debased techne." This is quite different from a traditional technology-versus-nature conflict, where environmental damage is regarded as the unpleasant, but seemingly reparable, result of collective negligence. Heidegger postulates that humanity has been numbed into a mental state where technical systems are no longer seen as manageable tools; rather, they have attained the corrosive effect of being perceived as beyond our control. From his philosophical perspective, when technology reaches this dangerous stage, it "lifts Mankind to a level where it confronts problems with which technical thinking is not prepared to cope." It is a mental plateau of temporality and resignation that psychically forces people beyond a point of no return.

In a strange way this atmosphere of universal malaise may ultimately prove to be one of the most influential forces in the development of architectural imagery over the next few decades. What form this will take is difficult to predict, but it is probably safe to speculate that some manifestation of what the Welsh call "hiraeth" or "a longing for the land," will characterize the deeper psyche of all civilizations and translate into the messages expressed by their buildings and the way people relate to the environment.

It would be misleading to end this discussion of organic and biomorphic architecture in the Age of Ecology by characterizing the universal mentality today as negative or depressed. Actually, contrary to the fatalistic resignation expressed by Thomas Lovejoy and the existential pessimism of Heidegger, the building arts are presently experiencing a resurgence of idealistic euphoria among young designers and students. Conferences on green technology, politics, aesthetics, and theory abound these days, and the older generation of designers is gradually being forced into the recognition that major changes are at hand. The climate seems anything but passive or resigned; but the issue of whether there is sufficient opportunity to embrace all this idealistic fervor is another matter.

The question is always the same in architecture – just how much idealism can the field support? To be prophetic has its price, and the history books are filled with non-building missionaries and messiahs – Étienne Boullée, Antonio Sant'Elia, Hugh Ferris, Frederick Kiesler, Iakov Chernikhov, John Hejduk, Peter Cook, Cedric Price and such groups as Archigram, Archizoom, and Superstudio – who pursued their visions with great integrity, but rarely constructed anything. The day-to-day survival mechanisms of architecture still require the designer to get up in the morning and make a living. This usually means one of two choices: resigning oneself to a teaching job in academia, or taking on the next available commission for some dreary commercial mall or anonymous office tower. In the general portfolio of job opportunities offered by conventional business or civic clients, the issue of higher aesthetic choices rarely even enters the picture, much less any sympathy for green initiatives (considered anathema in a world of short-term profit motives). It is obvious that such belligerent and commerce-driven attitudes collide head-on with visionary architecture. Still, there is plenty of hope for the architectural and ecological visionary today, with excellent role models for energetic perseverance and a successful record of built projects to be found in early Modernism – particularly in the work of that ultimate idealist, Le Corbusier.

In 1923, when Le Corbusier heralded the "new spirit" in architecture, technocentrism seemed to be the only liberating response to the perceived restraints imposed by nature.

After all, the seductive visual language and new materials of industrial production, plus the revolutionary ideas emerging in physics, were the absolute antithesis of 19th-century romanticism and methodological science. Technology promised the most luminous possibilities for the architect: an opportunity to develop a new aesthetic sensibility directly responsive to socialist ideals and Machine Age inventions, plus a theoretical foundation with which to rationalize this iconography as syn-

Railway station and airport
Antonio Sant'Elia
Project, 1913

Plug in City
Peter Cook
Project, 1964

Apartments on bridges
Hugh Ferris and
Raymond Hood
New York, New York, USA
Project, 1929

onymous with people's needs and architecture's functional responsibilities.

The scientist Francis Bacon set the stage for the Modernist revolution by declaring that scientific knowledge justifies a technological supremacy over nature and, since Man is the only species capable of exercising this option, it must be ordained by God. After 1850, there was no retreat from this position. The obvious advantages of Bacon's hypothesis for 20th-century economic development gave his credo a universal popularity, and one of its legacies became architecture wedded to the industrial dream. As long as the illusion of progress was equated exclusively to technology and economic growth, the shapes, volumes, and spaces of Modernism retained their energetically relevant content. Today the reverse is true. The Industrial Revolution is viewed by the majority of environmentally sensitized people on earth as the hereditary enemy of true progress. It has violated its basic ethical responsibility in what ecopsychologist Alan Thein has defined as each generation's obligation to "meet its needs without jeopardizing the prospects for future generations to meet their own needs." As a result, most architecture rooted in the industrial tradition could now be regarded as hostile to the best interests of people in the year 2010. At the same time the original fervor of the Machine Age optimism has been reduced to anemic formalism and academic theory. The focused idealism, the inspirational vision, the sense of purpose, the urgency of content – all of the qualities inherent in Le Corbusier's "new spirit" – are missing. In this stagnant climate there is a great deal for the eco-visionary to accomplish. Like the progressive tasks that inspired early Modernism, there is a job to be done and a social, economic, and moral demand to give it practical form and a convincing visibility. This century's technocentric architecture (not taking into account its environmental deficiencies) has been successful because it was always perceived as cheap, efficient, iconographically appropriate, and responsive to client demands. Green architecture will work

because it is cost effective, functional, aesthetically challenging, and responsive to nature's demands.

The pioneers of Modernism tended to over-dramatize their objectives by an "architecture will save the world" claim for their theories and manifestos. Le Corbusier, in particular, spoke of the bottom-line choice of civilization as being "architecture or revolution," with the implication that there was an inseparable bond between morality and building. In the framework of this dialectic, if the world did not respond to his clarion call for a new socialist

Field Guards House
Claude-Nicolas Ledoux
Project, 1792

**House of the
River Authority**
Claude-Nicolas Ledoux
Project, 1780

and industrial vision of the city, the heedless ruling classes would be doomed by a rise of the hostile masses demanding better housing (which would, naturally, take the form of one of Le Corbusier's own designs). The 1920s and 1930s were heady decades, when such passionate fervor could express itself without having to acknowledge ecological responsibility. At that time ecology wasn't even a word in common use. Today, anyone proclaiming salvation through the building arts would be looked upon as quaintly anachronistic. There is still a dynamic architectural mission – in fact, the greatest in human history – but the first qualifications for those designers addressing today's environmental challenges are humble reserve, thoughtful research, and quiet philosophical re-evaluation. The revolution is at hand, but its objective is not just a question of responding to the housing needs of disenfranchised communities or proclaiming architectural salvation through emotionally charged hyperbole.

Rather, the more inclusive task is to seek solutions for human habitats in the face of persuasive predictions for an unavoidable revenge on nature's part.

Nature will correct. It always has its way and, other than showing a certain tolerance for temporary aberrations, allows nothing to get out of control for too long. In the light of these corrective powers, there is serious speculation among ecologists that Homo sapiens may end up being the shortest-lived species ever to occupy earth – victims of its own suicidal misconduct. On the more optimistic side, the supporters of environmental reform and ecological stewardship tend to speak of saving the earth as though the planet were some kind of sickly patient in a recovery ward that should be restored to health for its own good. The earth is hardly the patient and certainly does not need saving. The only real beneficiary in any conservation program is the human race itself. From this perspective, the custodial role is just a faintly disguised version of the same anthropocentric premises lying at the core of all irresponsible behavior in the first place. There is no real sense of connectedness implied here, only the usual game of environmental opportunism to see if our deluded species can somehow trick nature into letting us conduct a guilt-free perpetuation of business as usual.

The only way this condition of disconnectedness can begin to change – particularly as related to architecture – is through a total revision of philosophical grounding and a deep commitment to regaining spiritual and psychological contact with nature. The consistent thread of apology that has run throughout this book is basically a reflection of doubt whether any viable new state of eco-centrism can be achieved in the face of so many conflicting realities. The entrenched systems controlling every aspect of human survival and its interaction with the environment are such that escape is virtually impossible without rejecting (or at least radically modifying) most of the high-energy demand conveniences associated with food supply, disposable products, temperature control, vehicular mobility, and communica-

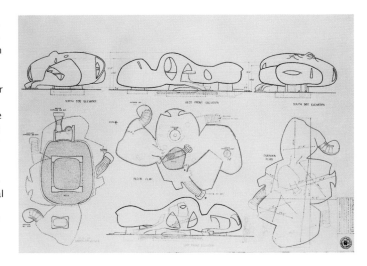

The Endless House
Frederick Kiesler
New York, New York, USA
Project, 1959

tions technology. It is doubtful that any significant trends toward reduced expectations are imminent, unless, of course, that final Armageddon prophesied by science actually takes place and settles the score for eternity.

In the meantime, architecture still has one of the most important conservation and communication roles to play in any new ecologically responsible vision of the future. The goals of buildings as examples of green policy and as monitors of the collective psyche tend to be compromised by architecture's dependence on the ponderous elements of construction technology. This physical presence alone communicates the opposite of serving the interests of nature, and most construction materials derive from ecologically reprehensible means of manufacture. Avoiding psychological and symbolic content, architecture still seems slavishly and inextricably committed to celebrating the virtuosity of how edifices are put together or how flamboyantly industrial materials can be manipulated. The iconographic significance, if any, is the antithesis of eco-centrism.

A great part of the solution is technological, but filtered through a study of the way nature solves its own engineering problems and how resourcefully energy and materials are converted to function. Two of the most astute observers of natural phenomena in the early 20th century were the great Catalan architect, Antoni Gaudí, and of course Frank Lloyd Wright. In both cases they studied how plants grow, analyzed land surfaces, evaluated seasonal change, researched geology, and learned from the interconnected processes through which nature achieves its miraculous states of evolution and perpetuity. Judging from their architecture, these observations were not just a nostalgic admiration of natural wonders or pragmatic analyses of ecological engineering; rather, they watched, learned, and created from the most subtle levels of earth-centered cause and effect. It is well known that Gaudí studied the intricate physiology of leaves, flower stems, and tree trunks as models for the structural systems used in his build-

ings. Wright, for his part, contemplated soil erosion, rock formations, and climatic influences as sources in determining the formal orchestration of his architecture and the way it established a dialogue with context. Both Gaudí and Wright were already envisioning an earth-centric future in the early 1900s; however, as a result of the more superficially appealing and overshadowing illusions of a Modernist-inspired technological utopia, very few architects were listening to their prophetic voices.

This book began with regrets concerning the eclipse of Wright's ideas and the majority of contemporary architects' lack of involvement with philosophical and conceptual ideas related to the ecological revolution. A frequently expressed conflict running through these pages has been a sense of pessimism concerning the options for changing a danger-

Parc Güell, viaduct
Antoni Gaudí
Barcelona, Spain
1914

ous state of complacency, versus moments of optimism inspired by evidence of a youthful wave of ideas, inventions, and commitments. Most texts of this kind are supposed to end with exhilarating reassurances and grand remedial plans. Because of its timing at the turn of the millennium, this book is more about questions than answers. Its primary message for architects in the Age of Ecology – meaning those who want to understand this era's complex philosophical implications – proposes asking all of the questions seldom raised by the design disciplines throughout the 20th century.

The most disturbing of these questions gnaw at the roots of cultural and theological development since the birth of the world's dominant religions. For example, how are we expected to evaluate and reconcile the environmental success of so many pantheistic ancient and aboriginal civilizations – when each element of nature was identified by its own divine spirit – versus the dominant monotheism of today, where an all-embracing (male) God is proclaimed in the human image, and the destruction of the earth is viewed as a privilege of Man's sovereignty in the universe? There is substantial evidence that a distribution of responsibility among multiple gods (of both male and female gender) related to the sun, rain, soil, rivers, crops, etc. has been a more productive theological vision, both ecologically and agriculturally, than the despotic ego-centrism associated with a single deity and the myopic delusions of "nature for Man's convenience."

Another question, asked earlier in this book, is why have 20th-century philosophy and linguistic studies produced so few persuasive voices whose sources of signs and symbols have been drawn from the natural environment? Instead, the majority of leading theoreticians have scavenged through the cacophony of pop billboards, the fetishes of fast-food psychology, and the digitalized rituals of consumer culture (actually, the shallowest elements of "surface structure") that block access to nature, while ignoring the richness of

earth-centered symbolism lying behind this junk-world detritus. Where, one asks, are the theoreticians and interpreters of an evolving eco-language? Where is the Baudrillard, Lacan, Foucault, Lévi-Strauss, Barthes, de Saussure, or Lyotard of a new "terrestrial signification?"

A third issue, directly connected to architecture in the Age of Information, involves the bothersome question of why the most sophisticated mechanisms of the cybernetic revolution – notably, computer-aided-design – are used primarily to describe buildings stylistically rooted in the early Machine Age. Why, instead, is the entire phenomenon of electronic communications not utilized as the inspirational resource for a new visual language? Part of the answer is obviously that 1920s Russian Constructivist architects did not have the luxury of software to articulate their complex formal innovations, so designers today feel somehow obligated to finish the job. Unlike the early Constructivists (whose work remained mostly unrealizable for the lack of computerized calculations and advanced construction technology), today's CAD-equipped architects can easily describe and erect the most exotic configurations. Still, it seems oddly regressive to resurrect ideas from the 1920s simply because they can be built in the new century. And finally, why have so few architects made

Living with the Computer
USA
1990's

the obvious conceptual and aesthetic connections between the integrated systems of the Internet and their ecological parallels in nature?

These questions point to the need for developing a visionary "eco-digital" iconography in architecture. By incorporating ideas from both informational and ecological sources, architects provide an opportunity to develop an imagery that echoes the mutable and evolutionary changes found in nature and the fluid and interactive flow of data through electronic communications. In spirit, this seems to indicate something more like trying to capture the intangibility of the wind passing through the trees than expressing the cumbersome mechanics of construction technology. It seems more like the quest for an invisible or virtual architecture, as opposed to celebrating the weight and density of industrial materials.

But there are also dangers in looking at architecture as an extension of virtual reality. Given the tendency of almost all technology in this century to isolate people in a "replacement for nature" context, then how are the interests of joining humanity with the environment served by the remoteness of computer communications? One supportive argument proposes that the capacity to bring an instantaneous ecological message to the global community has never existed before and must be allowed time to demonstrate its unique educational outreach. The opposition retorts that a perpetual isolation in front of screens all day – no matter how altruistic the messages being transmitted – represents the ultimate form of detachment from the environment and merely compounds people's alienation and their ever-increasing state of nature deprivation. These critics claim that electronic solitude is nothing more than a form of cyberspace pathology, where our species has managed to create an illusory and dangerously withdrawn digital incubator as a replacement for reality.

The conflicts inherent in these questions appear to have no resolution immediately at hand. The entire fabrication we think of as our "reality" must, in the final analysis, be re-evaluated from the standpoint of a return to nature

(some optimistic observers say we never left it, but that issue is up for debate). The ultimate enigma remains: is it too late, and does nature even want us back? Providing we could return – burdened with our warped perspectives of the planet – could we accept the qualifications for reunion and would we be prepared for the necessary sacrifices? Scientifically, the human race has never had a greater understanding about the functions and preservation of the environment than today. At the same time, without the world community's unified social and psychological grasp of the inestimable value of water, air, land, and atmosphere, this knowledge is not enough to assure survival. Without radical changes in economic and political priorities over the next two decades, the predictions of those ominous doomsayers may come true. Our species will decline and disappear – all of the noble ecological intentions and conservationist databases notwithstanding. The final challenge is not so much trying to understand nature, but re-learning how to intuitively, organically, and cosmologically live on its terms.

In nature, all things can be seen as a confusion of "seeming" and "becoming." It is a context where every assumption can become its own question, every evidence of a pattern can be a misleading illusion, and every attempt to impose human-initiated order can backfire as a higher level of disorder. At the same time nature demonstrates a rigorous, if incomprehensible, structure and symmetry, where violations of the rules are severely punished. There appear to be some practical and custodial levels of cooperation with the environment that can encourage its favorable response; however, in the formation of a relevant, ecology-based, architectural iconography, the challenges are definitely rooted in the most complex areas of conceptual gymnastics and the search for ways to relate aesthetic experience to conditions of indeterminacy and chance. But even the notion of chaos is rooted in man's perception that somewhere there must be order – a perception that is part of an illusion imposed by our human limits of reason. "Let

us beware of saying there are laws in nature," Friedrich Nietzsche has observed. "There are only necessities: there is no one in command, no one to obey, no one to transgress. When you realize there are no goals or objectives, then you realize, too, that there is no chance: for only in a world of objectives does the word 'chance' have any meaning."

Nature is primal, metamorphic, and endlessly ambiguous. It is rich in associations and the one totally universal source of ideas and symbolism in the arts. It is a genesis of communicative content that strips away redundancies and constantly reveals new information. Through its infinite complexity, nature is an

instructive and inspirational influence that can expand the aesthetic horizons of the building arts and confirm the inalienable right of humanity to try to salvage a place on this planet before its too late. The mission now in architecture, as in all human endeavor, is to recover those fragile threads of connectedness with nature that have been lost for most of this century. The key to a truly sustainable art of architecture for the new millennium will depend on the creation of bridges that unite conservation technology with an earth-centric philosophy and the capacity of designers to transform these integrated forces into a new visual language.

**Garden at the
Royal Palace of Katsura**
Kobori Ershu
Kyoto, Japan
1625–50

Bibliography

Ausebel, Kenny, Restoring the Earth: Visionary Solutions from the Bioneers. Tiburon, California: H. J. Kramer,1997.

Barnett, Diana Lopez, A Primer in Sustainable Building. Snowmass, Colorado: The Rocky Mountain Institute,1995.n.

Barrie, David, Architecture for a New Age of Nuclear Waste and Decommissioning. Peterborough, Great Britain: BBC, Cymru/ Wales,1995.

Bayley, Stephen, Taste: The Secret Meaning of Things. New York: Pantheon Books,1991.

Behling, Sophia and Stefan, Sol Power. Munich, New York: Prestel,1996

Berger, John J., Restoring the Earth: How Americans are Working to Renew Our Damaged Environment. New York: Alfred A. Knopf,1986.

Bourdon, David, Designing the Earth: The Human Impulse To Shape Nature. New York: Harry N. Abrams, Inc., 1995.

Brown, Lester, State of the World, 1999: A Worldwatch Institute Report on Progress Toward a Sustainable Society. New York: W. W. Norton,1999,1996.

Buchanan, Peter, Overview, Emilio Ambasz: Inventions – The Reality of the Ideal. New York, Rizzoli, 1992.

Buzzelli, David T. and Lash, Jonathan, Sustainable America: A New Consensus. Washington D. C.: U.S. Government Printing Office, 1996.

Carmody, John and Raymond Sterling, Earth-Sheltered Housing Design. New York: Van Nostrand Reinhold Company, 1985.

Carson, Rachel, Silent Spring. New York: Houghton Mifflin Company, 1962. (Introd. by Al Gore, 1994).

Calthorpe, Peter, The Next American Metropolis. Princeton, New Jersey: The Princeton Architectural Press, 1993.

Clocker, Robert and O'Brien, James, Ed.,Thresholds 14. Cambridge, Massachusetts: MIT Press, 1997.

Croft, David B., Australian People and Animals in Today's Dreamtime. New York: Prager Publishers, 1991.

Cronon, William, Ed., Uncommon Ground: Rethinking the Human Place in Nature. New York: W. W. Norton & Co., 1996.

Davern, Jeanne M., Lewis Mumford: Architecture as a Home for Man. NewYork: Architectural Record Books, 1975.

Dethier, Jean, Down to Earth. New York: Facts on File, Inc., 1983.

Francis, Mark, Community Open Spaces. Washington D. C.: Island Press, 1984.

Friedman, Stephen, Environments: Notes and Selections on Objects, Spaces, and Behavior. Monterey, California: Brooks Cole Publishing Co., 1974.

Gottlieb, Robert, Forcing the Spring: The Transformation of the American Environmental Movement. Washington, D. C., Island Press, 1993.

Gutheim, Frederick, In the Cause of Architecture – Frank Lloyd Wright: Essays by Frank Lloyd Wright for Architectural Record 1908–1952. New York: Architectural Record, A Mc Graw-Hill Publication, 1975.

Hawken, Paul, The Ecology of Commerce: A Declaration of Sustainability, New York: Harpers Collins Publishers, 1993.

Hayes, Jack, Ed., Cutting Energy Costs: The 1980 Book of Agriculture. Washington, D. C.: U.S. Department of Agriculture, 1980.

James, Peter, and Nick **Thorpe**, Ancient Inventions: Wonders of the Past. New York: Ballantine Books, 1994.

Kapelos, George Thomas, Interpretations of Nature. Kleinburg, Ontario: McMichael Canadian Art Collection, 1994.

Kaufman, Edgar, Selections, Frank Lloyd Wright: Writings and Buildings. New York: Penguin Group, 1960.

Kiesler, Frederick, Inside the Endless House: Art, People, and Architecture – A Journal. New York: Simon & Schuster, 1966.

Kroll, Lucien, BioPsychoSocioEco: Ecologies Urbaines. Nivelles, Belgium, L'Harmattan, 1996.

Levy, Matthys and Mario **Salvadori**, Why Buildings Fall Down. New York: W. W. Norton,1992.

Lobell, John, The Little Green Book. Boulder, Colorado: Shambhala, 1981.

Lynch, Kevin, Wasting Away, San Francisco: Sierra Club Books, 1990.

Makower, Joel, The E Factor: The Bottom-Line Approach to Environmentally Responsible Business. New York: Times Books, Tilden Press, 1993.

Marras, Amerigo, Ed., ECO-TEC: The Architecture of the In-Between. New York: Princeton Architectural Press, 1999.

Matilsky, Barbara C., Fragile Ecologies: Contemporary Artists' Interpretations and Solutions. New York: Rizzoli, 1992

McHarg, Ian, Design with Nature. New York: John Wiley and Sons, 1992

Michell, John, The Earth Spirit: Its Ways, Shrines, and Mysteries. London: Thames and Hudson, 1975.

Mills, Stephanie, Whatever Happened to Ecology? San Francisco: Sierra Club Books, 1989.

Mitchell, C. Thomas and Wu, Jungmei, Living Design: The Daoist Way of Building. New York: McGraw-Hill, 1998.

Myers, Dr. Norman, Ed., GAIA: An Atlas of Planet Management. London: Gaia Books Limited, 1993.

Naar, Jon, This Land is Your Land. New York: Harper Collins, 1992.

Noever, Peter, Die Grube/The Pit. Vienna: Aedes, 1991.

Omedeo Salé, Letitia and Serena, Architectura & Nature. Milan: Mazzotta, 1994.

Pearson, David, Earth to Spirit: In Search of Natural Architecture. San Francisco: Chronicle Books, 1994.

Pfeiffer, Bruce Brooks, and Gerald **Nordland**, Frank Lloyd Wright in the Realm of Ideas. Carbondale and Edwardsville, Illinois: Southern Illinois Press, 1988.

Pilatowicz, Grazyna, Eco-Interiors: A Guide to Environmentally Conscious Interior Design. New York: John Wiley and Sons, 1995.

Potteiger, Martin and Jamie **Purinton**, Landscape Narratives: Design Practices for Telling Stories. New York, Singapore, Toronto: John Wiley and Sons, 1998.

Roberts, Leslie, Ed., World Resources 1996–97. New York: Oxford University Press, 1996.

Romm, Joseph J., Lean and Clean Management. New York, Tokyo, London: Kodansha International Inc., 1994.

Roodman, David , Building Revolution – How Ecology and Health Concerns are Transforming Construction. New York: Worldwatch Paper #124, March, 1995.

Roszak, Theodore, Ed., Ecopsychology: Restoring the Earth, Healing the Mind. San Francisco: Sierra Club Books, 1995.

Roszak, Theodore, The Voice of the Earth: An Exploration of Ecopsychology. New York: Simon and Schuster, 1992.

Schubert-Weller, Christoph and Erhard **Wagner**, Earth and Cave Architecture – Peter Vetsch. Sulgen, Switzerland: Verlag Niggli, 199.

Solar Design Associates, Photovoltaics in the Built Environment. Washington D. C.: Department of Energy, 1997.

Sprague, Paul E., Frank Lloyd Wright and Madison: Eight Decades of Artistic and Social Interaction. Madison, Wisconsin: Elvehjem Museum of Art, 1990.

Steger, Will, Saving the Earth: A Citizen's Guide to Environmental Action. New York: Alfred A. Knopf, 1990.

Stone, Michelle, ON SITE/ ON ENERGY. New York: Distributed by Charles Scribner's Sons, 1974.

Thayer, Robert L., Gray World, Green Heart: Technology, Nature, and the Sustainable Landscape. New York: John Wiley and Sons, 1994.

Thompson, William Irwin, Gaia: A Way of Knowing. San Francisco: Lindisfarne Press, 1987.

Toy, Maggie, Ed., The Architecture of Ecology. London: Architectural Design Magazine Press, 1997.

Van der Ryn, Sim, Sustainable Communities: a new Design Synthesis for Cities, Suburbs, and Towns. San Francisco: Sierra Club Books, 1986.

Van der Ryn, Sim, The Toilet Papers: Recycling Waste and Conserving Water. Sausalito, California: The Ecological Design Press, 1995.

Vassilikos, Vassilis, And Dreams Are Dreams. New York: Seven Stories Press, 1996.

Wall, Derek, Green History: A Reader in Environmental Literature, Philosophy, and Politics. London: Routledge, 1994.

Weiner, Jonathan, The Next Hundred Years: Shaping the Fate of the Living Earth. New York: Bantam Books, 1990.

Zeiher, Laura C., The Ecology of Architecture. New York: Whitney Library of Design, 1996.

Credits

All illustrations not listed below were provided by the author.
l. = left | **r.** = right | **t.** = top | **c.** = center | **b.** = bottom

Acknowledgements

I am deeply grateful to the foundations and individuals that have made this book possible.

This book would not have been possible without the generosity of the Samuel H. Kress Foundation, the Graham Foundation for Advanced Studies in the Fine Arts, and the Design Arts section of the National Endowment for the Arts. I would like to express particular thanks to Marilyn Perry and Lisa Ackerman at Kress and Carter Manny and Richard Solomon of Graham. They have encouraged and supported my writing for more than a decade and have given me the opportunity to explore alternative – and sometimes dangerous – ideas in architecture.

This book would not exist without the endorsement of Philip Jodidio, Editor-in-Chief of *Connaissance des Arts*, who persuaded Taschen to take on this project in the fist place. His perceptive insights and sensitivity to the subject of green architecture have guided this publication from beginning to end.

I would like to thank my superb research team – Seth Cornell who gave passionate dedication to the historical investigation stages of this project and Kristin Rahn who focused her multiple talents on the section concerning contemporary architects. I also want to thank my wife, Kriz Kizak-Wines, for her research, devotion to the environmental cause, unlimited patience with my eccentricities, and endurance of the many sleepless nights spent finishing this text.

A very special thanks to Denise Lee and Zuzanna Karczenwska, the brilliantly talented young architects at SITE who guide our project to completion. Their presence fills every working day with joy and optimism and their encouragement to complete this book kept me glued to the computer.

My gratitude also goes to Kathleen Wright for handling the correspondence, to Sarah Ferguson for organizing the photo material, and to Max Böhler who saved the day at zero hour by pulling together all of the stray visual images.

I want to thank each of the contemporary architects whose work appears in these pages. They demonstrated a remarkable understanding of this book's objectives, gave generously of their time, and gracefully forgave my frequent delays in finishing the text.

My appreciation goes to Marion Hauff, the superb designer who has grasped the spirit of my book so well and translated it into graphic form. Thanks also to my editors at Taschen during the past years – Silvia Kinkel, Dr. Angela Pfotenhauer, Dr. Susanne Klinkhamels, Dr. Nicola Senger, and Caroline Keller – who steadfastly guided this project into reality.

And, finally, I want to extend an long-term expression of gratitude to Sydney and Frances Lewis, whose unique patronage launched my architectural career and the SITE studio in the 1970's, David Bermant who has supported my work and reinforced my spirit for more than two decades, and Malcom Knapp whose daily phone calls and perceptive advice have helped me keep the faith.